Reasons
to
Believe

Reasons to Believe

New Voices in American Fiction

Michael Schumacher

St. Martin's Press
New York

Design by Holly Block

Library of Congress Cataloging-in-Publication Data

Schumacher, Michael.
    Reasons to believe : new voices in American fiction / by Michael Schumacher.
        p. cm.
    ISBN 0-312-01811-8 (pbk.)
    1. American fiction—20th century—History and criticism.
    2. Novelists, American—20th century—Interviews.   I. Title.
PS379.S395   1988
813'.54'09—dc19   87-38246

First Edition

10 9 8 7 6 5 4 3 2 1

This book is dedicated to
My Parents
and
The memory of Dawn Ade, a true believer

Contents

Acknowledgments

The educational process is a quirky one, to which a variety of people contribute. You have teachers who feed you the facts, and you have an occasional kind janitor who lets you back into school so you can retrieve the book you forgot but which you need for your homework. There are people who give you a lift to school, and buddies who let you peek at their notes just before exam time.

There were a lot of people who filled such roles in the educational process that became this book, and it's difficult to say what grade I would have pulled without them.

Obviously, *Reasons to Believe* could not have been written if I had not been given the time and consideration of the people profiled herein. Many of these writers went the extra mile—or, in some cases, the extra twenty-six miles—to supply me information, suggestions, photographs, and, in some cases, tips on how to navigate my rube body through the Big City streets and come out in one piece.

Michael Denneny, my editor, spent a season going to bat for me when the game was on the line and, to his everlasting credit, he got a lot of hits when I might have struck out. I'm constantly amazed by the enthusiasm, as well as the patience and energy, that he brings to publishing.

Peter Spielmann and Judy Hansen offered me a place to stay during my extended trips to New York, but even more important, they were good friends who really came through when it mattered.

For their assistance in helping me handle miscellaneous physical and psychological logistics, I'd also like to thank: Ken Ade, Bill Brohaugh, David Black, Jim Sieger, Tom and June Landre, Bill and Lorraine Landre, Bill Strickland, Sue Rumachek, Al and Diane Schumacher, Tom Clark, Liz Darhansoff, Melanie

Acknowledgments

Jackson, Tess Gallagher, Linda O'Brien, Susan Magrino, Keith Kahla, and Darlene Dobrin.

Finally, I'd like to thank, most of all, Susan, Adam, Emily, and Jack Henry. They endured a year's insanity while this book came together and, without risking overstatement, I can say that they are truly my reasons to believe.

Foreword

Early in 1987, I approached my publisher with the idea of gathering some of my author interviews into book form. I had interviewed a number of highly regarded writers, including Kurt Vonnegut, Norman Mailer, Joyce Carol Oates, and Joseph Heller, and I figured that their insights might be useful to other writers or students of contemporary literature. Michael Denneny, my editor at St. Martin's Press, had seen a profile I'd written about Jay McInerney and countered with the suggestion that I write a book about some of the young fiction writers whose work was garnering so much attention today.

Who were these writers? How did they get their starts? How did they rise so quickly to public notice? What did they know that other young writers had yet to learn? Were they writing for posterity, or were they seeking to cash in on a publishing trend that favored youthful writers with megabuck contracts, high-profile publicity packages, and a sort of instant literary status that had previously taken writers many years (and books) to achieve?

One didn't have to be a part of the nerve center of the publishing establishment to see that something was going on in the world of fiction. Newspaper and magazine articles focused not only on the works but also on the authors themselves. There were articles about the lifestyles of the more visible—tales of the parties and clubs they attended, the clothes they wore, the advances their books commanded, and the Hollywood deals being made for their novels. There was talk of style, but very often it had more to do with their public personalities than their work.

I read these articles with skepticism. Before I had ever considered writing this book, I had enjoyed conversations with McInerney, Mona Simpson, and Jayne Anne Phillips, and it was fortunate that I'd done so. In the ensuing months, I read scores of articles about these new writers, and all too often they were presented as if they were a big, happy family (or, in the case of their detractors, as one big, overwhelming literary conspiracy). I found myself growing increasingly antagonistic toward these roundup reports, inasmuch as each of the three writers I'd interviewed was fiercely individualistic and part of no group, formal or informal, that I could think of. Perhaps their works could be viewed as examples of certain styles or concerns prevalent in a new generation of fiction writers, but lumping them all together seemed to me to be just another example of a loathsome journalistic practice of seeking common denominators and insisting that apples and oranges were more similar than distinct.

I was interested in their work—what it meant, how it was accomplished, how the individual writer's experiences contributed to his or her work. I had little interest in fame or notoriety, other than a curiosity as to how the writers' literary careers were affected by it. I had a feeling that straightforward conversation would teach me more about any existing trends in fiction than a hundred roundup articles. To add dimension to my study, I wanted to talk to publishing figures who, by influence and experience, were capable of discussing, with some authority, how new talent is discovered, developed, and placed in front of the reading public.

A 1987 conversation with Raymond Carver provided a sense of direction. Carver was a sensible and astute observer of the trends in American fiction, and over the course of several long conversations, he talked not only about his own work, which has had great bearing on the direction fiction has taken over the past twenty years, but also about issues such as the "Short Story Renaissance," writing schools, and the rise to prominence of brilliant fiction editors who have added their own spin to the way short stories and novels are being published.

Choosing the people to include in this book was difficult. In its initial stages, I had to consider if it was going to contain the voices of new, as opposed to *young*, authors. After much discussion and deliberation, a compromise was reached. I decided to include writers with breakthrough works published in the past decade, and while I didn't consciously set up an age limit, all of the included authors wound up publishing these works before they had reached the age of thirty-five.

At first glance, it may look as if I have honored certain biases. Most of the writers are from the East Coast, and many attended Columbia University's writing program. Four of the writers (Amy Hempel, Nancy Lemann, David Leavitt, and Anderson Ferrell) were taught by Gordon Lish, and four (Hempel, Lemann, Ferrell, and Raymond Carver) were initially published by Lish. Then there is the "*Esquire* connection": Lish and Tom Jenks served as fiction editors at the magazine. Many of the writers have published books at Knopf or Random House. The *20 Under 30* fiction anthology is well represented by its editor and four authors. Finally, some of these writers are friends and hang out together.

I'm not sure if this is an indication of my personal preferences or just a coincidence, or if it implies something stronger about the state of publishing. All I know is that when I embarked on this project, I was not motivated by any conscious bias toward any of these factors.

My criteria for inclusion were simple and innocent: I had to believe that the writers were compelling presences on the literary scene, writers who have made a difference, one way or another, in the way fiction is being published and read today—people who *may* (as opposed to *will*) help shape the future of American fiction. The same can be said about the editors and other publishing figures included.

Obviously, there are notable omissions, and to explain this I can only point to the limitations of time, space, money, circumstance, or an author's refusal to be interviewed for the book. You face such limitations every time you attempt a book of this nature, but this doesn't make the prospect of exclusion any easier to stomach.

The pieces in this book are conversations, not the final word. They are intended for readers who are more interested in discovery than in judgment. For me, good fiction has always come down to discovery of some form or another, and I'd be very satisfied if this book sets out some markers for readers seriously interested in contemporary writing.

—Michael Schumacher
April 1988

The only people for me are the mad ones, the ones who are mad to live, mad to talk, mad to be saved, desirous of everything at the same time, the ones who never yawn or say a commonplace thing, but burn, burn, burn like fabulous yellow roman candles exploding like spiders across the stars and in the middle you see the blue centerlight and everybody goes "Awww!"
— Jack Kerouac

*Struck me kinda funny seemed kind of
   funny sir to me
How at the end of every hard earned
   day people find some reason to
   believe. . . .*
— Bruce Springsteen

Reasons
to
Believe

Tess Gallagher

INTRODUCTION

After the Fire, into the Fire —
An Interview with Raymond Carver

Much has been written and said about the great interest publishers have been paying to fiction over the last decade. This is especially true of short fiction, with some observers calling the period a "Short Story Renaissance" in America, while others argue that readers have always been interested in quality fiction, that it is more visible today because publishers are marketing and promoting it more aggressively.

Either way, there is certainly no shortage of fiction on bookstore shelves today, and more of it is being purchased than ever before.

One cannot begin to seriously study the trend without looking at the works of the writers who paved the way—people such as Barry Hannah, Richard Ford, Mary Robison, Ann Beattie, John Cheever, Andre Dubus, Tobias Wolff, and, of course, Raymond Carver. Without the steady persistence of these and other writers, much of today's fiction would not be receiving the attention and serious critical notice that it is.

For nearly two decades, Raymond Carver was one of the best-kept secrets in the literary world. His short stories and poems, generally published by literary magazines and small presses, were read with great enthusiasm by a solid cult-following interested in the wonderful kind of work which never seems to gain a lot of attention. A large national following was slow in coming, but his work won awards and prizes, and was considered almost a staple in anthologies and "best of" collections. He was at the cutting edge of a resurgence of interest in the short story, but he was hardly a literary presence caught up in either book-biz glitz or the halls of academia.

Today, Raymond Carver is both "bankable" and well-honored. Large, high-paying magazines solicit his work, while students, writers, and interviewers solicit his time and opinion. He is considered to be one of the best—if not *the* best—of the modern short story writers. He is in constant demand on the lecture, teaching, and writers conference circuits. His papers and manuscripts are gaining value with collectors and university libraries.

To escape the brouhaha and constant work interruptions, Carver and Tess Gallagher, the poet and short story writer who has been his companion, critic, and inspiration for the past decade, have moved from upstate New York to Port Angeles, Washington. But even there, they have to unplug the phone or hang out a hand-painted NO VISITORS sign to elude the attention and get down to real work.

Carver admits that his past and present are two different lives, and his success has only sharpened his focus and perception of the past. He is lucky to be alive, he says, adding that his stories and poems "bear witness" to his past and, unfortunately, to all too many people's presents.

His life story, in fact, reads like one of his fictional works. Born in Clatskanie, Oregon, in 1939, Carver was the product of a father with a penchant for wandering and drinking—a sawmill worker who moved from paycheck to paycheck; Carver's mother supplemented the family's income by working as a waitress or clerk. Art and literature were the furthest things from discussion at the Carver dinner table.

Still, Junior (as Carver was called) wanted to be a writer, but it wasn't going to be easy: Carver married his high-school sweetheart and had two children before his twentieth birthday. Though he followed his father to the sawmills, Carver and his then-wife shared dreams of escaping their lives of blue-collar tedium.

Carver's writing career began when he moved his family to California and enrolled at Chico State College; there he took a creative writing class taught by John Gardner, the late novelist, essayist, and teacher who became a vital influence on Carver. From then on, Carver worked menial jobs to support his family, stealing time whenever he could to write. He published plenty of his work—much of it to great critical acclaim—but there was little or no money in it.

"We had great dreams, my wife and I," Carver wrote years later, remembering those hard times. "We thought we could bow our necks, work very hard, and do all that we set our hearts to do. But we were mistaken."

Their marriage ended and Carver took to drinking. Not even the 1976 publication of his first collection of short stories, *Will You Please Be Quiet, Please*, could reverse his slide. As his first life was reaching its end, Carver, like one of his fictional characters, was virtually powerless to alter his life's direction. Discussing this period with Mona Simpson in an interview for *The Paris Review*, Carver's assessment was brutal in its honesty: "You never start out in life with the intention of becoming bankrupt or an alcoholic or a cheat or a thief. Or a liar."

Carver's survival is testament to the resilience of the human and creative spirits. His second collection of stories, *What We*

Talk About When We Talk About Love (1981), was a sort of catharsis, a compilation of works stylistically stripped to the bone, an anthology of the pain and despair his life had become. At the core of the stories was Carver's modern version of Sisyphus—the working stiff, perched near the summit of the mountain, shoulder to the boulder, unable to push it to the top, too proud or stubborn to let it roll to the bottom, frozen in a seemingly endless test of strength and endurance. The book, like his first, was greeted with overwhelmingly favorable response, and Carver became recognized as one of the most powerful forces in short fiction since Hemingway.

Carver's second life fell into place two years later, with the publication of *Cathedral* and his receiving the prestigious Mildred and Harold Strauss Living Award by the American Academy and Institute of Arts and Letters; the former allotted Carver still more critical acclaim—a nomination for a National Book Critics Circle Award—while the latter afforded him the opportunity to devote all his time to writing. With this newfound freedom, Carver left his creative writing teaching post at Syracuse and turned his writing skills to poetry, publishing *Where Water Comes Together with Other Water* in 1985 and *Ultramarine* a year later. Like his stories, Carver's poems are dynamic and compressed, with each word a carefully chosen tool used to stretch tension to near-breaking point.

In 1988, Carver published *Where I'm Calling From: New and Selected Stories*. There has been talk of a novel over the years, but Carver is clearly in no hurry to write it—*if* he ever writes it. He has written a screenplay—for director Michael Cimino—and he hints that he would like to write another. He was guest editor for the annual anthology *The Best American Short Stories* in 1986, and he and Tom Jenks collaborated in editing *Short Story Masterpieces*, an ambitious collection of what they consider to be the best American short stories published between 1953 and 1985. He continues to write poetry.

Despite the demands placed on his time, Carver is a warm and cooperative man who doesn't seem caught up in all the hoopla surrounding his work and literary reputation. He is soft-spoken, even when he is talking about topics he cares passionately about. He is modest, yet confident in assessing his present status: "I feel that I *am* going to survive—I'll not only survive but I'll thrive. It hasn't been easy but, again, I'm sure other writers have had it as hard or harder. But this is my life and my experience."

Carver is rarely asked more than a few passing questions about his poetry—a situation I found peculiar, given the nature of his terse, exact writing style, which owes more than a nod of recognition to the craft of poetry. I began my questioning in this area, hoping it would fan out into a better understanding and discussion of his fiction. I was glad I did.

You've published more volumes of poetry than short fiction. How did your career as a poet evolve?

Back when I began to write and send things out, I gave an equal amount of time to short stories and poems. Then, in the early Sixties, I had a short story and a poem accepted on the same day. The letters of acceptance, from two different magazines, were there in the box on the same day. This was truly a red-letter day. I was writing both short fiction and poetry in a more or less hit-or-miss fashion, given the circumstances of my life. Finally I decided, consciously or otherwise, that I was going to have to make a decision as to where to put the energy and strength I had. And I came down on the side of the short story.

You continued to write poetry, though.

Yes. For many years, I was an occasional poet, but that, to me, was better than being no poet at all. I wrote a poem whenever I could, whenever I had the chance and wasn't writing stories. Those earlier books of poems were small-press publications that are now out of print. The best of those poems are preserved in the collection *Fires*, which *is* in print. There are, I think, about fifty poems that I wanted to keep from those earlier collections, and those poems went into *Fires.*

For the last couple of years, you've been more than an occasional poet. Your output of poems during this period has been prodigious. How did that come to be?

After the publication of *Cathedral* and the attendant hubbub, I couldn't seem to find any peace and quiet or a place to work. We were living in Syracuse. Tess was teaching and there was a lot of traffic in the house, the phone kept ringing, people were showing up at the door. And there was her school business, and some socializing. But there was little time to work. So I came out to Port Angeles, to find a quiet place to work. I came here to this little house with the intention of writing fiction. I had not written any poems in well over two years and, so far as I knew, I felt it was conceivable I might not ever write another poem. But after I'd gotten out here and had just sat still and was quiet for about six days, I picked up a magazine and read some poems, and they were poems I didn't care for. And I thought: Jesus, I could do better than this. *(laughs)* It may not have been a good motive to begin writing poems, but whatever the motive, I wrote a poem that night and the next morning I got up and wrote another poem. And this went on, sometimes two or even three poems a day, for sixty-five days. I've never had a period in my life that remotely resembles that time. I mean, I felt like it would have been all right, you know, simply to have died after those sixty-five days. I felt *on fire.*

So I wrote all those poems, many of which went into *Where Water Comes Together with Other Water,* and then I didn't do anything for a few months. We took a trip to Brazil and Argentina, to do some readings and lecture. In the meanwhile, the book of poems had been accepted for publication. When I came back from South America, I started writing poems again—and, again, I'm not sure if the motive was correct or not, but I thought: What if the book comes out and it gets a good pasting *(laughs)* and I'm told I should never write any more poems, that I should stick to my fiction? Whatever the reasons, I began writing poems again, and by the time *Where Water Comes Together* was published, I had a new book in the drawer. When I look back on this period of time, the period when I wrote those books of poems, I can't really account for it. This is the truth! All the poems seem now like a great gift—the whole period seems a gift. Right now, I'm back writing stories and in a way it's almost as if that time never happened. It did, of course, and I'm glad it did, and I don't want to make more of it than it is—but it *was* a wonderful time. It was a high time. I've written a few poems since the publication of *Ultramarine* last fall, but mainly now I'm concentrating on fiction. I hope that when I finish this collection of stories I'm working on I will go back to the poems because, for me, when I'm writing poems, I feel there's nothing in the world so important. You know, as far as I'm concerned, I'd be happy if they simply put "poet" on my tombstone. "Poet"—and in parentheses, "and short story writer." *(laughs)* And way down at the bottom someplace, "and occasional anthologist."

And "teacher."

And "teacher," yes. *(laughs)* Teacher would be at the bottom.

When I talked to Jay McInerney about having you as a teacher, he spoke of you much the same way you've talked about having John Gardner as your teacher. Did you enjoy teaching?

I did. See, my teaching career was unique for several reasons, one reason being the fact that never, in my wildest imaginings, could I have seen myself as a teacher. I was always the shyest kid in class—*any* class. I never said anything. So the idea of conducting a class or having anything to say or being able to help students was the furthest thing away from my mind. Coming, as I did, from a family where nobody had gone past sixth grade, the idea of being around the university in such a capacity, as a teacher, was important, I suppose, to my self-esteem. Most important was the fact that I had summers off, and I was earning a more or less decent living while I was doing it. I had done so many different kinds of jobs in my life; no work for wages that I had done before had ever paid me as much money and at the same time given me as much freedom to write. As you know, there are a lot of writers who teach and bad-mouth the schools and the writers who teach, all of that, but I never got into that situation; I was glad to have a teaching job.

When I began teaching, I think I did a decent job with it. The real role model I had, of course, was John Gardner. But there was also another fiction writer, at Humboldt State University, named Richard Day, and a poet in Sacramento named Dennis Schmitz. I tried to teach a writers workshop class the way they did. I tried to give people a lot of personal attention and help them to the best of my ability. There was a literature class that Jay took from me in which I might have been, you might say, a little ill-prepared, so I'd always call on Jay to get the conversation going. *(laughs)* "So what do you think about this book, Jay?" And he'd take off and talk for ten minutes. *(laughs)*

Do you think it's a good idea for aspiring writers to attend these schools or workshops?

Yes I do. Obviously, it's not for everybody, but I can't think of any writers or musicians who have just sprung full-blown without some kind of help. De Maupassant was helped by Flaubert, who went over all his stories and criticized them and gave him advice. Beethoven learned his business from Haydn. Michelangelo was an apprentice for a long while to someone else. Rilke showed his poems to someone early on. Same with Pasternak. Just about any writer you can think of. Everybody, whether it's a conductor or composer or microbiologist or mathematician —they've all learned their business from older practitioners; the idea of the maestro-apprentice relationship is an old and distinguished relationship. Obviously, this is not going to guarantee that it's going to make a great—or even a *good*—writer out of anybody, but I don't think it's going to hurt the writer's chances, either. There's a lot of flap and controversy and discussion and analysis of what's happening with the writers workshop concept —"whither are we going?"—but I think it'll all get sorted out by and by; I don't think it has to be a harmful situation for a young writer.

If nothing else, the encouragement is important.

Yes, exactly so. I don't know, frankly, what would have happened to me had I not run into John Gardner when I did. A writer can see that he's not in this alone, that there are other young writers around who care passionately about the same things he cares about, and he can feel heartened. Once you're out there in the world, on your own, nobody cares. I think a writers workshop situation is a shared endeavor, and an immensely important endeavor. It can be abused by students or teachers, but for the best teachers and students, it's a good thing.

Do you encourage your students to read a lot? How important do you see reading being to the writer?

I think writers—especially young writers—should want to read all the books they can get their hands on. To this extent, that's where it's helpful to have some instruction as to what to read and who to read, from somebody who knows. But a young writer has to make a choice somewhere along the line whether he's going to be, finally, a writer or a reader. I've known good, bright, young, putative writers who felt they couldn't begin to write until they had read *everything* and, of course, you simply can't read everything. You can't read all the masterpieces, all the people that you hear people talking about—you just don't have the time. I mean, I wish there were two of me—one to read and one to write—because I love to read. I probably read more than many people, but I don't read as much as I'd like when I'm writing full-time. Then I read very little if anything. I'm just writing, and that's all. When I'm not actively writing, I tend to read anything—history books, poetry, novels, short stories, biographies.

What do you encourage your students to read?

Flaubert's letters—that's one book I'd recommend. Every writer should read those letters. And Chekhov's letters, and the life of Chekhov. I'll recommend a great book of letters between Lawrence Durrell and Henry Miller, which I read some years back. What a book! But writers should read other writers, yes, to see how it's done, for one thing, how the others are doing it; and there's also the sense of shared enterprise, the sense that we're all in this together. It's been my experience that poets, especially, are helped by reading books on natural history, biography, in addition to the usual reading they do in the area of poetry.

You write in the American idiom and pay close attention to what's called the minute particulars, which brings to mind William Carlos Williams and William Blake. Were they influences?

William Carlos Williams certainly. I didn't come to Blake until a good long while after I had started writing my own poetry. But Williams—very definitely. I read everything of Williams that I could get my hands on when I was nineteen or twenty years old. In fact, I started a little magazine when I was at Chico State College. It was a little magazine that ran for three issues, and it was called *Selection*. I published an original poem by Williams in the magazine. I wrote him a fan letter and said I was starting a little magazine (of course, I couldn't promise anything but contributors' copies) and he sent me this wonderful poem. He scrawled his signature across the bottom of it. It was one of the great thrills of my life, and it happened shortly before he died. It was called "The Gossips" and it was included in that posthumous volume of his, *Pictures from Brueghel*.

How about his short stories? There's quite a similarity in his and your styles in short fiction.

I like his stories a lot, but I can't say for sure how much of what he was doing—the *way* he was doing it—got into my own stories. They may have, you know, because at that time it seemed like I was influenced by almost everything. I was just nineteen or twenty years old, and John Gardner was my teacher. He hadn't published anything at the time, but he seemed to know everything. He was directing me to authors—people I *should* read, books I *had* to look at—so, consciously or otherwise, Williams's poetry influenced me, and maybe the stories did, too. It wasn't long, as a matter of fact, after reading Williams that I wrote this little story I called "The Father." But he was a more direct influence on my poetry. I suppose the influence on my fiction would be the early stories by Hemingway. I can still go back, every two or three years, and reread those early stories and become excited just by the cadences of his sentences—not just by what he's writing about, but the *way* he's writing. I haven't done that in two or three years, and I'm beginning to feel like it's time to go back and reread Hemingway.

When you're in one of those periods when you're writing a lot of poetry, do you find your mind working like a camera, where you see things like a snapshot—everything's taken in instantly and you see the importance of what's before you?

I think so, yes. A lot of my poems begin with a visual image of some sort, like what you're talking about, a snapshot. These snapshots happen often. Most writers have trained themselves to be alert to these moments, but some of us, myself included, aren't always as alert as we'd like to be. Still, when these moments do happen—either at that moment or not too long afterwards—there might be a few words or a line that attaches itself to the image and brings this picture back again. That line often becomes the first line in the poem. Nothing that I write is inviolable—I often change virtually every word that's in a story or poem—but usually that first line, which is the thing that set me off to write the poem or story in the first place, that line remains unchanged. Everything else is up for grabs. But usually that first line stays intact. But I like the idea of the picture because there's a glimpse of something that stays fixed in your head.

When you have that first line in your head, do you know right away whether it's going to be in a poem or a short story?

I'm not making a conscious decision to use a line in a poem or story. When I'm writing poems, it's invariably, inevitably going to become a poem; when I'm writing stories, it's going to become part of a story. Some writers write poetry and fiction at the same time, they can move easily from this to that, but I don't seem to be able to work that way. When I'm writing fiction, I'm in a period of writing fiction; when I'm writing poetry, everything I touch seems to turn to poetry. So if that first line comes when I'm in a period of writing poetry, it's going to become a poem.

Some lines in your poetry have also appeared, almost verbatim, in your fiction.

I know. There's been a crossover like that in at least three or four stories and poems. There's a poem of mine in *Fires* called "Distress Sale," where the people haul all their gear out on the sidewalk and somebody witnesses this, and then that's in my story "Why Don't You Dance?" It's happened in a few other instances. There's a poem called "Mother" that has some lines that come up in a story called "Boxes." In every case, it was dealt with first in the poem. Then I must have felt it making such a large claim on my emotional life that I felt somehow it was unfinished business and went back to it and dealt with it in a larger, fuller way.

The poem "Mother" works very well by itself, but that incident —the idea of the mother calling on Christmas and saying she's going to kill herself if it doesn't stop snowing, that the only time she wants to see that place again is from her coffin—was interesting when it was part of "Boxes." It seemed to heighten the tension you established earlier in the story. I don't know if this was conscious or not, but in "Mother" the narrator's thinking of seeing a psychiatrist, while in "Boxes" the narrator is thinking of having his mother see a psychiatrist.

There's a different kind of spin to it, yes. Most of my stories and poems have a starting point in real life, in reality, but I'm not writing autobiography. It's all subject to change—everything is—in a story or a poem. Whatever seems to suit the work best, that's the direction I'll go in. The stories and poems may have, as their genesis, some lines of references to the real world but, as I've said, I'm not writing autobiography by any account.

Still, it appears that you're getting closer to the bone, more autobiographical, when you're writing poetry.

I think so. The poetry gives me a chance to be intimate or open or vulnerable—or even surreal sometimes—in a way that I don't often engage in when I'm writing fiction. I'm more removed, more at a distance when I'm writing fiction. I feel I'm much closer to the center, the core, in the poetry.

When you're writing a poem, does the content usually dictate the form your poem is going to take? Do you automatically know how you're going to write it?

Sometimes I work considerably hard in making it attractive—making it look "right" to the eye, and hoping it'll be right to the ear as well. I'll work with it on the page well after it's been finished. But other times, just the content alone will dictate how it looks on the page.

Let's turn to your work as a short story writer. Interest in the short story seems to be resurging lately, with more and more story collections published every year. How do you account for this?

I think it's the single most eventful literary phenomenon of our time. I don't think there's ever been a time like it for the short story, or for short story writers. Many short story writers today are not even interested in writing novels. As you know, some short story writers can command advances that are every bit equal to some of the advances being paid for novels. The bottom line is always how many copies are being sold, and books of short stories are being sold these days like never before. It's a most remarkable thing. There was a time when, by and large, the commercial presses looked on publishing short stories as an enterprise that would be better left to the small presses and the university presses, but now that situation is completely turned around. Short story writers figure prominently on publishers' lists. Their books are reviewed prominently and supported in important ways by the publishing houses.

You, of course, have been mentioned as one of the main reasons for this trend.

Well, anything I can say to that sounds a little self-serving, and I feel a little awkward talking about this. I feel that there are a number of other good writers who began working more or less at the same time I was starting out writing stories; any success that might have come my way, or someone else's way, has helped all this along. But, sure, the good things that have happened to me have been good for every other short story writer as well. But don't forget that the publication of John Cheever's short stories in 1978 helped things considerably, too. I think maybe a lot of young writers saw what was happening and felt heartened: They felt it was all right to write short stories exclusively and not worry about writing novels. This gave license to lots of short story writers. There were a number of short story writers at work, and I feel I'm one of many.

Who, of the short story writers, do you like?

Oh, I like Toby Wolff—he's a wonderful writer. Joy Williams is another. Richard Ford. Charles Baxter has published a couple good collections. I like Ann Beattie's stories. Alice Munro, the Canadian writer, has to be one of the great story writers. Jayne Anne Phillips. Andre Dubus. Mark Helprin is first-rate as a story writer. Barry Hannah. I like many of John Updike's stories and Bobbie Ann Mason's stories. Joyce Carol Oates. We're talking about living writers now; there are the great dead writers, too, like Chekhov and Tolstoi, Hemingway and Frank O'Connor and Flannery O'Connor. Isaac Babel. And there are so many others.

In addition to this interest in the short story itself, there has been a growing interest, even on the part of literary elitists, in tales of survivors, whether they're found in the stories by writers such as yourself, Richard Ford, Barry Hannah, Charles Bukowski, Tobias Wolff, and so forth, or in the music of Bruce Springsteen, John Cougar Mellencamp, and Tom Waits. Why do you think that is?

Well, in part, of course, it simply has to do with the fact that these people are bearing witness to what they have experienced; they're able to talk about it. There's a fascination with somebody who's been there and come back—lived to talk about it, as it were. You know: "I'll tell you what it's like. This is my song, this is my poem or short story. Make of it what you will." I think there's a rock-hard honesty about what many of these writers and musicians are offering up which is of more than passing interest to the public, so the public is paying attention.

When you wrote about your father in "My Father's Life" for Esquire, you mentioned the time you told him you wanted to be a writer, and his advice was "write the stuff you know about." That's great advice—which a lot of writing instructors have been giving out over the years. Can you explain how your blue-collar background helped you with your writing, both in terms of subject and approach?

For certain I had a *subject*, something to write about, people and events that I knew well. I never had to go around looking for material. Also, I think that blue-collar life put a premium on directness and being straightforward. In that life, there wasn't a whole lot of room for, or patience with, the Henry Jamesian kind of indirection.

I guess the reason I mention this is I've been to too many creative writing classes and workshops where you have people with back-

*grounds similar to your own, and they were writing about being
college professors or something.*

Yes, I know. They ought to be writing about what they know
about. There's a lot that they know about, other than the college
campus scene, and the professor-student situation. God knows,
that's a subject matter all right, and some people can make art
out of it. But a writer, young or old, can't fake it. He's got to
write with authority, and he'd do well to write about something
he's acquainted with and about the things that move him—not
the things that *should* move him, but the things that *do* move
him. There are significant moments in everyone's day that can
make literature. You have to be alert to them and pay attention
to them. That's what you ought to write about.

In Ultramarine, *there is a poem called "What You Need for Painting," which really struck me. It's a list poem taken from a letter
by Renoir, but used in the context of writing, it seems like your
advice on the ingredients needed to write a good poem or short
story.*

Especially those last three lines.

*Which read: "Indifference to everything except your canvas/ The
ability to work like a locomotive/An iron will." Those are great
instructions for the young writer.*

In the beginning, when I was trying to write, I couldn't turn
off the outside world to the extent that I can now. When you're
writing fiction or poetry—or when you're painting or making
music or composing music—it really comes down to this: indifference to everything except what you're doing. Your canvas, as
it were. Which, translated to fiction or poetry, means indifference
to everything except that piece of paper in the typewriter. As for
the ability to work like a locomotive and an iron will—by God,
that's what it takes. Anyone who has written anything knows all
of these things are necessary—requirements. Of course, those

lines that struck home are from the Renoir letter, and so it was a *found* poem. But a young writer could do worse than follow the advice given in those lines. I think all of those things are necessary. If the car needs to have an all-important service job but the Muse is with you, so to speak, you just have to get to your typewriter and stay there and turn the rest of the world off somehow, forget about everything else. I'm glad you remarked on that poem and those lines because that is my philosophy of writing, if I have one. You could put those words on my tombstone, too. *(laughs)*

In discussing technique in your Introduction to The Best American Short Stories 1986, *you listed the five elements you consider important in the short story: choices, conflict, drama, consequence, and narrative. Do you have these things mapped out in your head before you start writing?*

No. I begin the story and it takes a natural course. Most often I'm not aware, when I start a poem or story, of where it's going until I get there. Not while I'm writing it. There's a passage from a Flannery O'Connor essay, "On Writing Short Stories," where she says that when she began a story she never knew where the story was going until she got to the end. And I read a little essay by Hemingway called "Monologue for the Maestro," in which somebody asked him if he knew where he was going with a story, and Hemingway answered that he never knew, that he just wrote and the situation developed and unfolded. I don't have any kind of program in writing a story. The drama enters the story, and the consequences and choices present themselves. I guess I tried to separate them in the essay, but they're all connected together. They're not really separate.

You do have that opening line you were mentioning before.

Yes, I have that opening line, and then everything seems to radiate out from that line.

Very often, when reading one of your short stories, I get the impression that something very, very important has happened just before the story begins—or will happen after the story ends. Your stories, like Hemingway's, really deal with the tip of the iceberg. When it works, it's wonderful, but a lot of beginning writers have problems in this area: They assume that their readers know what's going on—occurrences that are never mentioned in their stories. What's the cutting edge to you? How do you teach that to your students?

Well, you can't keep necessary information from the reader. You can assume that the reader can put a face on some of these characters—you don't *have* to describe the color of their eyes, and so forth. Insofar as the stories are concerned, you have to presuppose some kind of knowledge on the part of the readers, that they're going to fill in some of the gaps. But you can't leave them drifting around without enough information to make them care about these people; you can't obfuscate what's going on. To this extent, I had problems with some of the postmodernist writers of the Sixties. You'd sometimes read the work and you never knew what the problem was—just that there *was* some kind of problem or difficulty. Everybody was out of sorts in the story, but the fiction was divorced from reality in every way, shape, and form. I'm much more interested in stories and poems that have some bearing on how we live and how we conduct ourselves and how we work out the consequences of our actions. Most of my stories start pretty near the end of the arc of the dramatic conflict. I don't give a lot of detail about what went on before; I just start it fairly near the end of the swing of the action.

Your stories begin at crisis point.

Yes, I think so. I don't have a lot of patience for the other, I guess. But there *is* a fine line—the cutting edge, as you put it —where you have to give the reader enough, but you don't want to give him *too* much. I don't want to bore the reader, or bore myself.

Kurt Vonnegut wrote that short story writers should just write their stories and then toss out the first few pages when they were done.

There's something to that. D. H. Lawrence made a remark to the effect that you finish your story and when it's all finished, you go back and shake the branches of the tree, prune it again.

About revision: Some of your early stories have really been overhauled between the time they were originally published in little magazines and their eventual publication in your collections. Sometimes the endings and even the titles were changed. In explaining these revisions in your Afterword to Fires, *you wrote that "maybe I revise because it gradually takes me into the heart of what the story is about. I keep trying to see if I can find that out. It's a process more than a fixed position." Could you explain that a little further?*

There was a time when I revised everything, and they were often quite extensive revisions. I don't know, maybe I didn't know what was around the corner, if *anything* was around the corner, so I was just more interested in messing around with the work I had on hand. At that time, I didn't feel that the stories were in any kind of fixed place, and I wanted to get them there—wherever that was. Now, I don't feel this need to do all the revising that I once did. Maybe I'm feeling more secure with the stories I'm writing, or more satisfied, or more confident. Something has happened, at any rate. Now I tend to write the stories and for the most part lose interest in them after they're written. In some way, after they're published, they don't seem to belong to me any longer. I don't mean to make more out of it than there is, but I guess I feel now like there's everything to do and little enough time to do it in, so I tend not to be so keen on revising the stories. Now I do all the revisions when I'm writing the story. I'm just not coming back to them after they're published, as I once did.

Maybe that's the result of your maturation as a writer.

Maybe so. I didn't have the confidence then that I do now. I didn't know too much of what I was doing then—I wasn't satisfied. And now, for whatever reasons, I feel more assured and I'm seeing my way more clearly. A lot of things that work now were not working for me six or ten years ago. Whether that's growing as a writer, or maturing, as you say, I don't know, but I feel good about it.

When you're revising, what are you looking for? What do you tend to change?

I want to make the stories interesting on every level and that involves creating believable characters and situations, along with working on the language of the story until it is perfectly clear, but still a language capable of carrying complex ideas and sophisticated nuances.

In a number of your stories written in the first person, you've written from a woman's point of view. When you were writing them, did you feel that the stories' impact—their "rightness," so to speak—was strengthened by the woman's point of view. Was it difficult to write a story this way?

The first time I ever attempted to write a story from the point of view of a woman, I was nervous about it. It was a real challenge to me. When I brought it off, it was like a rush. I was excited. I like to be able to write with authority in either gender. Now when ideas for stories come to me they seem to present themselves to me with the point of view as nearly an inevitable thing. But, again, I think the choices are being made for me because of the nature of the material, and because of the way I'm approaching it. I just gear up and do it, and I like it.

Point of view is so important to a story. I've heard of people who have changed from first to third person in a story after it's been written.

Well, my friend Richard Ford changed the point of view of one of his novels. He worked on it for two years, and he felt it wasn't right, so he spent another year changing the entire point of view. That's dedication. And real seriousness in what you're doing. You want it right and you don't have that many chances at it. I don't know how many books a person's going to take to the grave with him, but you want to have it right, or else what's the point?

When you're writing steadily, what's your typical workday like?

I get up early, somewhere between six o'clock and six-thirty, and have coffee and a bowl of cereal or something like that. I'm always at my desk by eight o'clock. If it's a good day, I'll just stay at my desk until at least eleven or twelve o'clock, when I'll break for a late breakfast. On a good day, I can stay at my desk and do something all day, because I like to work, I like writing. When I'm working, I put the phone on the answering machine and unplug the phone upstairs, so if it rings downstairs, I can't hear it ring. I can check in the evening to see if there are any messages. I don't watch much TV—I watch the news usually—and I go to bed fairly early. It's a pretty quiet life, generally.

Do you prefer to write a story from beginning to end in one sitting?

Yes. I'm afraid of interruption and losing the story—whatever it was that made me want to write the story in the first place. I don't think I've ever spent longer than two days writing the first draft of a story. Usually only one day. I spend lots of time after that typing it up and reworking it, but I think it's good to try to get that story down before you lose sight of it. It might not look so good tomorrow. So on the first draft, you have to put your trust in whatever, just hope and assume that something's going to come of it, just barrel on through and try to get the first draft quickly before you lose it. Then it's subject to change and what-have-you. Then you can be slow and thoughtful with it.

I remember reading somewhere that, in the early days, you used to steal away and write in your car.

It's true. I wouldn't recommend it as a place to work *(laughs)*, but it was necessary for me at that time of my life. I don't know if I got anything lasting out of it, but at least I was working on *something*. I was trying to do something and I had no place to go. I was young and there was just no room in the house. I didn't want to have to go out in the car—it wasn't that I wanted to go for a quiet drive in the country and park next to the river and muse. No, I'd just go out and sit in the car in the parking lot, just to be away from my kids and the turmoil and confusion in the house. That was my office, as it were. *(laughs)*

Do you warn your students about how tough the writing life is?

Oh, I talk about it a little sometimes, but you can't tell them how hard it is. Not really. You can't truthfully tell a young poet or fiction writer they have to have not only the utmost seriousness in regard to their writing but that they're going to have to devote the rest of their lives to it if they intend to be any good at it. But you can't tell them what they're going to have to go through. You can sort of tell them, but they'll have to live through it themselves; they'll have to survive that themselves. You don't have to say much to the best of them. If they're smart, they have an idea of what it's like, and they know it won't come easy to them; if they're not smart and they're not hard on themselves, then they won't be writing very long after they graduate.

I've always been curious about the relationship between the hunger to publish and the hunger to create. What do you think that relationship is? Is the hunger to publish a good motivating factor?

I think it is. Even when I was teaching, I always felt it was too much of a hothouse and rarified atmosphere if there was never any talk about the young writers submitting work to magazines.

And on occasion I'd take in some bound galleys, or show them page proofs I was working on, so they could actually see this stuff. They don't know the first thing about the process a book goes through from inception to manuscript, from letter of acceptance to copy-edited manuscripts and galley proofs. So I'd show them these things and talk about possible markets for their stories. I don't think it diminishes the work to talk about publishing that work. Quite the contrary: There's literary *creation* and there's literary *business*. Art and commerce do sometimes go hand in hand. When I first got something accepted, it gave my life a validation that it didn't otherwise have. It was very important to me. I think I got paid a dollar for the first poem I ever published, but that didn't dampen my enthusiasm. No, I was thrilled with that one-dollar check.

There are, however, a lot of serious writers out there who have to try to balance art with budget: You want to write good, strong work, but you also have to feed your family. Sometimes you feel like you're playing "Beat the Clock": If you don't get something out, you don't pay the rent next month. Did you find that happening to you?

My situation was similar *and* different. I knew I was never going to get rich writing poems, not when I was getting paid a dollar or five dollars, or else being paid in contributors' copies. And, for years, I was writing short stories, of course, and if I got paid at all, it was twenty-five or fifty dollars. So, in truth, I never faced that same dilemma. The problems were similar, in that the kids were there, eating me alive, and I had to make all those monthly payments—some of which we didn't make—but the fact that I was writing stories and poems didn't make any great financial difference to us. The first story in *Esquire* brought me six hundred dollars; but then, I didn't publish in *Esquire* for a very long while after I started writing, so I knew I wasn't going to get rich writing stories, either. Had I been able to write them any faster and still take the time that was necessary for them, I would have done so, but I seemed to be teaching or working or raising a family and so forth, so I simply did the best I could, on what I could.

When you were thinking about becoming a writer, you were hoping just to be able to publish your work in the types of magazines you had around your home, publications like True *or* Argosy. *They were paying markets with reputations of their own, but they were hardly known in the literary community as being places where great literature was created. What made you decide to devote your work to the more serious markets?*

Until I met John Gardner, I had no concept of serious literature. I simply knew that I wanted to be a writer and, of course, nobody in my family did any reading so there was no guidance of any sort whatsoever. I just had to continually follow my nose, whether it led to a historical novel or an article in *True.* Everything was more or less of equal merit, or value, until I met Gardner. This is one of the most important things about our meeting: He'd say something like "I'm not only here to teach you how to write, but I'm also here to tell you who to read." That was immensely important to me. I began to read Joseph Conrad and Isak Dinesen, along with so many other important writers. For the first time in my life, I had some direction. I was introduced to the little magazines by Gardner, and I became interested in the stories and poems they were publishing, so that's what I set out to do: to write well and publish what I wrote. I don't want to seem snobbish about the other magazines—it wasn't that I turned up my nose at things like *Argosy* and *True* and so forth—I simply didn't have enough time in my day to read everything and write everything.

One of your big breaks was meeting Gordon Lish, your longtime friend and editor. How did that happen?

Our relationship goes back to the mid-1960s. He was working for a textbook publishing firm across the street from the textbook firm where I was working, in Palo Alto. That's how we became acquainted. Then he went off to become the fiction editor for *Esquire*. The next I heard from him, he was writing a letter on someone else's stationery. It was from *Esquire*, and he'd crossed off the older editor's name. In the note, he said, "I've taken over the fiction editor's desk from the above-named good gentleman. Send me whatever you have." I was still working at the publishing company, and I proceeded to dispatch all the stories I had in the house—four or five stories—and, by God, they all came back by return mail *(laughs)* with a message saying "Try me again, these are not right." I didn't know what to make of this. If my close friend becomes the fiction editor at *Esquire* and I still can't get a story in, what chance do I have? You're in *real* trouble then. *(laughs)* But I pulled up my socks, sat down and began writing more stories, and he finally took one. It was a story called "Neighbors," and that was one of the turning points in my life. And then he took another one, and so forth. Then he left *Esquire* and became an editor at Knopf. He gave me a contract there for a book of stories. So we go back a long way.

He was always a great advocate of my stories, at all times championing my work, even during the period when I was not writing, when I was out in California devoting myself to drinking. Gordon read my work on radio and at writers conferences and so forth. I don't think I ever had a greater advocate for the work, when I needed it, than Gordon. He was like Gardner in the sense that he offered encouragement. He was also like Gardner to the extent that he would say that if you could say something in twenty words instead of fifty words, say it in twenty words. He was very important to me at a time when I needed to hear what he had to offer. He's still championing the work of young writers.

There seems to be a trend in the publishing business for greater writer-editor relationships. Have you noticed that?

Yes. I was talking about this with Tess the other night, as a matter of fact. We were talking about Robert Gottlieb and his move from Knopf to the editorship of *The New Yorker*. And as we talked, I realized that this is probably the first age in literary history where editors have become public personalities, in some cases even greater personalities, or figures, than many of the writers they are involved with. Gottlieb goes to *The New Yorker* and it's a front-page piece in *The New York Times* and news in papers and magazines all across the country. And the distinguished editor Gary Fisketjon: They've written an article about him in *Esquire*, and he's been profiled in other magazines. I know any number of writers who will go with their editors when they move from one house to another. Writers have established a close relationship with their editors, and they will go wherever their editors go. The first editor I ever heard of was Maxwell Perkins, and he had that relationship with Thomas Wolfe, Hemingway, and so many other writers. Editors are playing a larger role in a writer's life these days, and I don't know whether this is a good or bad thing. I don't know what conclusions to draw from it, but it's a fact that they have become public personalities in their own right, and this is quite remarkable, I think.

Your survival as a writer has been a source of inspiration to a lot of struggling writers. Somehow, you've been able not only to work your way past a number of imposing barriers, but you've been able to translate your experiences into universal stories. How do you feel about all this today?

I just feel like an instrument. . . . It *has* been a question of survival, and had I been able to do something else . . . I don't know, maybe I would have done something else. But I *had* to write. You know, the flame went out: I think it was flat-out extinguished there toward the end of my drinking days. But, yes, I did survive. In fact, after I got sober and had quit drinking entirely, there was a period of time, for a year or so, when I didn't write anything and it wasn't even important for me to write anything. It was so important for me to have my health back and not be brain-dead any longer that whether I wrote or not didn't matter any longer. I just felt like I had a second chance at my life again. But for about a year or so, I didn't write anything.

And then, when things were right, when I was well again, I taught for a year in El Paso, and then, suddenly, I began to write again. And that was just a great gift, and everything that has happened since then has been a great gift. Every day is a bonus. Every day now is pure cream.

▲▲▲▲▲▲▲▲▲

POSTSCRIPT:

Raymond Carver died on August 2, 1988.

This interview took place shortly before Carver learned that he had lung cancer. As is evident by the tone of the conversation, Carver was cheerful and hopeful, confident that some of his best work was still ahead of him. Despite joking about the words that would be chiseled into his headstone, there was no sense of finality in either the man or his words.

Nor would there ever be. Even after he grew ill and had much of his left lung removed, Carver remained optimistic. The last time I spoke to him, not long before the publication of Where I'm Calling From, *he offered no complaint of tiring radiation treatments or failing health; instead, he looked ahead to the new book, as well as to a return to writing poetry.*

In his final months, he married Tess Gallagher, was inducted into the American Academy and Institute of Arts and Letters, and finished his collection of poems, A New Path to the Waterfall. *Only hours before he passed away, Tess Gallagher told* The New York Times *Carver mentioned how much pleasure he'd taken from the stories of Anton Chekhov.*

Raymond Carver was a man with his own personal and artistic credo, much of which was stated in this interview, much of which is inherent in the title of this book, chosen with Carver very much in mind. Rather than change the interview or its introduction to accommodate the remainder of events in Carver's life, I decided to leave it intact—a slight expansion of the way it originally appeared in print.

The way Ray liked it.

Maude Schuyler Clay

AMY HEMPEL

We start out by talking about pain.

We're not talking about the little day-to-day aches and pains, the ones you shrug off or ignore while you're going about your business. We're talking about the pains that seize your body and mind and spirit at the same time, forcing you to make choices or take chances that you would never otherwise consider. The kind of pain that frames you, shows your colors, and ultimately leaves you naked, vulnerable.

We trade stories about death and cancer and nursing homes and serious automobile accidents. We discuss the fires and floods and mudslides in California, as well as the psychic costs of living under the constant threat of earthquakes.

Our conversation is a portfolio of *Life* magazine pictures converted to words. It seems odd to be talking about such topics only a few moments after you've met someone for the first time.

Still, if you have any intention of understanding the short fiction of Amy Hempel, pain is where you start.

⁓⁓⁓⁓⁓⁓

"I remember this group that I worked with in Berkeley," Hempel says, recalling a time when she worked in a counseling group for terminally ill people in California. "We met at least weekly, just to air everything out. When you joined, they expressed the importance of life-affirming activity in your life—something like jogging or going out dancing—which you needed to indulge in so you didn't burn out, although everyone burned out quite quickly. The ultimate life-affirming activity was sex, so you would hear the phrase and there'd be all this winking: 'What'd you do over the weekend? A little life-affirming activity?' "

Hempel laughs—something she does often and heartily—but she isn't finished with her story. She has assembled all the components and now it's time for the payoff.

"One of the first women I met was this young mother who had lost a very young daughter over two years of agonizing cancer. It was the most hideous thing I could imagine. And people always asked her how she got through it, how she survived it. And she said, 'Sex.' That's how she did it: She joined all those sex experiments in California."

This time she doesn't laugh. By telling one quick story, she has summarized the major theme running through the fifteen stories in *Reasons to Live*, her first published collection: Life can offer an unbelievable menagerie of pain, suffering, and loss, but people always seem to find a reason to live. Those reasons, as well as the way they are found and pursued, are the fiber which holds the world—and Amy Hempel's short stories—together.

⌐⌐⌐⌐⌐⌐⌐⌐⌐

She has been through a lot. She volunteers that much. Much of it has made its way into her fiction; a lot has not. She makes one thing very clear: The choices of what to include and what to leave out are not formed by the modes of confession or wisps of self-pity. There is no place in fiction for that. Nor does she use the short story as a vehicle to work emotions out of her system.

"Looking for catharsis or a way to salve pain is a bad reason to go into fiction," she believes, "but it's a good reason to keep a journal. It's a bad reason to go into fiction because: What does the reader care how you feel after writing about something? The point is to make the *readers* feel better, or to make them feel *more*, or to make them feel *something*. What's nice, as a side effect, is that I do, in fact, end up feeling better."

She goes on to explain that she has always been interested in people who have responded to stringent trials, people who have borne up to the test. "Extremity—that's what I respond to. I'm endlessly, endlessly interested in people who have *come through* something, and the more they have come through, the more interested I am in them and their stories. That's what it's all about: How do you get through?"

⌐⌐⌐⌐⌐⌐⌐⌐⌐

In a story entitled *"Beg, Sl, Inc, Cont, Rep,"* a woman who has had an abortion knits a wardrobe of clothes for a friend's baby. "In the Cemetery Where Al Jolson Is Buried" finds its narrator at her best friend's deathbed, where the two are unable to address the issue of mortality and are only capable of communicating in trivia. In "Nashville Gone to Ashes," a veterinarian's widow comes to terms with her husband's life by thinking about the animals he treated. The protagonist of "Pool Night," having watched her house burn down, offers a rather alarming but ultimately on-the-mark assessment of the damage: "I know that homes burn and that you should think what to save before they start to. Not because, in the heat of it, everything looks as valuable as everything else. But because nothing looks worth the bother, not even your life."

Each of the collection's stories concerns a type of loss—life, options, hope—yet each is distinctive from the others because of Hempel's use and control of minute particulars, by the way she stitches these details and events together, everything compressed to the point where the stories take on a poetic sense of the elliptical.

"The trick," explains Hempel, "is to find a tiny way into a huge subject. In my case, it's loss. Every story in this book, and every new story written since the book, has to do with some kind of loss. As I was writing these stories, I discovered that the way I write was like piecing a crazy quilt. I'd have scraps and little bits of information and phrases and so on, and I'd kind of piece them together. If I did it right, they accumulated and signified by the end of the story. This ties in with the notion I got from my editor, Gordon Lish, who was also my writing teacher: He used to say 'Do it right in the small and the large will take care of itself.' "

Most of Hempel's stories are fusions of autobiography, fiction, and scraps of information which she writes down, or clips out of newspapers or magazines, and saves. She begins with a moment—or a particular line—that she wants to use, and she builds her story from there. The juxtaposition of personal experiences with items she's heard or read about create fictional possibilities, and she arranges and rearranges the pieces of her "crazy quilt" until she is satisfied that she has reached the effect she was seeking.

Again, she points to the teachings of Gordon Lish to explain her methods. "He talks about finding that nugget in your experience that you can draw upon, the way a nuclear submarine is powered by a little nugget of fuel. I like that approach.

"I always start with the first line, or the last line or paragraph. You figure that your big moment will be in your opening or your ending, so you build around that line. In the 'Al Jolson' story, the very first story I wrote, I had 'Tell me things I won't mind forgetting' because she was dying, and I had that image of the mother chimp over the dead baby chimp. That, I felt, was worth building on. It was worth coming up with something to frame it."

In the best stories, Hempel's patchwork is done with such care that you won't see the stitches in the craftsmanship.

But, if you look closely, you can see the author's scars.

- - - - - - - - - -

No *pain, no gain*: Gordon Lish, eccentric teacher, insists that his students approach their fiction like bloodletting. No shortcuts, no shit. Writing—a form of self-flagellation, an exacting craft which makes damn near crippling demands on the spirit. You have to put some skin on the line, or how else will you rise above the ordinary?

A good student (who eventually dedicated her first book to Lish), Hempel followed the advice of her guru. The result is fiction that is written in a voice and style that is distinctly hers, stories that could not have been written by anyone else.

Hempel's prose, usually written in the first person, using present tense, is by itself not that different from the prose written by scores of other writers employing what has been branded "minimalist" style. However, too many minimalists have been slaves to form, often at the cost of substance; their stories come off as well-crafted but cold. In her most successful stories, Hempel has added skin and blood and bone to her craftsmanship, the pieces finding her surrendering personal vitality for the benefit of the printed page. This is where she gets her signature.

She confesses, through her fiction, that she failed a dying friend, that she was unable to offer support her friend needed when it really mattered. In "The Harvest," an uncollected story, she writes about a traumatic motorcycle accident which crippled her for many months, while in "The Most Girl Part of You," in perhaps her most stunning example of addressing personal pain,

Hempel (whose mother committed suicide when Amy was eighteen) confronts the horror of suicide with the darkly comic line, "Any place I hang myself is home."
Asked about self-revelation in fiction, Hempel keeps a poker face. "What's to reveal? What could I possibly reveal that a hundred thousand people on the street wouldn't have done, felt, or thought? I'm going to *surprise* these people? No, I couldn't really surprise people. What I'm worried about is writing something stupid or trite. That would scare me.

"Stanley Elkin once said that he would never write about someone who is not at the end of his rope. That's not a bad way to go into something."

———————

A decade or so ago, minimalist fiction was the stylistic darling of the literary critics, a writing discipline considered to be the ultimate test of a story writer's marriage of form and content; today, the same critics have declared the style passé. What was once praised as stripped-back and *essentially* bare is now dismissed as being simply short. The complaint against minimalism focuses on the idea that early minimalists devoted great consideration to what should be left out of a short story, while today so little is left in that one can only imagine what was eliminated. It is an argument with some merit.

Reasons to Live was published at the height of this debate, and its resulting criticism focused on the issue. Ralph Novak, writing for *People*, rejected the stories as "provocative teases," grousing that it was "a cheat to expect people to pay, rather handsomely, for the opportunity to hear an author say, in effect, 'Well, wouldn't this little idea make a fascinating story sometime?' " *Publishers Weekly* called the stories "spare, droll, elliptical" pieces with "surprisingly sentimental and moving interior(s)." In a long essay for *Harper's* magazine, Madison Smartt Bell, a contemporary of Hempel's, asserted that "Hempel shares with the most modish of our new story writers an increasingly familiar spareness of style which suggests, in the end, that there is not too much to be said but too little." Finally, David Leavitt, in an essay for *The New York Times Book Review*, called Hempel "certainly the most experimental and potentially the most exciting of the writers of her generation."

Hempel is understandably testy about complaints based solely on the length of her stories. ("How long *is* a story?" she muses.) In fact, she says, some of her stories could be compressed more than they have been.

"I still tend to put too much in a story. In one case, I handed my editor a story I'd just finished, and I sat in his office while he read it, with pencil in hand, and he would circle paragraphs and say 'This is a story,' 'This is a story,' 'This is a story'—*five* stories he found in the ten-page story I gave him. I went out of his office, reeling, but when I got home and worked at it I could see what he was saying. That story became four stories in the book."

Hempel's example illustrates an important distinction between her fiction and much of the minimalist fiction of her contemporaries: From a purely physical standpoint, her sentences look like the sparse constructions typical of minimalist prose but, contrary to the observations of Madison Smartt Bell, who opined that in "too many stories . . . nothing is at issue except the characters' groundless angst," Hempel's foremost skill is her compression of as much into a single sentence as possible. The risk, as was the case in her "several stories within a story" example, is in including too much, not too little, in a story.

Since the beginning of her career, Hempel has worked on this stylistic point. Writing in this mode has not been easy, but she offers a simple explanation for why she chose this route. "I would write poetry if I understood the mechanics of poetry and how the line breaks. I like the compression in poetry. I read poetry all the time to get myself revved up to write short stories. I really don't read other people's short fiction to get going. I think that what I'm doing, because of the compression and phrasing, has more to do with poetry than with conventional short stories."

In regard to her stories being too short, Hempel uses poetry to answer her critics. "People don't look at a poem and say 'Boy, is that short.' They're looking at how much has been compressed. Someone recently asked me if I was looking forward to writing a novel or longer work, and I said that I was looking forward to writing *shorter* work."

Still, such compression does depend as much upon what is left out of the story as on what is left in, the choices of omission being made solely on the merits of what is included. Success depends on the writer's skill, along with faith in readers' ability to fill in the blanks. In an unusual move, Hempel wrote a detailed, point-by-point illustration of this process of inclusion and exclusion. Published in the premier issue of *The Quarterly*, the untitled piece was longer than "The Harvest," the short story it explained.

"I leave a lot out when I tell the truth," Hempel wrote. "The same when I write a story. I'm going to start now to tell you what I left out of 'The Harvest,' and maybe begin to wonder why I had to leave it out."

"It was fun for me to do," she says of the story's companion piece. "Gordon Lish thinks that a lot of us are storytellers and we don't realize it. Something happens to you, and when you tell the story to somebody, you put a little better spin on it, just to deepen the irony or whatever. In the Addendum to 'The Harvest,' I show how I took the real story and changed it to make it work better. It's something that's been on my mind since I've been writing, and I thought I'd address it head-on in this piece."

Predictably, what was left out of "The Harvest" was nearly as interesting as what was included—the stuff of a half-dozen or more short stories. There was a story of an attempted jailbreak, another about shark attacks, and still another about a young reporter who wound up covering the Jonestown suicides—all connected to Hempel's real-life accident (which is the focus of the story), all left out because they would have detracted from the story. By compressing her stories to the point of squeezing out any unnecessary, distracting material, Hempel keeps the focus on the tale that is being told, the truth that powers everything she is writing.

~~~~~~~~~~

"One of the good things about writing" she continues, "is that I'm different on the page than I am in person. On the page, I get to be precise, cool, tough—things that I'm really not. In life, I'm all over the place: I'm vague, not defined, and full of fear. But what people see is the end result, this precisely honed story. You get to be known that way and it's wonderful."

~~~~~~~~~~

"Most of this," she says, holding up her copy of *Reasons to Live*, "is firsthand. I don't think I have a wide range of imagination, in the sense that people talk about it. What I have is a good sense of observation. In college, I was trained very briefly as a reporter, and that carried over into fiction because it's very useful to know what to see, to know what's important—the little perfect details. That's what I capitalize on because I don't have imagination in the sense that I will think up a whole new world."

For the purposes of the themes she pursues in her fiction, California provides an ideal setting. "In California, it's very easy to have your worst fears made tangible in the form of natural disaster. Every year, they'll have these fires. And then there are the floods and mudslides and the quakes. I've been through all of that."

And more . . .

Born in Chicago on December 14, 1951, Amy Hempel was the eldest of her parents' three children. Her father, a successful businessman, moved the family from Chicago to Denver when Amy was in third grade, and then to San Francisco when she was in high school.

Of her childhood, she says, "I had a lot of fun. I had terrific brothers, a terrific father. Any time there's a boy in anything I write, the boy is a composite of my two brothers, who are extremely entertaining fellows. The story 'Today Will Be a Quiet Day' is one of the most literal stories in the book. That whole

Amy Hempel

story was written to get to the last exchange, which is something my father really did. He was tucking me in, and he said, 'There's some good news and some bad news. Which do you want first?' That exchange. And then his answer: 'I lied, there's no bad news.' That was way, way long ago, but I knew that that was something important."

Her love of words came as a result of her rocky relationship with her mother. "About the only time we really talked and got along was when we were talking about books. I read above my level because my mother was a real, real reader. How we communicated, when we did, was to talk about the books we read. I read as a way to talk to her. She'd always use words I didn't know, and she wouldn't tell me what they meant. I had to read the dictionary to look up the words. I read it the way you'd read a book, just to keep up with her."

A fair student, Hempel excelled in English, and while she knew early that she wanted to be a writer, she waves off her juvenile writing as "pathetic." More important than her practice exercises in writing, she claims, were the experiences which eventually supplied her with a book's worth of material.

In Denver, a close friend's house burned down, supplying her with the genesis for "Pool Night."

"I was just so moved by what the neighbors did for them," Hempel remembers. "They had enough money and insurance to replace the furniture and rebuild and all that, but all of the photo albums of the children had burned. All the neighbors got together and went through their own albums to find pictures of their kids with the other children, and they put together and gave them this album. 'Pool Night' started with this. . . ."

Then there was a particularly bad stretch in California. In less than a year's time, she was involved in two serious accidents, one on a motorcycle and another in a car, and between the two accidents, her mother died. In an interview for *The Short Story Review*, Hempel characterized this time as "everything [being] traumatic: upheaval wherever you looked."

It was during this period that she began to form a personal philosophy that became her central theme in *Reasons to Live*.

In "The Harvest," she writes about driving to the beach after her second accident, which had traumatized her to the point where she was afraid to drive. Doing so was a personal victory. Though her leg was scarred and still bandaged, she wore shorts. In her fictionalized account, she recalls:

> At the edge of the sand I unwound the elastic bandage and waded into the surf. A boy in a wetsuit looked at my leg. He asked me if a shark had done it; there were sightings of great whites along that part of the coast.
> I said that, yes, a shark had done it.
> "And you're going back in?" the boy asked.
> I said, "And I'm going back in."

What was left out of that story—and the Addendum to the story—was any detailing of the recovery process that led Hempel to her testing of real or metaphorical waters. The accidents left scars, mental and emotional, as well as physical; recovery required extraordinary measures and self-preservation.

"I found myself in a pretty morbid state of mind for some time, which is pretty normal, I think. I was afraid of dying and being injured, and I wanted to get out of that. The whole concern was so self-absorbed in a really morbid way. I enrolled in one of Kübler-Ross's 'Death and Dying' classes and, through a doctor friend, I made myself watch several autopsies. I took an anatomy class and dissected cadavers. I just was not going to be afraid of the body and what could happen to it. I thought I'd be better off if I could make myself view the whole thing from a scientific side, instead of the way I was doing it. And it absolutely worked."

For Hempel, the essence of life is a willingness to take oneself, scars and all, back into potentially dangerous waters. It is the final aspect of recovery and, generally, the final aspect of any of her stories. It is not enough to endure or survive; there has to be a triumph, however small.

"Suffering isn't enobling, recovery is," she says, quoting Dr. Christian Barnard. That, she explains, is the first element to her personal philosophy. The second can be found in the last line of her story, "The Man in Bogotá." In a story-within-a-story, Hempel writes about a wealthy man who was kidnapped and held for ransom. Since he was in poor health and the ransom was long in arriving, his captors had to keep him alive in order to have any hope of collecting their money. When he was finally released, a doctor examined him and declared him to be in good health—the result of the kidnappers forcing him to exercise and quit smoking. In her story's parting shot, Hempel has the man wondering "how we know that what happens to us isn't good."

"There you have it," she now concludes. "In the midst of all of everything that's happened, how do we know that what happens to us isn't good? That's what I come down to."

Her stories, however, aren't the standard grace-under-pressure fare being served up by a glut of post-Hemingway fiction practitioners. Her characters bear up, not because they feel compelled to face and overcome personal challenges, but mainly because they need to survive. There are very few romantic delusions in the short stories of Amy Hempel.

The biting edges, though, are often smoothed over by comic lines. Dark humor lurks in the darker corners of tragedy. In "Celia Is Back," the symptoms of a father's mental collapse are manifest when he attempts to help his children create a slogan for a sweepstakes: "I like Jell-O pudding because it has a tough satin finish that resists chipping and peeling. . . . Because it goes on dry to protect me from wetness longer." In "Going," another story about an automobile accident, she opens with her protagonist, badly injured and in the hospital, reading a menu that includes a typographical error announcing that "the pot roast will be *severed* with buttered noodles." The humorous touches are light—just enough to keep pain from being intolerable.

"I've always put a premium on humor," she says. "In California, one of my closest friends was a stand-up, improvisational comedian. I knew a number of comedians, and they were the people I most wanted to be with. In 'The Most Girl Part of You,' the first story I wrote after I finished the book and went a year without writing fiction, there's definitely a mixture of humor and horror that kind of dances the reader around."

Listing her favorite comic novels, she names Stanley Elkin's *The Franchiser* and *George Mills* as favorites. She also cites two works by friends, Nancy Lemann's *Lives of the Saints* and Christopher Coe's *I Look Divine*. She goes on to mention that there are pitfalls to injecting humor into serious stories, especially when those stories are presented at readings.

"I once interviewed Grace Paley for an article, and I asked her about reading aloud, and she said she tended not to choose a very sad or emotional story to read aloud because her stories always have humor, and that doesn't always work aloud. People laugh and continue laughing, and it throws the reader. Then there are always these surprises: You think you'll knock them over and no one responds, or they'll laugh at an odd place. It *is* interesting how you move a reader from one emotion to another, but it's hard for me to do."

The use of humor is only one aspect of her writing that sets her apart from some of her contemporaries. Almost as interesting is the lack of profanity or sexual content in her stories—especially today, when the two are taken for granted in serious fiction. She also avoids writing on trendy topics which might help boost book sales. Doing so, she says, doesn't interest her.

"There are people who do it better. Nancy Lemann and I were talking facetiously about how we could 'up' sales of our next books if we had some sex in our books. We were joking that her next book could be called *Sex Lives of the Saints*, and mine could be *Reasons to Love*. We started out joking and I wound up thinking: Why *don't* I write about sex?

"Well, there are a couple of reasons. Everybody out there is writing about it and, for the most part, I find it really embarrassing because it's not very well done. Also, my editor used to sort of spurn these relationship stories—he called them 'Boys and Girls'—and I don't want to do 'Boys and Girls.'

"Then, too, one of my favorite lines in all of literature is one that's never been published. My little brother once tried to write an erotic story when he was about twelve. When I read this piece of erotica by my twelve-year-old brother, it contained the line: 'Then he unzipped her negligee.' That just stayed with me forever. If I ever write about sex, it will sound like 'and then he unzipped her negligee.' I just know it would. It's like this sign that comes up when I get toward that territory."

⁓⁓⁓⁓⁓⁓⁓⁓⁓⁓

She describes her entry into fiction writing as a matter of "coming in sideways."

She attended several colleges in California, studied journalism, and came away with little to help her in a writing career. There were odd jobs and three separate attempts to relocate to New York, the first two finding her retreating to California when the going got tough. She worked for less than a year as a publicist at Putnam's, booking author tours and trying to place writers on talk shows. She worked as an editorial assistant at Crown Publishers. She drifted out to Breadloaf, where John Gardner and Stanley Elkin were teaching. She was living in California, no closer to the writer's life than she had been years earlier, when she was a student at Whittier College, when her best friend became ill and died.

"The day my friend was buried, I was on a plane. I didn't go to the funeral—I mean, I barely made it to the hospital. What that was to me was this huge kick in the pants. It kicked me from California to New York, and I just dug in for the duration. I got serious."

It was at this point that she enrolled in Gordon Lish's writing workshop at Columbia. Her first assignment was to write about a moment of personal failure, and she responded with "In the Cemetery Where Al Jolson Is Buried."

Today, the story is included in *The Norton Anthology of Short Fiction*.

At the end of the "Al Jolson" story, there is a memorable image of a mother chimpanzee which had been the first chimp taught sign language:

> In the course of the experiment, that chimp had a baby. Imagine how her trainers must have thrilled when the mother, without prompting, began to sign to her newborn.
> Baby, drink milk.
> Baby, play ball.
> And when the baby died, the mother stood over the body, her wrinkled hands moving with animal grace, forming again and again the words: Baby, come hug, Baby, come hug, fluent now in the language of grief.

In another story, "Nashville Gone to Ashes," Hempel's protagonist, a widow grieving her husband's death, admits: "I would like to think bigger thoughts. But it looks like I don't have a memory of our life that does not include one of the animals."

It is no coincidence that animals play a large role in Amy Hempel's fiction. Next to writing, caring for animals has been one of the most consistent influences on her life. As soon as you enter her apartment, you are introduced to Nefer, an Abyssinian cat that seems just a tad younger than Moses and who obviously rules the roost. The next thing you see is the conglomeration of animal magazines which appear to outnumber other available reading materials: *Dog Fancy, Cat Fancy, Gorilla Newsletter, Our Animals' Animals*—the list goes on. A poster of Koko, the first gorilla to be taught sign language, occupies a prominent spot on the wall of her study.

In 1986, *New York Woman* magazine asked Hempel to write a profile of Warren Beatty, an assignment she turned down in favor of writing an article on Dr. Stephen Kritsick, the veterinarian seen on "Good Morning America."

"Anyone who knows and loves animals is my kind of person," she wrote in the article. "Especially a good veterinarian, someone who has put that love to work. Because if I were not a writer, I would be a veterinarian. Period."

In the past, she has actively supported animal protection groups, and she lights up when the conversation turns to her love of animals. Flipping through the pages of a magazine, she invites equal enthusiasm from her audience. "Look at this little baby, this chubby little puppy body." She punctuates her comments with laughter, but there's no doubting that she is almost as passionate about her concern for animal welfare as she is about her writing.

"I really *did* want to be a veterinarian all my life," she insists. "I always did little, peripheral-related things. For a while, here in New York, I did work as a veterinarian's surgical assistant. The part I loved about the job was when the animals were returned to the kennels after surgery. They tend to panic when they start to come out of anesthesia because they don't know what's going on. They kick real hard and they can hurt themselves. So I would walk around to the various kennels, and when the animals were coming out of it, I could scoot myself into the cages. I put some of that direct experience into the 'Nashville' story."

Her images in "Al Jolson" meant even more to her later, when she met Koko. A simple magazine assignment turned out to be a powerful experience.

"It was one of the most extraordinary things that ever happened to me. She had real *personality*. She made jokes and asked me questions: *Was I thirsty?* She had this personality, yet it kept washing over me, as I sat there opposite her, that Koko is a gorilla. I was relating to her just as this personality.

"Koko lives with another gorilla, a male named Michael, who's a little younger and doesn't have the vocabulary she does, though he's catching up. Koko was born in the San Francisco Zoo, but Michael was orphaned from Africa. He was born in the jungle and brought over here. After Michael was given language, he told his teacher of his fear, terror, and sadness when he saw poachers kill his mother. Think about that! The ending of the 'Al Jolson' story was nothing I thought up—it's something that happened, that I heard about."

There are still times, she says, when she considers getting her degree in veterinary medicine. She has also considered going back to San Francisco and working with Koko full-time. But she concedes that these ideas are mostly fantasy.

She has other work to do.

We wind up talking about fear.

Again, we're reaching for the core, not the fears that can be fairly easily overcome, such as Hempel's fear of standing in front of an audience and giving readings, but the fears that freeze you in front of the proverbial headlights.

Amy Hempel's recent writings have dealt with fear, as well as loss. It's a fine-line separation: Her characters are still *coming through* something, only now they are responding to something immediately present, as opposed to something lost.

And, as was the case when she was writing about loss, she draws from personal experience when she writes about fear. One of her most recent stories is a case in point.

"It started out as an apology. A magazine offered me a free week at this incredible health spa in Mexico for a thousand-word piece. They sent me the tickets and I packed, went to LaGuardia, and boarded the plane, but before the plane took off, I got off. I used to do this with some regularity, but it had been years, and what I didn't know—and found out immediately—was that, these days, when you chicken out of a flight, they think you're getting off because you left something behind.

"So I held up a plane of almost three hundred passengers while the baggage handlers went through the hundreds of bags to find my suitcase, while the pilot and flight crew searched the overhead compartments and bathrooms for the bomb they thought I left, while I was interrogated by an airline official. I was mortified. They were treating me as though this was my idea of a prank, when it was a tremendous personal failure. I was deathly afraid and humiliated, but they didn't get that at all. I was on the verge of tears, and finally a lie occurred to me: I said, 'Well, if it helps you understand this any better, my husband died in a plane crash!' *Bingo!* Suddenly they were nice to me and it was all over. So the story is an apology to the passengers who may have missed their connecting flights because of me."

She finishes her anecdote by quoting a passage from Adrienne Rich: "Better to know the ways we are accursed and stand up fierce and glad to hear the worst."

Even today, years after she has moved to New York, Amy Hempel sets all of her stories in California. It is an interesting choice coming from someone who calls California "restorative" and admits that she has developed a "rather nasty attitude on the street" in New York. The San Andreas Fault may offer symbolism or metaphorical possibility to the writer concerned with the ways people survive living under constant threat of loss, but New York has a way of making threats clear and present dangers.

"In the last six weeks," she mentions, "I was robbed twice. I was held up at gunpoint in the subway, a block from my house. He took about two hundred and fifty dollars, but he didn't shoot me. A few weeks after that, while I was in Boston, my apartment was burglarized and they took everything and traumatized my poor, lovely cat, and I came home to this complete wreckage. I'm going to become like my friend in the East Village who rents Sam Peckinpah movies and fast-forwards to the massacres. And then, last night, as I was walking home from a writing class I teach at the West Side Y, a drunk spit in my face—a big gob, all over my forehead, down over my eye, and on my hair. And I'm thinking: 'New York—do I need this? Do I need this?' "

She chuckles, not because she survived, but because she knows she'll stay, despite the trials of living in the city.

She has her reasons—reasons that, in due time, will be considered and passed along.

PINCKNEY BENEDICT

Pinckney Benedict's voice has a *sound* to it. It's the kind of sound you associate with a stop at an old garage in some Southern state, a garage still owned by the grandson of the first mechanic who picked up an open-ended wrench in the place, and maybe there's a little paint left on the garage but probably not, more than likely it's blistered and peeled by now, exposing old gray weathered wood, and there's Queen Anne's lace growing out of the cracked concrete next to the premium pump, and (probably best of all) the place still has an antique Coke machine up next to the torn screen door, where you can buy a bottle of soda on a day so damned hot and dry you'd swear a high-pressure system's anchored itself in the back of your throat, and the guy in the gas station is wearing greasy blue coveralls and an incredibly stained baseball cap which looks like it was once green, which he tilts back when you ask directions, and he answers you in the kind of voice Pinckney Benedict has: "Hoo, boy, I'll tell ya. . . ." It's a ramblin' voice. You'll get directions and you'll get a story—maybe not in that order—but you're mostly going to hear a *sound* in that voice that seems to be older than the sun beating off the Marlboro sign out by the road. A voice that always seems to have a smile at its edge, yet it's as rich as the smell of a damp spring breeze blowing over freshly plowed fields.

The resonance of Benedict's West Virginia voice, as he ambles through a tale, almost belies the substance of a tragic, poignant story which so impressed him as a boy that he eventually found room for it in "Town Smokes," the title story of his first book, a collection of short stories.

"We had a bunch of beef cattle that we kept out in a field, and the field had a pond in it," he recollects. "And the pond, you know, it froze pretty hard near the banks and was pretty thin out in the middle. A bunch of cattle went out onto the ice and broke through and then, whenever they tried to get their feet up on the ice again, that ice would give because they were moving toward the center. So they just kept breaking these channels in the ice like icebreaker ships, and they got away. They probably lived for a half hour to an hour because, you know, they're real big-bodied and have a lot of warmth and stuff like that. But they finally did die. It was kind of weird: You had these trails going through the ice, and at the end of the trail, there was this dead beef steer."

Real life as metaphor, worked into a short story dense with Faulknerian colloquialism: Benedict admits, "I'd been trying to work that into a story for a long time," and he did. The same goes for a childhood incident involving a runaway white pig, a tale spun into mythical proportions by the time Benedict had worked and reworked the incident into a story. The creature wound up being a wild, renegade hog wreaking havoc on un-suspecting farmers and livestock, hiding in sink holes and at-tacking with Melvillean, killer ferocity. Even the behemoth's name—Booze—placed in the confines of the story, had a rubbed-to-fading sound distilled from a front-porch oral history tradition.

The stories, like the voice, have a *sound*.

> Echols Doolittle is a bootlegger that lives up in the hollers a couple miles beyond us, up on Tree Mountain. He is all the time haven to go up to the farm at Huttonsville to do short stretches. I hear tell some guys call him Iron Eyes 'cause he got no light of the soul in his face when he looks at you but is just blank and cold as river ice. . . .

This brief passage, taken from the story "All the Dead," rep-resents several important elements of Pinckney Benedict's fiction. Most apparent is the seasoned, colloquial flavor to the actual storytelling, along with a polished, built-in rhythm which speaks to the mind's ear: Even though you're reading the story, it *sounds* like it's being read to you, spoken aloud. Also important is Ben-edict's use of legend; in Benedict's neck of the woods, what you hear is almost as important as what you see, and his stories are packed with secondhand information, complete with the exag-geration that accompanies the retelling of any tale. The stories sound like they've been told repeatedly over the ages.

"I'm pleased if they read that way," Benedict says, when this is pointed out to him. "They are the kinds of things that I have thought about for a long time, and chunks of them have come out in different ways. For a long time, I had an idea about a guy sitting at the base of a statue of the Confederate dead, and that's actually been in several stories that weren't in the book—stories that I wrote for a workshop or whatever. Finally, I did drop it in 'All the Dead' and it found its home there. The cattle were in other stories before they were in 'Town Smokes.' Everybody who knows me well has heard the stories I love three or four times, and some of them tell me I'm repeating myself, and some of them are kind enough to listen to me over and over again."

Benedict's characters are hard-bitten and fiercely individualistic, dwellers of a rural area hit by a wind much different from the one blowing up refuse on Broadway or Sunset Boulevard. Farmers, moonshiners, pit-bull breeders—these characters are capable of anything. Rusted cars litter their dirt lawns; they roll their cigarettes in papers torn from the Bible. In its review of *Town Smokes, The New York Times Book Review* reported that "Mr. Benedict's people are the skulls they see in their Sears mirrors; his turf is the dismal sludge underneath the cartoon strokes of Al Capp's Dogpatch."

In short, these are people with different lives, different voices.

Being concerned with the sound of his stories often puts Benedict in contention with what he knows is grammatically correct on the printed page. His words are often abbreviated, clipped, or misspelled, his sentences inverted to represent the way people talk. One of the big tests, he says, is when he reads a new story aloud, a practice he finds almost essential to his work. "You can feel yourself stumbling, no question about it," he admits. "I read my stories aloud, to myself and to friends, whenever I can get folks to sit down and listen to me. That's a really important tool. I find myself editing even when I'm reading in front of an audience. I'll be dropping words and cutting stuff out."

This practice not only lends authenticity to the dialogue, but it also adds a flavor of intimacy to the narrative which sets up the tensions in a story. In "Rescuing Moon," a new story that was not a part of *Town Smokes*, Benedict opens with a tense scene which captures the oral tradition of his strongest stories:

> Mrs. Tencher checks me up and down. She is the lady that runs the place, and there is iron in that gaze. "Visiting hours is over," she says. "You just come back another time during the day and we'll see about letting you visit Mr. Potterfield." She don't like my looks any too much, that I can tell. I am a big man and never have been real what you call presentable. Plus the ride over was hot and hard

and I have sweated through my clothes under my arms and down my back, and that never does do much for the way you look.

"I come a long way, Mrs. Tencher," I say to her. She looks over my shoulder at where my old Dodge Dart is setting in the gravel drive. If it was a nice new Buick out there, or some kind of foreign job, she'd let me in, but I know by the set of her mouth she don't like the primer paint or the places where the chrome is dead-looking and milky, like an eye that has got a cataract. . . .

In a few of his stories, Benedict eliminates quotation marks altogether, a practice which achieves the populist, storytelling effect gained in the best of William Carlos Williams's "Doctor Stories." Benedict uses this style to distinguish one type of story narrator from the others in his book, and while the distinction may be very subtle, it is one that he feels is important nonetheless.

"It gives the stories a kind of flat, filtered reading," he says. "The narrators in those stories are not particularly dramatic people, so everything is through their consciousness. There's nothing that they report that isn't the way they *think* it is, in addition to what actually *might* have been said. There's nothing apart from the way they narrate."

Even the misspellings are major points of style, present in some stories, absent in others, which Benedict believes add to their sense of being narrated aloud. "It occasionally has effects I really don't want, but I wanted them to get the sound. The word 'having' becomes the word 'haven,' and that's a problem, but I decided that it wasn't too much of a problem, so I kept it."

Finding the right combinations of style and voice ultimately boiled down to a lot of writing and experimentation. Benedict's early stories—"Booze," written when he was a sophomore in college, and "The Sutton Pie Safe" and "Fat Tuesday," written a year later—are much more traditional in narrative and style than the stories he wrote in subsequent years. The longer

Benedict wrote, the more his stories were carried by their own voices rather than by the author's own intervention. Part of this evolution can be traced to Benedict's maturation as a writer, which is especially apparent when you read his stories in chronological order, and part of it can be attributed to a "discovery" Benedict made during his junior year at Princeton. "Up until that time, I had been writing real straightforward stuff," he says. "Then I read Madison Bell's story 'The Naked Lady,' and I realized some of the possibilities of what you can do with voice and character. Then I moved into stories like 'All the Dead' and 'Town Smokes.' "

His continuing interest in the storytelling tradition, Benedict goes on to explain, is a combination of the literature he enjoyed as a student and reader, and his appreciation for the way stories were told in his part of the country. He lists Eudora Welty, Carson McCullers, Flannery O'Connor, and Robert Stone as favorite authors, but his main influence is Breece D'J Pancake, a fellow West Virginian and short story writer who, in 1979, committed suicide at age twenty-six.

"For a long time, I have thought of him as a kind of literary older brother," Benedict says. "I feel almost mystical about him in some ways, I guess, because we were from the same state and he died so tragically and people cared very deeply about his work. I've read his book a number of times, and so many of the places he writes about are so close to where I live, places where I've been. It's such powerful stuff."

Much of that power, Benedict thinks, might be attributed to the region. Benedict places most of his stories in mountain country—a ways removed from the flat, agricultural area where he was raised—mainly because there's a mythical quality to the former, as if its rugged terrain, typified by miles on end of deep forests, is caught in a bygone era. For Benedict, "the mountainous regions seem like wonderful places, where the structure of the life we've gotten used to in the late part of the twentieth century breaks down somewhat and it's easier for amazing, story-like things to occur."

Home, to Pinckney Benedict, is a dairy farm near Lewisburg that's been in his family for three generations. It is a place where he is comfortable, where he feels no urgency to be someone he's not. On the front cover of *Town Smokes*, he is pictured, in a photograph taken from the back and from a good distance, walking down a country road, a huge saw hoisted across his shoulders. Here, he seems as happy talking about his family as he is about discussing his fiction.

"There were a lot of tale-spinning relatives that came around," he says. "My mother's uncle was a guy named Uncle Hunter, and he was kind of a mountain man. He had a camp up above the Jackson River, near Covington, Virginia, and he lived up there and used to shoot snakes and stuff like that. He didn't have a wife, and when we were kids, that always seemed pretty strange to us. We didn't understand that. And Mom would tell us to go ask Uncle Hunter about what happened to his wife. He'd turn around and say 'The hogs et her.' He was really something. That's where the word 'et' comes from for me, and I put it in a line in 'Booze.' "

His father is the farm's chief mechanic and bookkeeper, his older brother its manager. Benedict jokes that he knows how to change a tire, but he's far from being mechanically inclined— a prerequisite for life on the farm. He was the creative one, the one with the book brains.

"Mom is from the Shenandoah Valley of Virginia, and she's very proud of that Virginia heritage," he says. "That is a large part of her makeup. She's very small—four-eleven and three-quarters or something—but she will tell you that she's five feet tall. She went to Hollins, which is a women's college in Virginia, and apparently they measured her down there and told her she was four-eleven and three-quarters, and she said, 'No, I'm *five feet* tall.'

"Now, Dad is just shy of six feet tall, and my concept of him has always been that he's very tall because when he stands next to my mother, he looks like he's a very tall person. He's real thin, and he's in good shape, boy. He runs all the time and, of course, he works on the farm. My brother's real skinny and very muscular. So I got to be the short, heavy one—which is hell, but I'm bearing up under it."

He laughs as if he'll never get over it. This is *his* story, after all, and he'll tell it with as much spin to it as he decides it warrants. Exaggeration, he'll tell you, is the color that storytellers from his part of the country like to add to their tales. As is a smattering of self-deprecation, which not only spices up a story but keeps its teller honest. He loves telling about people's reactions to his announcement that he was going to attend Princeton.

"To people here, Princeton is a town about seventy miles south of us. Now that's very strange, because Princeton in West Virginia is in Mercer County, and Princeton in New Jersey is in a county of the same name. So when you say you're going to Princeton, everybody says 'Oh, well, at least you're close to home.' " A little later, he'll get around to explaining that Princeton is his father's alma mater. He'll also mention that his mother wanted to be a writer, and that both parents, avid readers themselves, encouraged him to follow his dream, although it probably would have been in the family's best interests if he'd stuck around to work on the farm.

Benedict characterizes life on the farm as being a lot of hard work, often filled with the violence or natural cruelty that eventually took on metaphorical proportions in his fiction. "I had a tiny flock of Banty chickens, and I had to feed them," he remembers, starting up another story. "I used to go out in the morning, and there was always some new tragedy in the Banty community. Something was always dead or had had its toes chewed off or whatever. It was pretty ungodly. We used to have a lot of trouble with rats. At night, we had the chickens in a hutch with a wire floor to it. We didn't have a stick or anything for them to roost on, so they would grip the wire from the hutch. And the rats used to tunnel up under the hutch and nip off their toes. It took us a long time to figure out what was going on, so we had all these kind of stump-toed chickens out there."

A natural storyteller as a boy, he enjoyed spinning tales for his family and friends, though he filed away the more brutal examples of rural life; even today, he views these events as facts of life, attaching no particular significance to them until symbolic possibilities present themselves during the writing of a story. A writer, Benedict believes, cannot force his symbols without running the risk of watching them fail.

Rural childhood life, Benedict recollects, was also filled with simple pleasures which, he later learned, were considered less than sophisticated by writers brought up in the city. "Booze" includes a number of fragments from his childhood, including his love for hunting. Guns play a role in a number of Benedict's stories.

"When I was about eight years old, Mom and Dad gave me an old Savage Arms .22 pump. It had been my grandfather's, and I thought it was really cool, the way that pump made a sound. I used to run around with that a lot. In 'Booze,' I talk about two kids who had a pair of rifles, one a Savage .22 pump and the other a semi-auto. That was me and Scott Powell. We actually had those rifles.

"We had this thing called a sink hole, which we used to dump our junk and stuff into. You'd see dishwashers and lawnmowers in there, and at the very bottom of it, there was an old Pontiac. We'd shoot the hell out of this Pontiac—a lot of rim-fire stuff."

This became part of the setting for "Booze," Then, of course, there was the runaway pig itself, which Benedict used as a symbol in his "human versus nature" story. A white renegade pig did exist, running loose on the Benedict farm, but Benedict used all his powers of imagination and exaggeration to build it into the raging boar of his story. "First of all, it wasn't anything like that size, and we never really ran into it. It ran onto our farm and disappeared. People would talk about it and say that they'd give you money if you shot it dead, but we never did. We found the skull of a pig one day, and everybody swore that, by God, that was the one, that was the white pig." Not quite the same as a teenaged boy, standing in the middle of a field, waiting to fell a mad, charging beast, as detailed in "Booze," but the incident captured Benedict's imagination.

Like most people fondly remembering their childhoods, Benedict views these times as being innocent. Natural violence was taken for granted. To his dismay, it was not a sentiment shared by his colleagues at the Iowa Writers' Workshop, which he attended for postgraduate studies. "Pit," his gory tale about the murder of a pit-bull breeder, written early in Benedict's attendance at Iowa, was greeted with scorn.

"People thought it was far too violent," Benedict says. "They felt that there was a lot of gratuitous violence, and they didn't understand the juxtaposition of the violence and the humor. They didn't like the tone: They thought I wasn't serious enough about my subject."

The criticism was not unlike the negative remarks written about Robert Omstead's *River Dogs,* another collection of short stories set in rural areas and focusing on less-than-savory characters and events. Benedict bristles when it's suggested that stories of this nature may always be frowned upon by the academics who encourage truth in fiction as long as the truth is politically or socially correct.

"People didn't like the character of Brunty [the protagonist of "Pit"], and they thought, 'Well, if we don't like this guy, and we wouldn't want to *be* him or be *with* him, why should we care to read about him?' I'm sorry to see that kind of criticism. It's limited because you wonder what you would do with, say, Graham Greene's *Brighton Rock.*"

Benedict ranks "Pit" as one of his favorite stories, and he now regards the fact that it was published at all a miracle of fortunate timing. Shortly after he finished the story, he put it in the mail to Joyce Carol Oates and Raymond Smith, his eventual publishers at the Ontario Review Press, for appraisal. The story was in the mail the day it was critiqued at Iowa.

"I'm glad I put it in the mail before I took it to workshop, because I never would have shown it to them if I'd been afraid that I would get the kind of reaction I got from the workshop people. When I found out that Joyce and Ray thought the story was good, I wasn't as hurt by the negative criticism. But, you know, it *does* kind of leave you at a loss for equilibrium. I hope I'm developing that kind of sureness where I can look at something myself and say 'This is good and I don't give a damn.' But it's hard to do, and I'm not nearly as good at it as I would like to be or that I probably should be."

Pinckney Benedict's writing career really began when he enrolled in Princeton's writing program and took a fiction writing course from Joyce Carol Oates. She began as his teacher, and wound up being his publisher and mentor.

"I wanted to be in her class because I knew who she was," Benedict recalls. "To get in, we had to turn in a piece we had written. In my senior year of high school, I had done an independent study which was writing eight short stories, and I used one of those as a writing sample. I got into her class the spring of my freshman year, and we got along very well."

Benedict glows when he talks about having Oates as a teacher. Although she was brutally honest, she was sympathetic and encouraging to young writers, and her firm-but-gentle approach was what Benedict needed to develop the discipline necessary to write his fiction. He especially appreciated Oates's practice of assigning her students readings of young writers who were just breaking through. "Very often, she had us read the writing of folks who were not that much older than we were, writers who were in their twenties or early thirties, just so we could see that that it was really possible. You know: Crank it up a notch or two—fine-tune it that much more—and you're actually one of them.

"She's a phenomenal editor, and she's very clear about what she is looking for and what her criteria are. She does excellent line editing of a story, and she'll do it with you. She sits down in front of the class and runs through a story—sometimes on a very minute level—and explains what's good and what is not good. It's a little hard to take sometimes, because she can be *extremely* honest. Obviously, that's good because she's far more motherly than a lot of critics you're going to run into, if you want to write as a professional. You really do have to learn to deal honestly with your material or you don't stand a chance in hell.

"One time, I had a story that I had written, which she had critiqued and hadn't particularly liked, and I rewrote it and turned it in a second time. We were all sitting around before class one day, and she was talking to somebody and she turned to me and said, 'Pinckney, do you know the expression "money down a rathole"?' I said I did, and she said, 'Good,' and turned away again and left me to think about that. I didn't ever pick that story up again."

The stories she did like, however, were given unusual care. Benedict's first published story, "Town Smokes," was printed in the *Ontario Review*, the literary magazine edited by Oates and her husband, Raymond Smith; the magazine later published "Dog," Benedict's tale about a man having to confront and shoot a rabid dog, and the Ontario Review Press included "Town Smokes" in its anthology *The Ways We Live Now*. Oates also encouraged Benedict to enter his work in literary competitions. Two stories, "The Sutton Pie Safe" and "Town Smokes," won consecutive *Transatlantic Review* awards—which Benedict calls "a real shot in the arm" to his early career. For three straight years, Oates encouraged Benedict to enter the Nelson Algren Award competitions; he won the first place prize in 1986, on his third attempt, for "The Sutton Pie Safe," his tale of a wealthy woman's attempt to purchase an heirloom from an impoverished country family. Benedict was twenty-two years old at the time. Before he had even graduated from Princeton, Benedict found himself a sort of literary celebrity.

The short stories, he says today, don't come easy. ("I'm not a particularly fast or prolific writer," he mentions. "Sometimes I feel like I'm moving in slow motion.") He mulls them over in his head for a long time before he sets out to write, making sure he has everything the way he wants it, fitting all the components together with all the care and precision his father might apply to fixing a large piece of machinery.

"I'll spend weeks or months kind of *pretending* that I'm writing," he says, laughing. "I'll think about what I'm going to do and change my mind a lot and take notes and read people who I've heard are similar to what I'm thinking about doing, and then I'll do a draft in about two days. I'll try to get a good foothold on it in one sitting—you know, five or ten pages—and then I'm not scared to sit down to it the next time."

Benedict is hard-pressed to explain where his ideas come from. Despite the planning, he never enters into the writing with all of a story's events and symbolism planned, and he never works from an outline. The best stories, he says, are the result of a "subconscious process" working in tandem with his writer's instincts. An overheard conversation at a restaurant, a few scraps from his childhood, a couple of quick stories that have been stewing in his mind for a while—all come together almost spontaneously, giving a story its direction and sense of purpose.

"It's always great to ride a train or sit in a restaurant and listen to what the people behind you are talking about," he says, adding that such eavesdropping can set the writer up for an embarrassing scene if he's caught in the act. "It's astonishing to me how often whatever is being said around you conforms to what you're working on or what you're planning to work on. You'll think: 'My God, that's the line I've been waiting for!' "

The most difficult part of writing, he continues, is finding the endings for his stories. Unlike many writers, Benedict does not have his beginnings and endings planned before he starts a story—or, if he does know how a story's going to go, he has to resist the impulse to put a quick ending on a story that has been giving him trouble. Doing so, he says, not only makes an ending look contrived or rushed, but it upsets the sense of the story's being *told* by a narrator who has all the time in the world to tell his story. "It's a terrible impulse," he admits, "and I do find myself doing that. I never get an ending right the first time—I generally don't get it right the third or fourth time, either. It takes me forever."

Benedict still solicits opinions about his short stories. He continues to submit his work to Joyce Carol Oates and Raymond Smith, and he checks with his father whenever he has a question about the technical matters which play such a great role in his stories. "I will never question what he has to say, because he has this incredible knowledge of the physical and mechanical worlds. If there's a rifle or a tractor or something in the story, and it gets past him, then I know I've got it right."

Benedict was a senior at Princeton when Joyce Carol Oates and Raymond Smith decided that he had nearly enough material for a book of short stories. Benedict had written seven stories that they felt were worthy of a collection, including the two that had been previously published and had won awards. "Water Witch" and "Pit," stories written while Benedict attended graduate school at the University of Iowa, are the last two additions to the collection, and they are two of his most technically accomplished works, combining Benedict's obsessions with the "sound" of the printed word and the theme of rural violence. The flat declarative sentences, coupled with Benedict's ear for dialogue, create an unflinching look at people who manage to survive, if only for a while, without any hope:

> "You ought not to of called me a dead man," he said to Sue. It was the first time this thought had occurred to him, that he should be insulted by her calling him that. She had her back to him, putting together an egg sandwich for him. She knew he liked an egg sandwich when he was hungry.
>
> "I ain't dead yet," he said to her. He took the plate with the sandwich on it out of her hands. He felt more like eating now. He hadn't been sure he wanted to eat before, but with the sandwich in front of him he felt like he could put something down after all.

"I guess not," she said, looking at him. "But what kind of future you figure you got, the man that put the knife into Paxco?"

"I might do okay," he said. He took a bite of the sandwich and it tasted good to him. He figured that a man that had an appetite was a man that could go on living for a while. . . .

Published in 1987, *Town Smokes* received strong notices from those who read and commented on the book. "Beware the wise who are young and gifted," wrote Russell Banks in a blurb for the book. "They become irreplaceable. And with these first stories, Pinckney Benedict, who is not merely precocious, shows convincingly that he is one of them." In another blurb, Eudora Welty opined that "we are beyond question in the presence of a strong talent." Diane McWhorter, reviewing the book for *The New York Times Book Review*, commented that "Mr. Benedict has taken big risks—particularly in using a dialect that, failing perfect pitch, could have badly got on one's nerves—and his prose achieves excellent harmony between voice and virtuosity"; she concluded that *Town Smokes* was a "fiercesome debut."

Now at work on a novel, Benedict feels no compulsion to quickly follow up his first book, nor is he worried about finding a larger publisher for his novel. He's quite pleased with the way the Ontario Review Press published his book and by the reception it's picked up, and he's content to work at his own pace without concerning himself with plans for mapping out a long-term career or topping his previous efforts.

"My favorite stories aren't necessarily the ones that pulled down the awards," he points out, adding that he prefers certain stories for their literary accomplishment, others for the way they sound when he reads them. "I intend to keep going at the pace I'm going at, and maybe two or three years from now I'll have something else done. I don't see myself in terms of having to write five novels or anything like that. I'm having trouble seeing beyond the next short story."

The sound of his laughter, like the sound of his voice or his stories, reaffirms associations in your mind. You can picture

Pinckney Benedict carrying a load up a rural dirt road. He doesn't mind the weight of the burden, and he doesn't mind the journey, wherever he's going. If you hurry and catch up to him, he'll stop for a rest somewhere up ahead.

Then he'll tell you a story.

SEYMOUR LAWRENCE

Seymour Lawrence loves to tell the story about the day a tall, thin novelist approached him at the Iowa Writers' Workshop. Lawrence had read the author's work, and he had sent the man a letter saying that he would be happy to publish him if he was ever looking for a publisher.

"I'm a bad financial risk," Lawrence remembers the novelist telling him. "None of my books have ever sold in hardcover. Are you sure you want to publish me?"

The novelist was Kurt Vonnegut, and Lawrence was certain he wanted to publish him.

"We gave him a contract, and we published *Welcome to the Monkey House*, his book of stories, before we published the novels. The first book of his famous three-book contract, which enabled him to leave Iowa and return to Barnstable on the Cape, was *Slaughterhouse-5*, and that was his breakthrough book. We advertised it heavily and we had good reviews. We then bought back, with his help, the earlier titles—*Player Piano*, *The Sirens of Titan*, *Mother Night*, *Cat's Cradle*, and *God Bless You, Mr. Rosewater*—and we reissued everything in Dell paperbacks. We had posters with his picture which went to all the college bookstores and other bookstores that had all the titles. That's how the 'Vonnegut sweep' happened: The underground was already there, on the colleges; we simply took advantage of it."

Nearly a decade later, a young West Virginia writer approached Lawrence at the St. Lawrence Writers' Conference. She had a small collection of one-page stories, entitled *Sweethearts*, which had been published by a small press. She was hoping that Lawrence, working then as an independent publisher for Delacorte Press, would take a look at the collection, and while Lawrence told her he didn't publish story collections if he could help it, he took the book.

"I thought they were wonderful," Lawrence says of the stories, "and I told her, 'Why don't you write a novel, and maybe we'll offer you a contract for a novel and a book of stories.' But she's a very determined woman, so I asked her to send me her book of stories in manuscript."

He recalls her sending him the manuscript, titled *The Heavenly Animal*, toward the end of the summer, shortly before she was to leave for a teaching job in Humboldt, California. He thought the language and imagery in the stories were extraordinary, "virtuoso sweeps of imagination," and he was eager to publish her.

However, he was still less than thrilled with the title of her book, so he and the author, Jayne Anne Phillips, looked over her list of potential titles and settled on *Black Tickets*. Another career had been launched.

There seems to be a story behind each of his authors. As an editor and independent publisher for over thirty-five years, Seymour Lawrence has discovered or worked with some of the most highly respected writers of contemporary fiction, including Vonnegut, Thomas Berger, Robert B. Parker, Tillie Olson, Katharine Anne Porter, and a number of others who will be mentioned below. He had his publishing imprint with Delacorte from 1964 to 1982, and published through Dutton from then until 1987. He currently works through Houghton Mifflin. At the time of our conver ation, he had ten authors on his current publishing list: Barry Hannah, Jayne Anne Phillips, Thomas McGuane, Tim O'Brien, Mary Ward Brown, Jim Harrison, William Kotzwinkle, Susan Minot, Frank Conroy, and Richard Currey.

In its "Who's Who in the Cosmos 1987," *Esquire* listed Lawrence as one of the "editors more important than their houses." It is a label that Lawrence disputes.

▴▴▴▴▴▴▴▴▴▴

You don't consider yourself an editor?

I'm not an editor. I'm a publisher, and that's a whole different thing. I look at an author's work and try to figure out the best way of launching it. I think of editors as line editors, or people who edit manuscripts, and I was an editor twenty-five years ago.

I never really enjoyed editing. What I always enjoyed was the discovery of talent and the launching of it—the promotion, if you will, of the book and an author, and all of the details such as choosing jacket art and bindings and flap copy.

People often ask me how I choose the authors, and I'll say that it's very hard to explain. Often, I don't explain it. I'll say that it's an intuitive thing. Well, it *is* intuitive, but it is also really based on two things: language and vision. Vonnegut and Donleavy and Brautigan are all very different—they all have unique visions—yet they're all concerned with language. That's what interests me—language and individual vision. I'm not interested in having a lot of volume. I'm looking for quality. We have ten authors, and I think they all are, or will be, literary stars, if you want to call them that. I wait, for months at a time, without signing any new author. Occasionally, the agents will offer them to us, but in a lot of instances, the authors will come to us. Or they'll be referred.

For example, we just signed up an author named Richard Curry, who has written a beautiful book about the Vietnam War. It has marvelous, cadenced language, but it also has the brutality of war. Jayne Anne Phillips knew him and referred him to us. He had the same background as she: He wrote a book that was published by a small press and had an underground reputation. We read it about two years ago, and we were sort of half-and-half about it. It was very short, and we asked him to expand it. He did, and it just bowled us over. Everybody who's read it is very excited. This is the discovery of a new talent.

I met Susan Minot at a literary reception. I was introduced to her by Morgan Entreken, a young editor who knows Gary Fisketjon and who works with him as an independent editor. They introduced her to me. They told her, "You better watch out, if he reads your story in *Grand Street* he'll give you a contract." And I said, "I'll give you a contract right now." *(laughs)* But I did read the story, and I felt that she was a really perceptive writer able to compress a great deal of what she was writing about—family life—into one story. I thought she could write a novel based on that, so we gave her a contract. Shortly after that, another story appeared in *The New Yorker*, and then another, and the book developed. She wrote the chapters, or the stories, into a book called *Monkeys*, and she had one of the most highly praised books of the year. It sold very, very well, which is unusual for a literary first novel.

A lot of writers come to me. Tom McGuane liked what I'd done with his friend, Jim Harrison, so he said he'd like to publish with me. Jayne Anne Phillips really wanted to be on our list because I'd published Tillie Olson, whom she admired so much, and Katharine Anne Porter. Tim O'Brien came to my office one day and said he wanted to be on my list because he admired Vonnegut and Donleavy and Brautigan. He just walked in with a manuscript of *Combat Zone*.

How did you get involved in this business in the first place? How did you move from being an editor to being a publisher?

When I entered Harvard, at eighteen, two of the first people I met were Robert Creeley and John Hawkes, and we took over a magazine called *The Harvard Wake*, which had not been doing very well. I became the editor-in-chief at the end of my freshman year, because the others were not that interested in editing and publishing and I was. We began to publish people of national reputation. We had poetry by Marianne Moore, Wallace Stevens, and William Carlos Williams. Issue Five was an e. e. cummings issue. Creeley's first works were in *The Wake*, as were the first poems by Richard Wilbur, who became our laureate. It got an international reputation because of the new young authors, as well as the established writers, that we published. I edited that for the whole time I was at Harvard and that is how I actually became interested in publishing.

After I graduated from Harvard in '48, I decided I wanted to continue the magazine as an annual, and Harvard allowed me to do so provided I drop the "Harvard" from its name. So it was called *Wake*, and I was responsible for any debts and printing bills. I did that until '52, when I was hired by *The Atlantic Monthly* as a special assistant to the editor. My mission, as it were, was to bring good American fiction to *The Atlantic*, and I did. One of them was Richard Yates, who was an "Atlantic First."

But I was more interested in the book publishing end of *The Atlantic* than the magazine, so they decided to make me an associate editor of the Atlantic Monthly Press. I brought in *The Last Hurrah*, by Frank O'Connor, which became a number-one best-seller and made a lot of money, and a year later, when I was twenty-eight, they made me the director of the Atlantic Monthly Press. I published Yates's *Revolutionary Road*, and we published the work of Brian Moore. I worked for several years with Katharine Anne Porter on her big novel, *Ship of Fools*, and we became very close; she became my daughter's godmother.

And then we did other books. We published Howard Nemerov's novel and his poetry. We published John Malcolm Brinnin. We did Nobel Prize winner George Sefaris, whom I had published earlier in *Wake*. And Donleavy . . .

There was quite a controversy about your publishing him, wasn't there?

Yes. The owner of the Atlantic—a very rich woman who was an absentee owner—felt that he was an obscene writer, and she didn't want me to publish A *Singular Man*. She didn't want an author like that on the Atlantic list because she felt it would besmirch the image of Atlantic in the schools and colleges. I was the youngest member of the Board of Directors then, and I fought against her and the rest of the board. I said, "This is a work of literature. It's not immoral or amoral." I won the battle but lost the war: I published A *Singular Man* and it was highly praised, but she then curtailed my whole list. She didn't want me to publish foreign writers, or writers like Donleavy, so I had to resign. That kind of restriction was just unacceptable to me.

Then, lo and behold, I got a phone call from Alfred Knopf, who'd heard about this. He and his wife, Blanche, asked if I would be their vice president. Alfred Knopf had been my role model when I was at Harvard—he and Maxwell Perkins. I knew I was going to be a publisher when I was eighteen or nineteen, and I had read all the letters of Perkins, over and over again, and I thought Knopf books were just the best, in terms of design and production and the quality of the list.

So I commuted between Boston, where I lived, and New York. But I really didn't enjoy corporate life. I didn't want to work for a corporation—I wanted to work independently—so, after six months, I decided to resign. I went back to Boston and, for three or four months, I tried to get a joint publishing arrangement with a publishing house. Donleavy, in fact, was the one who urged me. He said, "What you have to do to be a publisher is have one room, a phone, and one author—and I'm that author."

That's how I began. I made an arrangement with Delacorte and Dell to be copublishers, and my first book, in 1965, was the unexpurgated edition of *The Ginger Man*.

Thomas Victor

JAYNE ANNE PHILLIPS

Still, you and I will go on and on, despite whatever differences, whatever quarrels. For me, we are what's left. How are we different? Body and soul, I know—but some things don't change.

—from *Machine Dreams*

"There's nothing more moving than hearing somebody talk," Jayne Anne Phillips is saying. "To hear a beautician talk about what happens during the day is more interesting to me than a well-crafted short story. I guess I've always been more interested in that kind of oral history than in anything else."

Phillips is talking about Studs Terkel, a writer and oral historian she greatly admires. But she could just as easily be describing her own work. Her three books—a novel, *Machine Dreams*, and two volumes of short stories, *Black Tickets* and *Fast Lanes*—are as much oral history as they are fiction. The voices of her characters are authentic, speaking with conviction. Instead of playing back and transcribing tapes of recorded conversations, as Terkel does when he prepares a book, Phillips listens to the dialogues of her imagination—American voices which have remained constant through the ages, despite changes in the world. In Phillips's fiction, you get a sense of history in terms of people and voices, rather than through dates and events. What her characters are telling you is urgent, moving.

"I think it has to do with the idea of bearing witness, of having someone tell about having lived through something," she says, explaining her preference for telling her stories through voices over presenting them in more traditional narrative style. "It's only in that kind of first-person voice that you get the type of detail that begins to set up associations in your mind. It makes what happened *real*. That's what fiction can do for history."

It's strange what you don't forget. . . .

So begins *Machine Dreams*, a stirring, lyrical novel about the disintegration, over a three-generation span, of a West Virginia family. There is something familiar about Phillips's Hampson family: Their voices, though far from being imitative, carry at their edges a ghostly presence resonant of the voices found in works by William Faulkner, Carson McCullers, Eudora Welty, or even Tennessee Williams. The Hampsons are confounded by the loss of tradition, by the voices of machines, whispered or screamed, ushering in a new way of life which depends more upon technology's futuristic view than on images of the past. The Hampsons represent a changing of the guard: Their children's children, rather than sit on the porch and talk long into the night as their elders did, will fall asleep before a VCR showing a movie they've already seen. One reads this novel with the same vague uneasiness you feel when you hear that they have to layer bodies at the cemetery because they're running out of room.

Jayne Anne Phillips has not only found an important seam in the fabric of American consciousness, but she seems to have defied the odds in doing so. As part of the rock 'n' roll generation, she is a witness to a popular philosophy that insists that we live for the present because the Nuclear Age has deprived us of our past and future. Her literary peers are assembling an impressive body of work which reflects this concern, and while her fiction —with its thematic interest in the rootlessness and aimlessness of modern America—surely underscores some of those same concerns, her strength lies in the sensibility to juxtapose past and present in work which defines *and* defies the future.

The epigraphs to *Machine Dreams* bring this into clear focus. One, taken from Hesiod's *The Theogony*, speaks of the force of Pegasus, the winged horse in Greek mythology; the other, drawn from a song by performance art musician Laurie Anderson, talks of the power of the jet, modern civilization's new god of space-age technology. There is particular irony in the use of Pegasus, for there was a time, when people traveled coast to coast by car more than they do today, when a Pegasus was the logo for one of the country's major oil companies, as common on roadsides as the now-extinct Burma Shave signs were. Even the symbols of progress eventually become historical footnotes.

There is no question that Jayne Anne Phillips possesses a powerful sense of historical perspective in her fiction, especially in longer works such as *Machine Dreams*, and her novella, "Fast Lanes." Her characters *are* bearing witness, though in an unconscious way, to the ways their lives and times fit into a historical spectrum.

It is a crucial issue to Phillips, personally and artistically. In a *New York Times Book Review* essay on the future of fiction, she wrote: "American writers in particular must concern themselves with a history of the spirit in personal and (intrinsically) national terms, with an exploration of what survives as American, with what continues, with matters of loss and strength."

When asked if she sees a writer's role as that of a historian, she explains that she believes "writers are observing and incorporating history into their work whether they set out to do so or not. I don't think being a historian should necessarily come first in priorities. What I meant is that when I read a piece of fiction, I like to have a sense of its relating in some way to the world, not simply to some kind of inner angst. And I'm not saying that inner angst is necessarily a bad subject, because something like *Notes from the Underground* is a totally interior piece, but it reflects very directly on a whole society.

"If a work is good, it will automatically address the times. I see time and history as a continuum, so if you present a realistic, understandable picture of a period of time, it's going to relate directly to where we are now. Your own vision of how you fit into the world, and your vision of how the world works, is what should be in the piece."

Written partially in the style of oral history, *Machine Dreams* contains the nuances, dialects, and poetry of natural speech in a manner similar to the voices heard in Faulkner's *As I Lay Dying*. Phillips accredits Faulkner as a major influence—"I think Faulkner was an influence to anybody who grew up in or near the South"—along with writers like James Agee, Eudora Welty, and Katharine Anne Porter, but she also believes the storytelling tradition of her youth, the colloquial tradition of oral history, was instrumental in her obsessive interest in the sound of spoken language.

"I've always been really interested in voices and the way they sound," she says. "I'm interested in telling a story with voice alone, rather than with a kind of train of events. I very much wanted that to be in [*Machine Dreams*], in a sense of hearing people talk—and the *way* they talk—in a kind of circular motion, rather than in a beginning-middle-and-ending way. I think it's a challenging thing for a writer to try to get down on paper."

A reader might approach *Machine Dreams* the way one pages through a well-kept family photograph album: You sense the passage of time by what is contained in each framed moment, and how the faces and styles change from frame to frame, and though it is impossible to completely capture entire lifetimes in this context, you still feel as if you have witnessed them. Phillips's snapshots are verbal "takes" filtered through the selective memories of her characters:

> I had my thirty-fifth birthday on the train—cake with candles, and ice cream. Red Cross girls kept all that information on us, must have been their idea to celebrate. They were nice girls. The men got a kick out of it and joined in with the singing. The train was hitting rough track about then, and one of the girls (she was from Ohio, I believe) came walking down the aisle carrying a big square cake, lurching from side to side and trying to keep the candles lit. The way the car was jolting and shaking made me think of the boat crossing to the Philippines. . . .

In *Machine Dreams*, Phillips's use of holidays serves several purposes, all suited to unite the various aspects of Phillips's main theme—falling away from tradition, using the crumbling of the Hampson family as the book's major symbol. Holidays, and the traditional celebrations surrounding them, tend to stick in the selective memories of people, and Phillips used them not only as reference points but as a means of contrasting the changes taking place over the years. Almost all holidays are recalled in *Machine Dreams*, yet they are presented in different years, at varying time gaps, affording Phillips and her characters an overview of the time continuum.

"Those kinds of rituals connect one year to another," Phillips explains. "I mean, people observed Christmas in 1910, and in 1930, and in 1950, and those observations changed. I think those rituals are our culture in America, and I wanted to put some of those rituals down on paper because, in a way, they are changing a great deal and disappearing.

"Different things that are in the book have changed. For instance, some town festivals and parades have changed. They have gotten bigger, with this whole trend to get bigger and better. It's become less of a representation of the local thing, and other

small-town entertainments, like drive-in movies and drive-in restaurants, don't exist anymore."

There are, however, plenty of fast-food restaurants, which serve,
more than any examples immediately coming to mind, as symbols
of the way marketing has become a dominating factor in day-to-
day existence in the latter part of the century. American fiction
has not been exempt from the country's obsession with product
identification. Brand names conjure up instant reader associations with the product and what it stands for, and more and more
fiction writers are using brand names to achieve the association
effect—often at the cost of what Phillips calls "shutting the lens
too tight." The readers wind up focusing too much on a quick
flash and not enough on the sense of the importance behind the
flash.

"I think part of what fiction can do in the twentieth century
is offer access again to the kinds of mythology that really underlie
popular culture, to the gigantic ideas and images that are boiled
down and mass produced until they begin to lose a lot of meaning.
As a writer, you have to look at it as though you were a child
and it's new and the reader doesn't understand it, as if these
things had never been seen before. If you're writing with a child's
mind about, say, a Coca-Cola sign, you're talking about it in a
way that elevates it to something more than just an emblem. It's
new to the voice that's speaking, in the context of being viewed
by an outsider. If you use what's real and get beyond it, you make
all those emblems serve the material you're writing about."

What makes Phillips's works especially effective is the way they
balance contemporary or topical themes with a sense of timelessness. Phillips thinks timeless qualities can be found in nearly
every event, that topicality need not hinder a serious writer seeking to create lasting fiction.

"You address timeless values within political events," she ad-
vises, when asked how one avoids writing material that looks
dated a few years after it's written. "Questions about right and
wrong, what is humane and just, are not questions that ever
become dated. It would only be dated in the way you wrote about
something: If the piece was dated, it would be because the writer

didn't really penetrate to the historical symbol he or she was using."

————————

That Jayne Anne Phillips is absolutely serious about her work is evident in her fiction, as well as in the way she addresses questions concerning it. Like many artists who have unexpectedly found themselves on the best-seller lists, she seems genuinely puzzled by her commercial success; good fiction, she points out, is not something that is designed to fit a formula for mass appeal.

"It's my feeling that a literary writer, as opposed to the commercial writer, never writes according to a formula, and never writes with any thought to an audience," she says. Her spoken words, like the ones she strikes onto paper, are chosen slowly, deliberately, each question given pause before it is answered. "If you're writing with an audience in mind, it's going to limit what you do in a certain way. You may think that some things are acceptable and some things aren't. You may feel that some risks are acceptable and some aren't. I don't think a literary writer should be concerned with those things.

"It's always pleasantly surprising when a literary book gets any kind of wide audience," she continues, "but even in terms of the kind of effect *Machine Dreams* had, when you think of how many it sold, compared with how many books are sold, say, of the romance genre, or how-to books . . ."

Her laugh is quick and ironic, offered with the realization that an entertaining book is almost always more popular than a literary one. Still, it's as difficult to argue with success as it is to account for, or gauge, public tastes and interests. In her introduction to *The Pushcart Prize: Best of the Small Presses*, the annual anthology of the best fiction and poetry from literary magazines, she asserted that literary writers expect to go unheard, that they labor "unsure of a potential of effect beyond what they have achieved in themselves."

Why, one wonders, would anyone write if he or she didn't expect to be heard?

"Well," she answers, "when I said 'expect to be heard,' I meant in a larger sense. Most writers know about the culture we live in—about the media and the fact that we are largely a pictorial, image-oriented society at this point. A lot more people watch television than read books. That cuts down the effect, by a wide margin, right there, because it's only a tiny minority of the population that reads serious fiction. So I think that when you expect to be heard, you may be expecting to be heard by a few of your peers. You don't expect to have the kind of wide-ranging effect that writers had before the advent of television."

Like many writers, Phillips has published—and continues to publish—much of her fiction in "little magazines," the literary quarterlies and small-press publications that pay little or nothing to the author, operate on miniscule budgets, and are irregularly distributed throughout the United States. These publications, Phillips believes, are not only good places for serious writers to practice their craft and gain modest reputations, but they also present otherwise unavailable forums for literary and stylistic experimentation.

"My work wouldn't have been published anywhere else," she offers. "It wouldn't have been thought acceptable. It was either too innovative in technique or subject matter. Stories like 'El Paso' or 'Lechery'—or even stories that were more conventional, like 'Home'—were simply too strangely written, too different, or their use of language was not something you see in commercial magazines, even by well-known writers.

"Commercial magazines have very specific ideas about their audiences. There are still a great number of magazines that don't publish certain curse words, for instance. They don't print certain explicit sexual themes, even if these themes aren't in the piece to make it sexual. I think there were only a couple of stories in *Black Tickets* that were published by commercial magazines and, in one case, they deleted references to nudity and things that aren't even risqué. It's a good illustration of why *not* to think of an audience when you put together a book."

Phillips admits an allegiance to the small presses which published her early work. While *Machine Dreams* enjoyed its hard-cover success in 1984 (a *New York Times* best-seller and alternate selection of the Book-of-the-Month Club which sold for record prices in England, Germany, Italy, Denmark, Holland, and Sweden), she quietly published "Fast Lanes," an illustrated short story (which became the centerpiece for her Dutton/Seymour Lawrence book of the same title), for Vehicle Editions. The small-press edition offered a dramatic example of the differences between small- and large-press publications. At sixteen dollars, the booklet is as expensive as many hardcover novels, yet its craftsmanship is impressive, from the layered, three-dimensional look of its cover art to the quality of paper it is printed upon and the typestyle selected to the lavish illustrations. Collectors, along with Phillips's "hardcore" following, found the book well worth its price, and the author was pleased with the way it was published.

"I'm interested in books for books' sake—what books look like and the kind of paper they're printed on," she says. "It's good to have some kind of say about the design of the book, which is often the case with the small-press book."

Phillips would like to see writers gaining more control over the "packaging" aspects of books published by larger commercial houses, but she is skeptical of its ever becoming a trend. "I don't think they'll ever put that in a contract," she says. "It really has to do with the kind of relationship you have with your editor, and how powerful your editor might be within the publishing house. I had expressed very strongly that I didn't want some kind of artist's representation of the book on the cover [of *Machine Dreams*]. I asked them to use a Pegasus. They asked me what I thought of the cover, and I specifically asked them not to use an illustration, just to use something that would be typography."

All this might be designed to please the author and her projected limited audience, but in *Machine Dreams*, whether she consciously designed to or not, Phillips hit a universal chord extending far beyond the interests of a few of her peers. Not only was the book a critical and popular success, but its movie option was purchased by Jessica Lange, the actress whose eclectic cinematic tastes were presented in movies like *Country* and *Sweet Dreams*. Success on the big screen could afford Phillips an even larger audience.

Phillips believes the book's universal appeal may be attributed to her uncompromising efforts to make the story as realistic as possible without sacrificing her intentions of presenting a novel through authentic voices.

"I try to make my work absolutely specific, and if there is a reality about it, it will be universal in some sense. You have to be true to the work itself. That may mean, in many instances, that your work won't be popular, or that you may be saying more than people may want to hear, especially if you're experimenting in some way with technique. But the real debt that you owe to an audience is to be completely true to the material you're working with; if you do that, despite whatever personal risks it means taking, you're doing the best thing you can do for an audience."

The risks, personal and artistic, in Jayne Anne Phillips's fiction are prodigious. Her first published work, *Sweethearts* (a small booklet, published by Truck Press in the summer of 1976, later incorporated into *Black Tickets*), was a collection of twenty-four sketches reminiscent of the short pieces in Ernest Hemingway's *In Our Time*. Rather than create an interlocking series of incidents with the traditional beginning, middle, and ending, Phillips wrote fictions that attempted to capture a voice or emotional aura. These early stories were more like prose poems than stories, the weight of Phillips's success or failure resting on her ability to align the music in language with a picture painted in sparse, descriptive prose. In "Wedding Picture," a one-paragraph sketch which takes on the dimensions of an incredibly compacted short story, Phillips describes a photograph as seen by a grown daughter:

> My mother's ankles curve from the hem of a white suit as
> if the bones were water. Under the cloth her body in its
> olive skin unfolds. The black hair, the porcelain neck, the

red mouth that barely shows its teeth. My mother's eyes are round and and wide as a light behind her skin burns them to coals. Her heart makes a sound that no one hears. The sound says each fetus floats, an island in the womb. . . .

"I sort of came to language as a poet," says Phillips, further explaining her method of writing. "I still write by ear, to a large degree. I don't work by ideas so much as by trying to create believable characters of a mesmerizing voice, because I think everything else will follow from that.

"I hadn't read *In Our Time* until after *Black Tickets* came out, when someone mentioned to me that it was similar, but I had read a lot of fiction that was short—condensed pieces from Rimbaud, Baudelaire, and from this country, Merwin. I had read Hemingway, certainly, but I hadn't read those short, short pieces."

Most of the pieces from *Black Tickets* were written within a short period after Phillips's 1974 graduation from the University of West Virginia. As an undergraduate student, she had studied under two teachers who acted as mentors in her early development as a writer. Judith Stitzel, a women's studies instructor, was "very, very important in that she was a role model who took an interest in me from the beginning." Winston Fuller, a poet who taught poetics classes which Phillips took four times, was instrumental in furthering Phillips's appreciation for the sound and possibilities of language.

At that point, she knew she wanted to devote her life to writing, yet to Phillips the idea of a writing career was a foreign concept, at least in terms of its being a way of making a living. "I was writing seriously from the time I was eighteen," she remembers, "but I didn't think of it as something that I was going to be doing as a career. I called myself a writer, but I didn't think of that as having anything to do with making money. It seemed to me to be a totally private thing, and that's the way it still seems."

While at the university, Phillips wrote poetry for small literary magazines; her evolution into fiction was the result of a need to capture what she calls the "massive ennui" of the 1970s in a form focusing more on the work than on the writer's own identity.

"I became more challenged by the difficulty of writing fiction," she recalled in a 1984 interview with *Publishers Weekly*. "I was really attracted by the *subversive* look of the paragraph. In a poem you're always having to confront the identity of the writer. In fiction the reader becomes less defended against that identity and more open to text."

For Phillips, absence of author identity is a critical point. Though some of her stories—and much of *Machine Dreams*—are autobiographical in nature, their characters, to be effective, have to possess a life of their own, divorced by necessity and Phillips's own strong need for privacy from the known experiences of the author. They must flow *through* her more than originate *from* her. Phillips views the loss of author identity, coupled with her habit of writing without regard for a specific audience, as conducive to the experimentation in style and voice for which she is best known.

"I have a very definite separation between myself and my work," she says. "I think the reason most people write has to do with getting beyond the limits of one's personality—doing more and knowing more than one person could do or know. If you make some sort of connection that affects other people—and it comes through in your work—you should be grateful that it happened, but I don't consider it as having anything to do with me personally.

"In a way, it's a compliment if people think your work is autobiographical, because that makes it seem as though you've really lived the work. In fact, it would have been impossible for me to have done all those things, been all those people, seen all those periods of time in my books. But I certainly wanted to give the impression that the voices of the books were totally authentic."

Many of the characters in *Black Tickets* originated from people Phillips saw and heard while working a series of odd jobs. After graduating from college, she drifted across the country, moving first to California and then to Colorado; she encountered the aimlessness that became a major theme in her first collection of stories. Phillips insists today that this drifting had nothing to do with "researching" her book of short fiction, despite the fact that this assumption was made by critics reviewing her book. "When *Black Tickets* came out," she says, "one of the things the press kept saying about it was that I had hitchhiked across the country in order to meet a lot of weird people so I could write this shocking book. This whole take on it was so silly because everyone I knew was traveling a lot, and it didn't have anything to do with *forcing* experience. A lot happened to me before I ever started traveling, and I would have written by using voices no matter where I might have been. I applied the voices to wherever I was, more than the other way around."

The voices in *Black Tickets* are nothing if not compelling. The longer pieces are uncompromising, gritty tales, told in stark or colloquial language, confronting readers with the forceful, unsettling impact of a Diane Arbus photograph: You are driven to look, to witness the black heart of America, represented by the hopeless, the drifters, the brokenhearted—all clutching for that which cannot be grasped. Phillips believes the success of the characters in *Black Tickets* rises out of reader empathy, if not actual reader identification, for the people she is writing about. Her characters are flawed, some fatally so, and while it would have been asking too much to expect readers to embrace such characters, Phillips counted on readers' seeing the human aspects in even the most unsavory voices in her book.

"The point is to make the abhorrent or repulsive character sympathetic in some way to the reader," she says. "It has to do with making those lives understandable, forcing the reader to really take on a voice or understand that character's world so that the reader develops a kind of compassion for the narrative voice, even though that voice represents an abhorrent human being or whatever."

Response to *Black Tickets* was very positive. In a cover blurb, Tillie Olsen called it "the unmistakable work of early genius." Reviewing the book for *The New York Times Book Review*, John Irving wrote that "Miss Phillips shines brightly enough in this collection to interest me in whatever she might write next."

To write *Machine Dreams*, Phillips returned to her roots. Born in 1952, she grew up in Buckhannon, a small rural town in West

Virginia, where her father worked in road construction and her mother taught school. Much of the material for *Machine Dreams*, especially Phillips's interest in family traditions and rituals, originated there, as did her regard for the way average people tell their stories.

"Growing up in West Virginia was really rich for me because it's one of the few places in the country that doesn't lend itself to mobility. People there didn't live the same kind of mobile lives as people in Los Angeles or Baltimore or wherever. We lived in a world apart from what we saw in the news or on television shows or in magazines. I think there's something, too, about the geography and topography of the area: The mountains are very old and sort of worn down, and it's a place with deep valleys and brambly, overgrown hills. In a sense, it's Rip van Winkle country, a place that time forgot. It's not a place that belongs to anywhere—it's not Northern and it's not Southern. I guess it belongs to the mountains and the idea of Appalachia."

Such an environment, Phillips continues, lent itself to the oral storytelling tradition. "Every story is different and interesting and has some merits," she points out, adding that the area instills in one a sense of individualism. "I was accustomed, from a very young age, to seeing a broad range of people and knowing more about them than I would have known if I'd grown up in a city. Everyone knew everyone else's story, and they talked about each other. They told a lot of stories, although they didn't really tell stories about themselves because my family was very closed-mouthed. There was also a great sense of pride, a sense that people could affect what happened to them on a day-to-day basis. They've known each other's families for generations and have seen the kind of cross-patterning that happens from generation to generation. I tried to replicate that, in a way, in my novel."

Phillips admits that many of the feelings and characteristics of Danner Hampson, the novel's main character, originate from her own childhood. The other major figures in the book are also based on Phillips's family, the parent figures sharing the same occupations as their real-life counterparts; Danner's brother, Billy, being a composite of Phillips's two brothers, one older and one younger. Despite the autobiographical aspects of the novel, Phillips insists that her characters are fictional, that the private lives of real people were not violated.

Of her parents' reaction to the way she depicted them in the book, Phillips says, "They weren't disappointed, they just thought I didn't get it right. Of course I didn't, because it's not really *them*. It was a very limited, small part of them. I think you use the reality of your *feeling* about something, sort of like method acting. Even though I didn't have a brother who went to Vietnam, certainly the feeling in the book for Billy was the feeling I would have had, had one of my brothers gone. It was based on my feelings for my own siblings. It's the feeling—the *ambience*—of the climate of the book that needs to be autobiographical. All the rest can be, and usually is, invented."

Inherent in the statement, though unspoken, is an antithesis to the opening line of *Machine Dreams*: It may be strange what we don't forget, but it's interesting what we choose to remember.

––––––––––

The chronology of Jayne Anne Phillips's early writing life reads today like the archetypical scheme for a successful serious literary career. In the summer of 1976, she published *Sweethearts*, and that fall she enrolled in the Iowa Writers' Workshop. A year later, she was studying fiction in one of Frank Conroy's workshops, and in 1978, *Counting*, her second small-press collection of very short fictions, was issued. The book won the St. Lawrence Award for fiction, which led indirectly to her meeting Seymour Lawrence, who would become her publisher.

During this period, however, Phillips was still uncertain about her function as a writer, even if the signs were good. Her choices were almost instinctive, based primarily on how she wanted to work as a writer, and how those roughly sketched goals had been successfully reached by other writers. The Iowa Writers' Workshop had been functioning since 1936, boasting of teachers and students that included Flannery O'Connor, Philip Roth, Nelson Algren, Raymond Carver, Andre Dubus, Wallace Stegner, Kurt

Vonnegut, John Irving, and Robert Penn Warren; virtually every serious student of fiction had heard of the workshop and the way it helped shape and launch literary careers. She chose to study under Frank Conroy because she was appreciative of his work.

"He was a model for me because he's a writer whose writing is really central to his life," says Phillips. "He was someone whose writing I really admired, who happened to be a very good teacher. By that, I mean he was a very good editor. I don't think writing programs can ever teach anybody to write, but they can teach you how to edit your work, and they can authenticate one's sense of oneself as a writer. From the time I was an undergraduate, I had temporary mentor relationships with people and, at that point, Frank was one of them. One of the good things about writing programs is that they allow those relationships to evolve with people who are real, who can speak back and teach you to edit your work."

This kind of relationship, Phillips goes on, is similar to the one she currently enjoys with Seymour Lawrence. The story of their meeting and Lawrence's decision to publish her book is the stuff of publishing industry folklore. After she won the St. Lawrence Award for *Counting*, Phillips traveled to the St. Lawrence Writers' Conference on a literary fellowship from Houghton-Mifflin. Seymour Lawrence was at the conference, hoping to lure Margaret Atwood to his publishing house, and though Atwood decided to stay with her publisher at the time, Lawrence met Phillips and asked to see her short fiction. Though he was less than enthusiastic about publishing short stories, Lawrence took the booklets, but he didn't get around to reading them until much later. At that point, Phillips had accepted a teaching post at Humboldt State University in California, and she was literally pulling out of her driveway, about to embark on another cross-country jaunt, when Lawrence called and told Phillips's mother that he wanted to publish Jayne Anne's book.

Phillips had hoped to publish with Lawrence, who then had his imprint at Delacorte, because she liked the way he approached writing as a serious literary undertaking rather than just another commercial venture. "I felt that he published *writers*, rather than publishing books," she says. "He had almost always published quality, timeless fiction. He wasn't in the business of merchandising a certain book or pushing somebody to be the next young phenomenon. It had to do with a writer's life and a writer's body of work. He was a publisher in the best sense of the word."

The relationship developed into a classical writer-publisher relationship. When Lawrence left Delacorte for Dutton in 1982, Phillips followed him to his new publishing house. *Fast Lanes*, her first book of stories there, published in 1987, was a slender volume of seven stories, most of which had been written shortly after the publication of *Machine Dreams*. In praising the book, *Newsweek* characterized it as "a collection of loose ends: first-person monologues revolving around barefoot girls, post-hippie gypsies and other street-smart naifs," while *Publishers Weekly* concluded that "judging from this collection, it seems as though there's nothing Phillips can't do."

The book is a startling example of a writer's placing quality over quantity, each story being so precisely crafted with dense, yet rhythmic language that a reader can easily imagine the hard labor devoted to every piece. There is plenty of evidence of Phillips's evolution as a writer, from the post-punk language of "How Mickey Made It," a story reminiscent of "Lechery" in *Black Tickets*, to the poetic images of "Rayme," which recalls the prose-poetic voices of the shorter pieces in the earlier collection of stories. Two of the stories in *Fast Lanes*, "Bess" and "Blue Moon," feature the characters Phillips wrote about in *Machine Dreams*. So, in many respects, *Fast Lanes* had the quality of being a connecting work to Phillips's previous two books.

The inclusion of more stories about the Hampsons was an especially interesting choice, particularly in the case of "Bess," which spans a period of time overlapping that covered in *Machine Dreams*. Phillips explains the story as being originally part of the novel, a section cut for reasons of continuity and clarity.

"I wrote 'Bess' as the second section of the book, before I wrote 'The Secret Country'—that section about Mitch's childhood. I ended up taking it out because Bess did not turn out to be such a central character that the whole section needed to stay in the book. It would have misled the reader into thinking that she was going to be a major character. But I wanted to publish it because I thought it was one of the strongest pieces of writing that I'd done. I also liked the idea of shedding light on the novel after the fact.

" 'Blue Moon' was not an outtake. It was written two years after the novel came out, and it was actually the newest story in the collection. I wrote 'Blue Moon' out of an interest in the kind of bonding that goes on between girls of that age—the kind of bonding that was going on between Danner and Kato that had to do, really, with both of them loving Billy."

Phillips confesses a certain obsession with these characters, and though she won't predict whether she will be writing about them again, she won't close the door on the possibilities of working with them, or similiar characters (such as those West Virginians in *Black Tickets*), in the future.

"There's definitely a group of characters that I work with that come from the same place," she says. "Even in the material I'm working on now, I can see that they come from the same place, though they're not the same people. I think, in a way, I have the greatest fidelity to that place and those people. It's my deepest material."

Work on a new novel, she continues, is going slowly, and it's a process she describes as "painstaking and difficult." Writing, she explains, has never been easy for her; the material she is writing about, along with her own method of writing, determine the pace and direction of all her work.

"I think material should always dictate form, and that's a rule I've always followed. I'm a very slow writer, but I think that has to do with how you compose. I really compose line by line, the way a poet would: It's a good day if I can get a page. I'm a very self-censoring writer, so my revision has to do with very small things, like moving words."

For Phillips, this is the only way to write. Even today, with three well-received books behind her, she chooses not to approach writing as a long-term career with carefully planned objectives;

the sheet of paper in the typewriter, on any given day, *is* the objective.

"It remains completely private," she says. "Regardless of how many books you've written, you have no guarantee that you'll write another one, and just because one novel turned out well, you have no guarantee that the next one will. You know? It's just something that goes completely from moment to moment, and the only thing you have for sure is the process of doing it, and the fact that you choose to go through that process and it organizes the world for you somehow. That's why people should write."

Norman Seefe, courtesy of Esquire magazine

JAY McINERNEY

"**Y**ou are not the kind of guy who would be at a place like this at this time of the morning. But here you are, and you cannot say the terrain is entirely unfamiliar, although the details are fuzzy. . . ."

These words, thoughts of the unnamed protagonist in Jay McInerney's best-selling *Bright Lights, Big City*, also describe the author's own Road to Damascus. For McInerney, there were no flashes of light or auditory displays—only fading neon lights in early Manhattan predawn and an internal whisper telling him he was on the wrong path.

It was 1981. McInerney was a twenty-six-year-old aspiring novelist with a list of failed attempts in his near-past. His first wife, a model, had packed her bags and left. A nine-month stint as a fact checker at *The New Yorker* had been a very unhappy tenure, winding down with a "quit or be fired" understanding. The short stories he wrote were returned with form rejection slips. After *The New Yorker* fiasco, he took a job at Random House as a manuscripts reader, but the position only fortified his growing doubts about his sense of direction: The manuscripts, although often offered by respected New York agencies, were losers— worse, he felt, than his own work, efforts which were being turned down everywhere. He didn't have an agent, any published credits or, by all indications, much of a future as a writer.

What he did have was a good sense of where the party was. He had a taste for alcohol and "Bolivian Marching Powder," both of which helped propel him through his binges in New York's after-hours clubs. His idea of a goal was finding the right table in the right club where, plied with the right drugs, he could bulldoze his way through another night.

But he wasn't *really* that kind of guy. The thought gnawed at him, off and on, over the months, but it struck home particularly hard one evening—make that *early morning*, five A.M.—as he prepared to leave the now-defunct Berlin club in Manhattan. His drinking buddy had already left with a woman he'd met on the dance floor and McInerney, sick and dazed from the self-abuse, realized that he was again about to step from a night's partying into daylight. Time was not being kind to him, but all it really was, after all, was a vicious payback.

You are not the kind of guy. . . .

The words formed in his head and he went home and wrote them down. They would eventually be the opening words of a short story entitled "It's Six A.M. Do You Know Where You Are?" The story would then become the first chapter of *Bright Lights, Big City,* one of the most astonishing and successful first novels of the decade. In the novel, written entirely in the second person, the protagonist, like McInerney, drives himself to the brink of self-destruction before he sees the light.

There is a koan-like quality to McInerney's "dark night of the soul": To find the way, one must be lost beyond hope, caught in a territory without guideposts or map, where sheer survival becomes a test of will.

It's a road, McInerney now believes, that most writers travel, though the way is usually a lot less extreme.

"There are no guarantees," McInerney says of the writing life. "When one goes to law school, one pretty much knows he is going to practice law at the end of it all, whereas in setting forth to be a writer of fiction, not only aren't there any guarantees, but the route isn't even mapped out. You know, do you work as a lumberjack, or do you go to creative writing graduate school, or do you try to go to Paris to see if you can discover the ambience that Hemingway sought out?"

Success has afforded McInerney the opportunity to look back and reexamine the options with less-frenzied, more-detached insight than he experienced while he was living the Question. Though confident, he is far from being cocky, and you get the feeling that his failures, personal and professional, serve as reminders. He admits to his somewhat hedonistic past, but he's eager to point out that not only has he reformed, but he was never as extreme as the protagonist of *Bright Lights*. He had, he claims, a romantic's view of the writing profession which years of trial and error, coupled with his experiences in the magazine and book trades, honed to a far more realistic attitude.

"When I first got out of college, I had a sort of unfounded faith that I would be a self-supporting writer. As the years went by, I felt that I had to be more realistic about it. I never lost *faith* but, at the same time, this whole idea about becoming Hemingway or something, of being a writer who had a big audience and could support himself, was one that seemed a little unrealistic to me.

"I can't help but be tremendously grateful that my long apprenticeship paid off in sort of precisely the way I'd always hoped—but never believed—that it would. I had worked in New York in publishing long enough to know that authors' adolescent fantasies were very seldom fulfilled. I'd seen friends publish books and almost expect, despite their better instincts, to be mobbed on the streets the day after publication. Of course, this hardly ever happens. So I had lowered my expectations to a point where I was just eager to publish a book. I hoped to reach some readers and get some critical attention, but I wasn't expecting to reach all that many."

Ironically, he hit the jackpot with both readers and critics. *Bright Lights* has sold over 150,000 copies—a remarkable achievement for a first novel, the feat becoming even more impressive when you take into consideration the fact that the book was a paperback original. As for the critics, who tend to ignore both first novels and paperback originals, their reviews were slow in arriving, but once the word was out, they virtually fell over each other in praising the book.

The Washington Post: "McInerney is an extremely gifted young writer, and it is a pleasure to see the beginning of a career like his. One waits with anticipation for whatever comes next."

Mademoiselle: "McInerney has an incredible ability to pack more substance into one sentence than most writers are able to convey in ten. . . . He is, in short, a born writer from whom, I hope, we'll be hearing more and more."

Publishers Weekly: "The best part of this promising debut is McInerney's humor—it is cynical, deadpan and right on target, delivered with impeccable comic timing."

Even today, McInerney is cautious in his assessment of the publicity and critical acclaim. He points out that it was quick in coming and could depart as easily—that, indeed, it *wasn't* as lavish in its reaction to his second book, *Ransom*—and while he's now being courted by magazines that wouldn't have considered his work or returned his phone calls a few years ago, he remains realistic in light of the country's recent tendency to have its stars flare like supernovas, only to fade from sight a few years later.

"There's a terrible tendency in this country to consume art and culture, to try to package it in the same way that all our other familiar products are packaged, and that can be terribly distorting to the work, to objects of art and culture. Every once in a while, a writer does get processed by this machine. All of us can think of writers who have been distracted and who, perhaps, have taken the publicity more seriously than their writing. I feel like it could all be gone tomorrow, so the only sensible approach is not to take it too seriously. What counts is the writing."

Not that it's been an easy road to travel. As one of the media-labeled "literary brat-packers," McInerney's every move has been pursued and reported by gossip columnists eager to cash in on a "hot" name. People began to see him as a figure as much as they viewed him as an author of serious fiction. It got to the point where he had to retreat to Yaddo if he ever intended to finish his third novel.

The humor of this literary rags-to-riches story is not lost on McInerney. A few years ago, when interviewed by *USA Today*, McInerney quipped that the success of *Bright Lights* even affected the way people looked at his age: All of a sudden, he had been transformed from an aging, unpublished writer to a young, published one.

As if, when the dues are paid, one forgets the cost.

⁓⁓⁓⁓⁓⁓⁓⁓⁓

"Writing is something that I've wanted to do since I can remember, aside from a brief notion of being a trapper in the Hudson Bay, or a mercenary, or something. . . ." McInerney laughs, the unspoken understanding being that writing a book, to a child, might have seemed as accessible as the life of Lewis and Clark. "When I was a kid, we moved a lot, and I'd find more companionship in books, when I was the new kid in school, than I would find elsewhere. I was also an insomniac, so I read an awful lot. I read the Hardy Boys and that kind of stuff. I sort of stumbled on Dylan Thomas—he was the first literary author I discovered, I guess. What he did with words seemed incredibly imaginative to me. He's a natural for adolescents because he's so word-drunk and romantic. At that point, I fell in love with the image of being a writer—you know, this Dylan Thomas, this roustabout, this bad boy, this perennial adolescent. . . . I guess I've just gotten more pleasure from reading than from almost anything else, and it seemed that the most interesting thing I could do would be to be a writer."

Other writers, particularly Hemingway and Fitzgerald, strengthened McInerney's romanticized vision of the writing profession, as well as influencing his own work. McInerney explains that he had recently read a Hemingway biography and discovered that, as an apprentice writer, Hemingway had considered moving to Japan. He chose to go to Paris instead, but to McInerney, who spent two years in Japan as a young expatriate writer, the story bore unexpected poignance.

"The myth of Hemingway, the writer, is very powerful," he says. "I think it's hard to be at least an American male writer, even now, and not feel the shadow of Hemingway. The myth shapes one's conception of the nobility of the calling. I also learned a great deal about storytelling because Hemingway's work is so clean and stark in a way. It's very easy to learn from him, to overcome some of the traditional defects of apprentice writing, which are being very florid, overly emotional and underly concrete, showing off. It's easy to imagine and build your conception of how a sentence works if you start with Hemingway."

Ultimately, though, Fitzgerald proved to be a greater influence. As he was with Hemingway, McInerney was intrigued by Fitzgerald's public image as a powerful figure in the imagination of American literature. But more than Hemingway did, Fitzgerald offered more stylistic possibility to McInerney. "I love Hemingway's prose, but it doesn't do as many things as Fitzgerald's does. In one sentence, Fitzgerald can be wistful, intelligent, funny, and sad—that's pretty remarkable. I love Fitzgerald's lyricism and his ability to see the poetry at the same time as he somehow maintains his critical faculties.

"I recently reread *The Great Gatsby*, which I hadn't read in a long time, and one of the things I admired, about the book and about Fitzgerald, is how, in a book like *Gatsby*, he can show the massive illusion of Gatsby's dream, which is essentially a version of the American Dream, and expose it as an illusion while, at the same time, he lyrically celebrates its power. He once said, in an essay, the mark of a great mind is the ability to hold two contrary and opposing ideas at once, and I think *Gatsby* is like that: It's a critique of Gatsby's dream and, at the same time, a sort of celebration of it. Fitzgerald figures specifically in *Bright Lights, Big City*, I think, in that the young Fitzgerald is exactly who the protagonist wants to be: He wants to be successful, good-looking, and sort of jump into the fountain of the Plaza—and do it all with his left hand."

In some respects, this was what McInerney hoped for in the literary life. Writing, he felt, could be a romantic adventure with both temporal and immortal qualities that even failure couldn't diminish. (The tragic demises of Hemingway, Fitzgerald, and Jack Kerouac—another influence, to a lesser extent—were generally treated kindly by biographers and critics.) Wealth and fame were the rewards for creation, a fact that seemed to be underscored when McInerney studied fiction at Williams College. As he would learn, the struggle to reach any level of success was one that had to be experienced, not read about, to make a lasting impression. If the spirit of good literature was pure, it was nonetheless far from perfect.

"When I was in college," he recalls, "I wanted this literary world to be immune from the kind of petty motives and short-sightedness that, to me, characterized the world of commerce. I subsequently grew up and learned that the literary world is imperfect, too, that some of the same principles operate here as operate elsewhere. I realized that I might not ever make it as a writer, that it might be because I wasn't good enough, or that it might be because the odds were just too long and I didn't get the right kind of help or attention."

Upon graduating from college, McInerney packed his Volkswagen and, with Gary Fisketjon, a classmate and eventually his editor, embarked on a Kerouackian journey across America. He intended to write a novel about the experience, but nothing ever came of it. When his money ran out, he returned to the East, taking a writing job with a weekly newspaper in New Jersey, the *Hunterdon County Democrat*. His apprenticeship had begun.

"It was a small newspaper, where I did everything from school board meetings to dog shows. I could write features on anything interesting that I could dig up. My editor used to weigh copy bags at the end of the week, and mine would always be really light. Other people would have, like, ten pounds of stories that they'd written, and I'd have three or four stories."

McInerney tells the story with good humor, preferring to write off the job as ancient history with a benefit or two. "It was very good for me, I think, in that it loosened me up a lot at a time when I was sitting and rewriting first sentences, over and over again, like some kind of precious poet. It forced me to think about beginning and ending something which, at the time, I was not very good at."

Though he is now in a position which gives him much more time to plan his projects than his weekly newspaper deadlines once allowed, McInerney still finds the two ends of a project—the beginning and ending—the most difficult aspects of writing. "I'm always afraid, when I sit down, that nothing is going to come out. That's a scary feeling when you're about to embark on a novel or short story, wondering if you're ever going to finish, wondering how you're going to get started and what you're going to do. If I'm in doubt, I'll sometimes make myself go farther along a certain road, to see if it will work. I find that I actually have to write in order to discover my ideas. I think you could allow yourself to never get started if you tried to guess in advance what was going to inspire you.

"I also find it very difficult to let go of my fiction without worrying about whether I'll be revising it for another three years. I like to tinker. Every sentence is potentially revisable in thirty directions, and it's tough to stop doing that, to know when you've ended."

The newspaper business taught him the discipline of working under deadlines and since, by his own admission, he is by nature the type of writer who needs the pressure of a timetable, he continues to work under artificial, self-imposed deadlines. The first draft of *Bright Lights* was written in six weeks to accommodate one of these deadlines.

Newspaper writing, however, was not McInerney's idea of the proper program for the future novelist. As his tenure at the paper wound down, McInerney began looking around for another type of employment and was told of a fellowship, sponsored by Princeton, which would send him overseas for two years. He applied and was granted the fellowship. Since, in 1978, he had yet to be exposed to the formalities of the publishing world, he still had his idealistic attitudes about writing and the expatriate writer who finds his voice, while gaining valuable experience and the time to write, in an exotic setting.

It was a time when a lot of Americans were still looking to the East for self-realization and discipline. The Sixties had challenged an individual's perception of his or her moral obligation to the whole, but the country's internal violence, along with the slaughter in Vietnam, had turned attention inward. McInerney found himself caught in the backwash.

Like Christopher Ransom, the expatriate American character in *Ransom*, his second novel, McInerney found assimilation into Japanese culture impossible, despite his efforts. He pursued the trappings—going to the public baths, studying karate (for which he received a black belt), and taking Japanese courses at the Institute for International Studies near Tokyo, but he soon realized that he was as much a prisoner of the myths about Japan as others were of the myths surrounding New York. He wound up teaching English to Japanese businessmen—an irony that didn't escape him.

The experience gave him plenty of material to write about,

even after his two-year stay expired and he moved back to New York, and he spent the next five years, off and on, trying to write a novel which proved to be as elusive as the one about his cross-country trip. Both journeys had found him searching, but he wasn't prepared to write about what he might have found. In many respects, his taking a job at *The New Yorker* was also a quest; what he gained was an education unlike any he had received in his formal schooling.

"When I came to New York, I was looking for the center of the literary world," McInerney quips, adding that "*The New Yorker* is a sort of stand-in for the center of the literary world, although it's a very insular place. It seemed like the closest thing I could find."

It was a logical, if not accurate, assumption. Long regarded for its almost limitless commitment to excellence in prose, *The New Yorker* offered a literary history especially attractive to the serious fiction writer. One could not walk the halls without feeling the tradition of Salinger, Thurber, Updike, and E. B. White; if, as has been suggested, buildings trap the spirits of everyone ever entering them, the offices of *The New Yorker* had to seem like nirvana to the aspiring writer.

McInerney, however, was not employed to write, nor was he similar to his *Bright Lights* alter ego, who sends unsolicited short stories to the magazine's fiction editor, only to find them rejected in stiff, formal terms. McInerney was a fact checker, and that carried an unwritten yet enormous responsibility. Prior to the Alastair Reid scandal in 1984, *The New Yorker* was considered a bastion of journalistic accuracy. No fact was too small or un-important to check, and the tedium of the job eventually worked on McInerney's nerves.

"It was interesting, and I enjoyed the experience very much," he says, "but fact checking was not for the aspiring fiction writer and an absentminded space cadet such as myself. Its demand for strict attention to detail just wasn't my forte." According to

McInerney, he made a mistake—like his *Bright Lights* character yet, again, with far less consequence—which led to his demise. When he left, he had an abundance of material for what would be his first novel, plus a growing knowledge of how publishing really works.

His next job, as a reader for Random House, focused the knowledge. It was a useful job for a future novelist, McInerney believes today, noting that E. L. Doctorow also held a similar job for two years when he was just starting out.

"It was interesting to see what was being submitted and, in a negative way, it was probably instructive because most of what I read I did not feel was eminently publishable. Some people told me that if something wasn't too good, you didn't have to read the whole thing. But I can hardly ever start a story without finishing it, so I would always finish these things and then think about what I would do with them if I were writing them. That was an interesting exercise. There was a way, in seeing these completed manuscripts and seeing how they worked or didn't work, that I could view the novel as not quite such a daunting object. With these less than perfect manuscripts, it was easy to see the seams."

McInerney will always remember this period as bittersweet. He was learning the ropes of the publishing business, establishing contacts, and supplementing his income by helping read manuscripts for *The Random Review*, a literary anthology, originally intended to be an annual publication, which died after its initial issue. But there was less discipline than McInerney had encountered in his newspaper and magazine days, and he began to take advantage of his less than rigid work schedule. He began his "partying period," and he recalls now that there were many days when he barely made it to work. His brief marriage failed. No good writing was being accomplished.

Shortly after his "revelation" outside the Berlin, he caught his first big break. Raymond Carver, who had a story in *The Random Review*, was in New York, and McInerney met him and spent an afternoon discussing fiction with him. At the time, Carver was teaching fiction at Syracuse.

"We developed a correspondence," says McInerney, "and he said to me, 'Living in New York and working in publishing doesn't look like it's doing much for your fiction. Why don't you come study with me at Syracuse?'

"I was very torn, but I applied. It was a way of going for broke, for making a decision to stop straddling and trying to have it both ways—have a publishing career and write. I figured that sooner or later you had to make a commitment, one way or the other, and I decided that removing myself from New York City and going to upstate New York, to a campus that I had never seen before, leaving a lot of things behind, was a way of going for broke and demonstrating my commitment to fiction. Not having developed my writing habits and having to work somehow to make a living in a very expensive city, it was important for me, at that stage, to get into an environment which was more conducive to writing, where I didn't have a high overhead which required a full-time job."

When he returned to New York City four years later, he was the literary toast of the town.

E. L. Doctorow once compared the process of writing a novel to driving at night. It's an analogy that Jay McInerney remembers and likes to repeat. "You can only see as far as the headlights," McInerney recalls the saying, "but you can make the whole trip that way."

The idea describes McInerney's method of creating a novel. He explains that he is presently working on another novel, and that he's plowing ahead, not totally certain where he's going. "I think a set of themes or an intricate plot design which preexists the work itself is not going to result in an organic work of the imagination. I'm not saying that I don't *try* to figure out what I'm doing, but usually I only figure it out by doing it. That's the excitement of writing. If I didn't constantly get surprised by the material and the configurations I was stumbling onto in my writing, I don't think I'd be able to keep my interest up to finish a book."

McInerney's life, like his writing, might be seen as a matter of his driving at night, and when he followed his instincts to Syracuse, he was heading in the right direction. Raymond Carver turned out to be a remarkable teacher and friend.

"He's a very, very patient teacher," notes McInerney. "He believes in finding the strength in everyone's work, because he says he can never be sure: One of his worst students, when he first started teaching, he subsequently came across fifteen years later and recommended for publication. It's somebody who's quite well-known as a short story writer now. . . . Carver's approach is to try to encourage everyone's strengths, and since there's so little encouragement out there when you're trying to become a writer, having someone like Ray—encouraging you and egging you on, pointing out your potential strengths—can be psychologically invaluable. One of the great advantages of creative writing programs is that you're in an environment of support, and you're with people engaged in the same enterprise—people you don't have to explain yourself to."

Like Hemingway, Carver writes prose concentrating more on dramatic presentation of material than on expository narrative, the work gaining its power through understatement. The influence is unmistakable in McInerney's work—though McInerney employs humor and Joycean wordplay more than either Carver or Hemingway—and Carver remains one of the few people to whom McInerney will show a work-in-progress.

Despite the more tranquil, academic enviroment, McInerney continued to feel frustration when he submitted his short stories for publication. "I think I had the kind of luck that many aspiring writers would be familiar with—not much," he laughs. "I would send out stories to magazines and I always got form rejections. I once got a nice note from *Redbook*, but I never had any luck.

"The first story that I did have published was in *The Paris Review*. I'd had something rejected by them right before that, but they said, 'We liked this story, but we're not quite sure it's right for us. Do you have anything else?' That was my first real break, officially."

Encouraged by the response from the magazine, McInerney looked around for a story to submit. In one of his drawers, he found the fragment he had written, a one-page scrap about a young man, dazed and lost in the wee hours of the morning. Intrigued by the second-person voice, he decided to expand the story, and within two days he had completed "It's Six A.M. Do You Know Where You Are?" *The Paris Review* accepted it immediately.

"I just flipped," McInerney says. "It was the first positive response I'd had from an official source. I'd had my friends and teachers encouraging me all along—which, I think, is the only thing that keeps a young writer going. It's crucially important to have people you can show your work to, people who are sympathetic."

Writing an entire book in the second person, present tense, was an especially noteworthy risk for a first novelist, but McInerney claims the actual writing presented no special problem. "It's a very common form of interior monologue which, I think, somehow makes the story more ironic. I tried rewriting parts of it in the first and third person, but some aspects, like humor and irony, disappeared entirely. The voice must have been appropriate for that character in that situation. What actually happened was it became difficult for me to start writing in the first and third person again when I finished the book."

McInerney's irreverent humor, placed in the mind of his protagonist, smoothed out the rough edges of what might have become, given the nature of second-person narrative, an exercise in excessive self-consciousness. The result was a character of sharp wit and insight who is never dragged down by the undertow of his predicament:

> You wake up with a cat on your chest. You are on a
> couch, wrapped in a quilt. After a few minutes you rec-
> ognize Megan's apartment. Her bed is empty. The clock

on the nightstand says 11:13. That would be A.M., judging by the sunlight. The last thing you remember is an amorous lunge at Megan somewhere in the P.M.; presumably unsuccessful. You have the feeling you have made a fool out of yourself.

To the unpublished writer, using this style is like working without a safety net: You will be applauded for your courage while being criticized for being foolhardy. There are, after all, easier ways to publish a first novel.

⸺⸺⸺

Success has a way of making the logistics of writing and publishing look simple, but even today, with the benefit of hindsight and a mountain of newspaper and magazine articles speculating on the reasons for the phenomenal success of *Bright Lights*, McInerney is still surprised not only at how well his book was received, but by the different reasons for which people found it so appealing.

"We didn't anticipate what people would focus on," he says. "We really thought it was going to be a kind of small, literary book that was first excerpted in *The Paris Review*, and we thought people might get interested in the stuff about *The New Yorker*. But this whole public image that *Bright Lights* took on was a surprise to us. I saw it as a book that grew out of a voice and the Hemingway epigraph, and then other people thought it was a guide to nightlife. We were surprised by that reaction."

That reaction, for the most part, was governed more by an enormous, word-of-mouth factor than by critical acclaim. The early reviews of *Bright Lights* were generally favorable, but since it was a first novel—and a paperback original at that—the reviews were slow in rolling in. Good timing, sensible marketing, and word of mouth snowballed sales to the point where, by early 1986, the book was selling five thousand copies a week.

Ironically, McInerney was initially less than enthusiastic about publishing his first novel as a trade paperback original. In the beginning, the McInerney-Vintage Contemporary marriage was as touch and go as McInerney's writing career. When Gary Fisketjon, McInerney's old college buddy and then-editor at Vintage, was given a line of trade paperbacks and asked McInerney to contribute the first original to the series, McInerney was hesitant. Publishing tradition called for a book to be published first in hardcover, then in paperback, and McInerney worried that bucking the trend might mean that his book might not be taken seriously as literature by critics and readers, and that its sales to libraries might suffer. Fisketjon argued that readers just couldn't afford to buy a lot of hardcover books each year—especially first novels—and that the trade paperback format might afford McInerney more readers than he would otherwise have if the book were issued in the traditional hardcover-paperback format. McInerney finally agreed.

In hindsight, McInerney sees the idea as being brilliant. "It's applying some good marketing sense to an industry that hasn't changed in a hundred years," he says. "We're in a very vital period of fiction, and it's important to reach general readers—not just the five thousand who are always going to pick up a book that's reviewed by *The New York Times*. If you think of the way you read Dostoyevski or Hemingway, it was in paperback edition. That's the way we consume books now. It's impossible to second-guess what would have happened to *Bright Lights* if it hadn't come out that way, but it clearly worked and I'm really glad to have been a part of it."

The Vintage Contemporaries, along with other trade paperback lines, were dubbed "Yuppie-backs" by the press; and McInerney, as the year's most successful breakthrough novelist, found himself inundated with requests for interviews. From the press's point of view, he had star-quality: He was young, good-looking, caught up in an American Dream success story. McInerney profiles appeared in *The Wall Street Journal*, *The Chicago Tribune*, *New York*, and *Advertising Age*. Photographers camped out in the doorway to his apartment and snapped his picture in some of Manhattan's trendiest clubs. McInerney's name turned up in newspaper gossip columns—often, McInerney claims, in assocation with people he wasn't with or at events he didn't attend. In short, he had become a literary celebrity. If F. Scott Fitzgerald was a symbol of literature of the Jazz Age, McInerney became, whether he wanted to or not, a symbol of the literature of the Eighties Yuppie Era.

McInerney has heard the talk comparing him with Fitzgerald, and while he admits that "one can't hate being compared to the man who wrote *The Great Gatsby* and *Tender Is the Night*," he also says he resents the focus on lifestyle, as opposed to the literature.

"These people are going to have to look at the work and not get all excited about what kind of clothes I'm wearing, or whether or not I go to Nell's," he says. "Fitzgerald's life, very clearly, had a tragic shape and he suffered, to some extent, from his own personal tragedies, but he also suffered from some exogenous factors—the fact that the country became disgusted with the era that he chronicled so well and therefore became somewhat fed up with him. All I can do is my best to stay ahead of myself and just take on my own challenges as a writer, and one of the ways I can do that, I think, is by continuing to think about my work in relation to books of the past. As long as I'm keeping my mental and physical health intact and am continuing to write, if I really sustain a high level of dialogue with my past work and the work of those writers I admire, my work is not going to be limited in appeal to those who are interested in the chronicle of a certain era. It will also have rewards for people who are interested in American fiction—and maybe even world fiction."

The notion of the writer-as-public-figure, McInerney continues, is a mixed bag. Any press, good or bad, tends to boost book sales, he notes, but he is also annoyed by those who suggest that he doesn't behave like a serious writer. "I'm always being told what I should and shouldn't do and, frankly, I'm not interested in following the rules. If I were, I wouldn't have written a novel in the second person, and I wouldn't have published it in paperback. I don't want to be told what writers do—I want to tell *them* what writers do. I'm going to do shit that hasn't been done before, or what else is the point—except to write well. Mailer made up this outrageous career that nobody would believe. Hemingway did the same thing: I mean, writers shouldn't be running around, catching marlin and wasting all their time getting drunk at bullfights, but Hemingway did it, and he created an enduring myth alongside his fiction. I like to improvise as I go along, and I live in a way that also feeds my observation of the culture. Insofar as writers, as a class, remain interesting, I hope they're not *all* doing the same thing—teaching at universities or hacking in Hollywood or appearing in *Interview* magazine.

"You have to have some of Oscar Wilde's attitude—'I don't care what people are saying, as long as they're talking about me'—though I wish the level of discourse were a lot higher than it is. I wish the people who made up the groupings and labels wouldn't talk about us as if *we* had made them up. Actually, though, my press has been good, and I've enjoyed the benefits of a lot of press, so it's a case of taking the heat if you want to stay in the kitchen. It's up to me to be careful because it would be easy to make a lot of the mistakes that, say, F. Scott Fitzgerald made—or, for that matter, that Jim Morrison made. The temptations to do a lot of dumb or easy things are there, and I hope I don't do any of them."

Ransom, McInerney's second novel, was published as a Vintage Contemporary almost exactly a year after *Bright Lights, Big City*. In part a fictionalization of McInerney's experiences as a young expatriate in Japan, the book was written in a more traditional style and narrative than its predecessor, leaving McInerney open to comparisons he didn't have to face with his first book. Many reviewers wound up writing as much about *Bright Lights* as about *Ransom*.

This may bother McInerney more than he lets on, but he's not showing his hand. He shrugs off the response to *Ransom* as being more or less expected.

"There's a way that a book that has any sort of success assumes an identity over which you don't have any control, which becomes something that people feel they have to take a stand on," he says. "I *did* publish *Ransom* pretty quickly, right on the heels of *Bright Lights,* when people were just getting around to reading *Bright Lights,* so a number of the reviews of *Ransom* were actually reviews of *Bright Lights,* written by people who had wanted to review *Bright Lights. Ransom* will probably be reviewed more when I publish my third book."

Ransom—or a book very similar to *Ransom*—was intended to be McInerney's first novel, but progress on the novel stalled and McInerney turned his attention to expanding his short story "It's Six A.M. Do You Know Where You Are?" That story, along with another titled "Amanda," also written in the second person, grew into *Bright Lights,* while *Ransom* was put on hold.

"When I finished *Bright Lights,* I went back and started *Ransom* again. At that time, it had some other dreadful title. So it was really written afterward, but I had started some before I wrote *Bright Lights.* It's hard to say," he mentions, laughing at the confusion, "what the real chronology is."

Thematically, *Ransom* is a much more ambitious book than *Bright Lights.* Set in Japan, where the novel's namesake protagonist is studying karate and attempting to assimilate into Eastern culture, *Ransom* continues McInerney's obsession with the personal quest for contemporary values, but in *Ransom,* the quest finds Christopher Ransom considering the clash between Eastern and Western values, as well as the ultimate confrontation between good and evil. Muddying the scene are flashback scenes which place Ransom in Afghanistan, a sort of no-man's-land where survival is the only dictum, but also where, curiously, more human compassion is displayed than in Japan. As the novel winds down and Ransom rushes headlong toward his final confrontation with evil forces, the reader is drawn toward the inevitable conclusion that spiritual values are often laid to waste by social Darwinism. In this regard, *Ransom* is not so different from *Bright Lights, Big City.*

"Both books are concerned with the search for values in an era in which there seems to be no moral or cultural consensus for intelligent and well-meaning people," says McInerney. "In

Bright Lights, the pursuit of Rolex watches and the right table at the right restaurant is a substitute for goals. *Ransom* is about a particular historical period between the Sixties, when there seemed to be that kind of cultural and moral consensus, and the Eighties, when a very cynical set of values had almost replaced the search. Ransom finds himself in between: There isn't any big cause at home any more, yet he was touched enough by it to be looking for one. He was *looking* for a confrontation between good and evil."

McInerney admits that he drew from aspects of his life when he was writing *Ransom*, as he had with *Bright Lights*, and that elements of Christopher Ransom's psychological makeup, as well as those of the *Bright Lights* protagonist's makeup, reflect some of his own philosophical concerns, but he's quick to point out that not only are the two characters polarized (thus showing the complexity of any human mind), but that they have been exaggerated for fictional purposes.

"My own feeling about life in general is a little more optimistic than Christopher Ransom's," he says. "At the same time, I don't think that things always work out for the best in the end, that we're living in a benign universe. It's a dangerous universe, and one of the things I was interested in, with a character like Ransom, is that he's someone who refuses to make the compromises we all do. Ransom seems to be someone who can't help but take personally the imperfections of the world, and rather than bending, he breaks."

And that, McInerney concludes, is a major distinction between author and character.

⁂

At times, McInerney's career could be characterized as a series of false starts, jump starts, and interrupted journeys, despite all his planning and working to stay on the open road. The writing of his first novel was interrupted in favor of his writing a second, and the pattern is almost identical for his third and fourth novels. And while he has been working on the novels, he has been interrupted by several forays into screenplay writing. Short stories, which McInerney hopes to collect for a fifth book, further cut into his time. McInerney jokes that he has been depicted as "running my own literary corporation," typing out reams of paper, traveling back and forth between coasts (and points between), and somehow managing to maintain his lifestyle; his literary ambitions keep him on the run. He may not write or pursue his career in a straightforward, linear fashion, but much of that can be attributed to the fact that his projects never seem to work out the way they were planned.

Such was the case with the making of the movie of *Bright Lights, Big City.* Shortly before the book was published, McInerney—his $7,500 book advance long spent—was working in a liquor store when he took a call from a motion picture studio executive interested in making a movie from the book. McInerney was commissioned to write the screenplay, to the tune of a reported $200,000, and rumors had Tom Cruise playing the lead. All systems were go, and McInerney appeared to be a "Young Writer Goes to Hollywood" in the direction he was taking.

He recalls those times with amusement. "I had the classic sort of Hollywood experience. I was the 'Flavor of the Week,' being wined and dined by every studio in town. The first limo they sent to meet me was eighty feet long, but the cars kept getting smaller and smaller, and then they stopped coming. On my fifth trip, I called them from the airport after an hour and they said, 'Yeah, why don't you catch a cab. We're busy. *What's* your name?' "

The experience only got worse. After writing three screenplays, McInerney suddenly found himself out in the cold when the film property changed studios. Time passed. A new director and screenwriter were hired, but they didn't work out and were subsequently dismissed from the project. Michael J. Fox was hired to play the *Bright Lights* protagonist, and Twentieth Century-Fox then contracted James Bridges, director of *The China Syndrome* and *Urban Cowboy*, among other movies, to direct *Bright Lights.* By the time Bridges became involved with the movie, a number of screenplays (McInerney estimates six) existed and, after reading through the different versions, Bridges decided that McInerney's original draft was the best of the lot. It was, McInerney remembers, the most faithful to the book. Bridges contacted McInerney, who was in Milan working on a new novel, and the two met to work out the final shooting script.

"He and I put together a hybrid of my very first draft," McInerney says. "Where I departed from the novel, he went back to it. It became an extremely faithful rendition of the book in sequence, tone, and everything else. I was on the set almost every day, and I participated in the editing of the film. So I had a very interesting movie experience, and I'm glad that, in one movie, I had the full range of the 'Writer Goes to Hollywood' experience, from being laughed at and spit on, to being treated like 'Queen for a Day.' It was fascinating, and I'm going to do it again. I like getting into the fighting and the fray, and I like reaching out to that bigger audience. By the time I'm sixty, I'm probably going to do what Norman Mailer has done recently: direct. But there's a lot of time for that.

"In the meantime—and *always*—I'm more interested in the novel. Given my abilities and ambitions, the novel will always be of more interest to me than film. As a novelist, you're sole monarch of a realm which you can invent and modify at will; as a screenwriter, you are, at best, a member of a committee, and at worst a galley slave. I had a taste of both feelings. Like most people, I am interested in film, and I wouldn't be surprised if I remain involved in the movies in some capacity, off and on, over the years, but frankly, I take literature and books more seriously, in their claims to art, than I do Hollywood movies. My priorities are quite clear to me. I'm a novelist first; my heart is with fiction. For me, there's no comparison, in terms of creative satisfaction, between writing a novel and writing a screenplay."

McInerney's third novel, *Story of My Life*, had its own peculiar evolution—a development not unlike that of *Bright Lights, Big City*. Almost as soon as he had finished rewriting *Ransom*, McInerney began what he calls "a very long, panoramic novel with seven or eight narrators," a presently untitled book which is easily his longest and most ambitious novel to date. While revising the book in Milan, McInerney became intrigued by one of his female characters—a voice that has already been heard from in a short story titled "Smoke," published by *The Atlantic Monthly* in 1987. He liked the challenge of writing from a woman's point of view.

"I became very interested in trying to imagine the whole psychosexual transaction from the opposite side," he says, "and, as a novelist, I was interested in trying to stretch my imagination to where it didn't have firsthand psychological data to fall back on. I found it a fascinating challenge to the imagination: For one thing, as an author you eventually start to deplete your immediate autobiographical material; for another thing, if you have any ambitions at all—and I do—you want to do other things than tell some version of the story of your own life. As with *Bright Lights*, I got interested in a voice. *Bright Lights* is a book that started with a tune and a mood and a voice, and it's the same thing with *Story of My Life*. It's a novel that relies heavily on voice."

And, like the voice in *Bright Lights*, the voice of Alison, the protagonist of *Story of My Life*, is hip, contemporary:

> I'm totally pissed at my old man, who's somewhere in the Virgin Islands, I don't know where. The check was not in the mailbox today, which means I can't go to school Monday morning. I'm on the monthly payment program because my Dad says wanting to be an actress is a flaky whim and I never stick to anything—this from a guy who's been married five times—and this way if I drop out in the middle of the semester, he won't get burned for the full tuition. Meanwhile he buys his new bimbo, Tanya, who is a year younger than me, a 450 SL convertible—always liked young girls, haven't we, Dad?—plus her own condo so she can have some privacy to do her writing. Like she can even read. He actually believes her when she says she's writing a novel, but when I want to spend eight hours a day busting ass at Lee Strasberg, it's like, another one of Alison's crazy ideas. Story of my life. . . .

Jay McInerney

"I was in a hotel room in Milan when I started this one night," McInerney remembers. "I wrote part of a short story in my journal because I was hearing this voice from this girl. I was between second and third drafts of my long novel, but when I got back to the States, this journal entry grew into a short story. Then, when I went to Yaddo for the summer [of 1987], I was faced with the third draft of this very long, very heavy manuscript, and I decided to fiddle with the characters in the short story. Before I knew it, they were talking their heads off, and that became my third book. But," he adds, enjoying the confusion of his literary chronology, "you could call it my fourth."

When looking back on his apprenticeship and pitting who he was then with who he is now, Jay McInerney finds no conflict. He is happy with his professional and private life. "I suppose, in a lot of ways, I've experienced a very radical change," he remarks, "but at the same time, I don't feel that I've changed as a person or writer. One doesn't develop a new personality after thirty years. The other years are the important ones.

"What has changed are my material circumstances. I'm now in that very enviable position of being creatively unemployed, devoting all my time to writing. That's the greatest benefit. I no longer have to pretend to be something I'm not—whether it's a Ph.D. candidate in English or a bartender or a newspaper reporter—when all I ever wanted to do was write fiction."

GARY FISKETJON

If Gary Fisketjon were a professional basketball player, he would be considered an "impact" or "franchise" player—the individual who can turn a team's fortunes around and drastically alter its place in the standings. Such players not only are very good at what they do, but they are also so dominant that they can literally change the direction in which the game is played.

There is no doubting the impact Fisketjon has made on publishing in recent years. In fact, he could be viewed as a symbol of the way literary fiction is being published and marketed today: As an editor, he has an excellent eye for quality fiction, especially those books written by unknown, unappreciated, or new writers; as a businessman, he knows how to aggressively market those works to readers who are generally overwhelmed by the sheer number of titles published each year.

His impact was initially felt on September 17, 1984, the day his Vintage Contemporaries series made its debut in the publishing industry. The original list of titles included trade paperback reprints of Raymond Carver's *Cathedral* and Peter Mathiessen's *Far Tortuga*, as well as a paperback original by a first novelist named Jay McInerney. *Bright Lights, Big City* went on to sell more copies than even the industry's biggest optimists could have predicted, and the Vintage Contemporaries series won the 1984 Carey-Thomas Award for creative publishing.

Not that the VCs (as they came to be known) were the first of their kind. Fisketjon had long admired British publishers that put out their contemporary fiction in series, and in 1979, Kathryn Court, an editor at Penguin and a former British editor, introduced a line of books, still in existence, called the Contemporary American Fiction series. Other publishers followed suit—all believing, as did Fisketjon, that the less expensive trade paperback format might entice otherwise reluctant readers into buying reprinted quality fiction that generally had shown slow or mediocre sales figures in hardcover.

The enormous success of the VCs can be traced to the way Fisketjon (along with Melanie Fleishman, another editor at Random House, and Jeff Stone, who worked in Random House's sales and marketing division) applied contemporary marketing sense and practices to the idea of publishing a trade paperback series. Believing that uniformity could be applied in the series's favor, Fisketjon asked his art director to design a standard cover format which would be used, with a logo, on all books in the series. Fisketjon also believed that his books would probably appeal to a fairly young audience, so he decided that the VCs' cover artwork should more resemble the artwork seen on record albums rather than the more traditional work seen on books. The artwork had to be dignified, but it also had to command attention. Finally, Fisketjon felt that his series shouldn't be limited to quality fiction reprints; instead, he chose to republish out-of-print fiction (such as Harold Brodkey's *First Love and Other Sorrows*), reprint current hardcover fiction (such as *Cathedral*), and publish paperback originals (McInerney's *Bright Lights, Big City* and *Ransom*). The strategy was to get the books to play off each other: A reader who liked Richard Ford's *The Sportswriter* (another VC original) might be tempted to purchase another book in the series, and then another. . . . The strategy worked. In a 1986 *Esquire* profile of Fisketjon, E. Graydon Carter wrote: "For a generation raised on baseball cards and Barbie costumes, Vintage Contemporaries have become the latest thing to collect." A few months later, *Publishers Weekly* proclaimed: "It seems that the trade paperback series, with an imprint name and a uniform cover format, has become *the* marketing vehicle for contemporary quality fiction."

Fisketjon is modest in his assessment of his role in helping initiate the trade paperback trend. "I'm happy with the way it's worked," he says, "but like most good ideas, it *is* obvious and pretty simple."

Fisketjon left Vintage in spring 1986 for the position of editorial director of the Atlantic Monthly Press. He has since instituted a trade paperback series for Atlantic, and he continues to search for fresh, new voices in contemporary fiction. He has mixed feelings about the publishing industry's almost obsessive interest in young writers, though he is not about to condemn the influx of books by young or unknown writers. "It's a fad, to a degree —'How young are *your* authors? Do you have a lot of good writers?'—and I think a lot of the books that have been highly praised are not all that good. But I'm happy even when books I think aren't successful in literary terms do well, because it proves that there's room for those books to succeed, that it's not all big commercial fiction or the usual stuff you see on the best-seller list."

How did you get involved in this business?

Publishing is something I sort of drifted into. I really didn't think about being an editor when I was in college. I worked on literary magazines, and I liked it, but I didn't think about doing that as a career. But I think that's true of a lot of people: You just fall into something, and if you like it, you stay with it.

I like reading and editing, and I like figuring out ways of selling things, which is a large part of publishing. You have to have enthusiasm for your work, and if you have the enthusiasm you read a lot of it and you can figure out what the best work is. Then you try to figure out ways of selling it.

That's my job. I mean, writers can have a lot of friends, but if they don't have people looking after their affairs—people who pay attention to the *business*—they're not being well-served. It's great to get a book published—it's better to be badly published than not published at all—but for too many people, the book is thrown away. It doesn't get promoted. It isn't reviewed. That's the responsibility an editor has when working for a publisher. We work for writers. Anybody who has it any other way is foolish, because without writers, we don't have anything to publish. We've got to explain what we're doing and why we're doing it—make the writers part of the process.

I like the life: I like working with writers, and I like the people in publishing. It's a good combination. If you have a dozen people who are really interested in contemporary fiction and they're good people, they can make a huge difference because if each of them publishes ten books a year, that's over a hundred good books a year.

Publishers would rather publish good books than bad books. There's no doubt about that. It's a question of coming up with a way of making it financially possible. It's an advantage if you can offer books at a price people are willing to take a chance on—it helps the writers, and it helps the readers—but publishing was never set up to work that way. Publishers would say "Well, we'll make a lot of money on these hardcover books, even if we sell a few, and then we'll make more money on the paperback." But that wasn't happening.

Book publishers, I think, for too long felt that what they do is special and so wonderful that not everybody should understand or enjoy it. They also said that people like hardback books. Well, people will buy hardback books if they really like an author or if they're really deeply interested in a subject; otherwise, a lot of people will wait and buy the book in paperback. No other business seems to postpone the sale of a product. They don't say "Wait a year and these tires are all of a sudden going to be cheaper."

Jay's first two books posted very well, and Richard Ford's book *The Sportswriter* is another case. Richard is very established critically: *The Sportswriter* was up for the PEN/Faulkner award, and it made other lists, like *Time* magazine's top-ten of the year poll. I don't know what that book would have sold had it been in hardcover; it got very good reviews but, again, people can always say "I'll wait and buy it later." This way, they say "This is the time to buy it." That generates a lot more excitement around the publication of a book, rather than splitting it up, getting reviews for hardcovers and then trying to sell the book all over again a year later.

The marketing and packaging of books have helped, because they tried to make books seem interesting and not boring. There are probably people in the business who think it's gone too far, but my view would be that if it's good packaging and good design, it hasn't gone too far. A well-designed book should make somebody pick it up and look at it. That's all it's intended to do.

What do you personally look for? What do you want to put your stamp on?

I don't know. Mostly it's a case of having people submit work and my recognizing what's good and what isn't. There have been a lot of books that I've turned down—books that other people have published and done well with, but I would never have published them because I didn't get them. What any editor should do is read a book as closely as he can, but never interfere with the book itself. All of my books are very different, but I liked them all, each in its own way. Books work on their own terms: There are "aren't like something" books, and books where the sentences are good, and books that are about something that catches you up. They could be virtually anything, but a book that doesn't have any of these things can't be turned into one that does. Editing takes me a long time, because I'm very slow at it and I do it carefully, but after I send a book back to a writer, I never look back at it and say "Oh, you took this suggestion and not that one. You didn't agree with me on this. . . ." It's the writer's book, and what I do is try to show where the book seems to fall down on its own terms. That's when you really get to know a book, because you read it so carefully that you see how the plot works and what makes the characters work. But I don't think anybody takes a sprawling mess of a book and makes it a perfect, wonderful thing. I find this whole Maxwell Perkins line of thinking sophomoric.

Ian Gittler

BRET EASTON ELLIS

B ret Easton Ellis, baseball fan, has a Los Angeles
Dodgers baseball cap which he likes to wear around
his apartment. A lifelong resident of California, he only recently
moved to New York, but he's learning the ropes: When he goes
out on the street, he dons a Mets cap. There's no use asking for
trouble, he jokes.

As a writer, he has also learned to wear more than one hat.
On some occasions, he is Bret Easton Ellis, Public Figure and

Writer, highly visible author of two controversial novels, occasional talk-show guest, and (even less frequent) subject of a photo shoot for magazines such as *Interview* and *Vanity Fair*. Usually he is Bret Easton Ellis, self-proclaimed Shy-Guy and Writer, a man who spends a lot of time alone, writing, and bears very little resemblance to the self-absorbed party animals he writes about. He prefers to wear the hat of the private professional, just as he still roots for the Dodgers. But he's flexible, and he's not one-dimensional.

This has created problems for journalists, critics, and readers who figure that fiction is basically autobiography seen through a veil. They expect Ellis to be a coked-out Holden Caulfield, and by the time they've finished talking to him for the first time, they wind up feeling like the bee that stung itself to death.

Amanda Urban, Ellis's agent, summed it up well when she once noted that Ellis has a tendency to get bad reviews but very good press. There is a marked distinction between the man and his work, and anyone expecting Ellis to be one of the spoiled, cynical, decadent rich kids he chronicles in his fiction is going to be in for quite a surprise. It takes no effort to dislike the characters in his novels, but it's hard not to like the man himself.

Ellis is aware of the surprise he elicits from people, but he shrugs off the misconceptions as being part of the territory. "I can imagine other people having a really bad image of what I'm like," he says. "I could understand people picking up *The Rules of Attraction* and thinking that I must be just like all the characters in this book—a total asshole. It's very disorienting. After reading *Less Than Zero*, people expected me to be this arrogant, coke-snorting bisexual from California. At a party, I'd talk to people who had read the book, and they'd go, 'Oh yeah, when I was in California, I met *your* dealer—the dealer in the book.' And I would have to defend my personality: 'I'm sorry, I don't *have* a dealer in California; I don't know who you're talking about.' I finally learned that when you read other people's books, you cannot always look at the book jacket, see the writer's picture, and say that *that's* the person who's in the chapters. You realize that a lot of writing is big leaps of the imagination and not diary scribbles that get published. That was an important, maturing process for me."

Call it the learn-while-you-earn procedure to understanding the publishing industry. In Ellis's case, it's surprising how much he has learned (and earned) in so little time. At twenty-one, he became one of the youngest best-selling authors in recent memory when *Less Than Zero* hit the charts, as they say, with a bullet. A couple years later, by the time *The Rules of Attraction* garnered huge displays in New York's midtown bookstore windows, Ellis was a seasoned veteran taking his criticism and fame in stride, still enjoying the life of the writer, and, perhaps most important, not taking himself too seriously. All this from a guy who probably still gets his ID checked in some out-of-town bars.

One of his earliest lessons focused on literary politics, East Coast style. In some literary criticism circles, great weight is placed upon a book's being "politically correct," and Ellis is only one of many writers who have run into negative reviews written by critics who take the attitude that if a reader doesn't like a book's characters and can't sympathize with them, there should be no reason to read about them. The criticism following this line of thinking was not only exceptionally hostile, but it all started to sound alike. "The stream of consciousness . . . snakes along the gutters, strictly urine," a *Vanity Fair* reviewer griped about *The Rules of Attraction*. "There's nothing in the stream except the toxic wastes of narcissism," groused another from *The Chicago Tribune*.

The wasted young characters of Ellis's two books *are* a loathesome lot, especially when you consider that the future of the country could conceivably be in their hands: They do, after all, have the money, which is only a short skip and a few odd years away from their possessing the power. Still, Ellis finds dismissals of his books, based on the likability of his characters, perplexing.

"These people aren't supposed to be likable," he insists. "I get this gnawing suspicion sometimes that people assume that I really do like and care about these people, that I'm putting them out for my readers to embrace. That's not the case at all.

"To me, it's not a valid criticism. I've loved the way a lot of characters have been presented in fiction, but that doesn't mean I like them or would want to hang out with them or have dinner with them. There are a lot more interesting things going on in a novel than if you love a character—technical things about the book, or the way a narrative unfolds or *doesn't* unfold."

One of the more interesting reviews, combining contempt for Ellis's subject matter and a detailed discussion of his method of presenting it, was published in *The National Review*: "As a novel, *Less Than Zero* is less than satisfactory. As a piece of journalism, though, it is provocative and disturbing, even valuable." This argument refuels the debate over techniques used in fiction (as well as how those techniques are applied to subject matter), as opposed to nonfiction—especially when you consider *The National Review*'s admission, earlier in the review, that "the actual writing is quite accomplished."

Ellis believes his fiction occupies a gray space, which seems to be widening each year, between the writing techniques in the traditional novel and a newer style of journalism. "I was hugely influenced by a lot of journalism, especially the New Journalism that came out in the late Sixties and early Seventies," he says. "I started out wanting to be a nonfiction writer, and I still like writing a lot of nonfiction. I hope my nonfiction sensibility is meshed with my fictive sensibility in my books, that I'm using the tools one uses for reportage and journalism, and meshing them with the tools one uses to construct a satisfactory holding block for a novel. I'm influenced by both sides."

The huge success of *Less Than Zero* also reopened a problematic literary argument concerning the duty of the fiction writer: With more and more journalism seeping into American fiction —and, hence, a more detached air to the writing itself—what is the moral obligation of the novelist?

One school of thinking, championed by the late John Gardner, maintains that a strong moral stance is the duty of the novelist, while another school, typified by the writings of Jack Kerouac, insists that the writer's objective is to tell the truth, regardless of the beauty or ugliness of the subject matter.

Reaction to *Less Than Zero* was largely based on this debate, the novel praised or damned not so much for its literary merit as for its journalistic approach to reporting the lives of its characters. Sex, drugs, and violence were as common and incidental in the book as was its use of various artifacts of pop culture. Listening to a record, snorting cocaine, brutally raping a teenaged girl—any could have happened during a three-minute stretch, on any given day, in the lives of these aimless people.

Ellis contends that "moral fiction" is not necessarily the novelist's main objective, although his books leave little doubt, he says, about his disapproval of his characters' lifestyles; even if this were not the case, he assumes that the journalistic aspects of his fiction should lead intelligent readers to draw their own conclusions.

"I like posing situations and questions, and having people react to them. I'm not a psychologist or sociologist. I feel that, in lots of ways, what I'm doing is documenting much more than answering questions or giving reasons why people misbehave in this fashion."

Misbehave is, at best, a charitable assessment of the actions of the characters in *Less Than Zero* and *The Rules of Attraction*. On a good day, the various characters in the two books are merely trashed or rowdy; on bad days, their behavior is satanic. Between the two books, readers are treated to orgies, suicides, gang rapes, a snuff movie, drug overdoses, sexual promiscuity of all types, and assorted violence and mayhem. Most of these kids will never know despair because they don't have hope to lose. Ellis's characters live in a world of wilting green, where rock 'n' roll plays like a soundtrack for the dispossessed. In Jay Gatsby's squalid environs, a sign, "The Eyes of T. J. Eckelberg," oversees the wasteland; in Ellis's version, a billboard on Sunset Boulevard invites passersby to "Disappear Here."

Instead of following a traditional, linear plot, Ellis circles his story, telling it in quick takes intended to build a story by cumulative effect. This cinematic sense, Ellis says, was purely intentional.

"It was really important to make the book cinematic, to integrate the language of film into the writing. I remember being heavily influenced by the films of Robert Altman—especially *Nashville*, and its powerful, wandering technique.

"I have a real hard problem with constructing plot: More often than not, it seems like an imposition, something that's forced, and I prefer not to work that way. That is not to say that I don't enjoy novels with plots; you can have novels that are very, very accurate and honest, novels that do have stories. They're a crucial part of literature. But a person who had a big influence on me, when I was starting to write, was Ann Beattie. Her first two collections completely opened my eyes because of the lack of the classic short story structure. They made me realize all the things you could do with the form. Narrative didn't have to be this straight, linear thing."

Ellis, who has written a number of short stories which, at one time, he wanted to publish in book form, used James Joyce as a model in his efforts to expand the nonlinear narrative to the novel. At the time he was writing the first draft of *Less Than Zero*, he was studying Joyce—particularly *Ulysses*. "The most important parts of *Ulysses* were not in terms of storyline," Ellis says. "It was more of the random little moments that impressed me so much." Ellis's other early influences were wide-ranging, including Joan Didion, Nathaniel West, and Raymond Chandler.

And Ernest Hemingway. Virtually every young writer, male or female, working today, will list Hemingway as an influence of some sort or other, but when you look at the flat prose style in *Less Than Zero*, the influence is very direct:

> Rip says you can always find someone at Pages at one or two in the morning at Encino. Rip and I drive there one night because Du-Par's is crowded with teenage boys coming from toga parties and old waitresses wearing therapeutic shoes and lilacs pinned to their uniforms who keep telling people to be quiet. So Rip and I go to Pages and Billy and Rod are there and so are Simon and Amos and Le Deu and Sophie and Kristy and David. Sophie tells us about the Vice

Squad concert at The Palace and says that her brother slipped her a bad lude before the show and so she slept through it. Le Deu and David are in a band called Western Survival and they both seem calm and cautious. Rip asks Sophie where someone named Boris is and she tells him that he's at the house in Newport. . . .

The style in *Less Than Zero* is deceptively disciplined. The structure of the long, seemingly aimless sentences can have an annoying effect on readers who find distasteful any writing resembling stream-of-consciousness writing, but as the book moves on, you realize how much care has been put into the individual sentences.

It is here that Ellis cites Hemingway's influence. "I owe a lot of my 'control' to Hemingway, at least in this piece of work. I read him relentlessly all during high school—he became, like, my god when I was first starting to take writing seriously. It was Hemingway in high school, and Joyce in college—which is so weird because they're two wildly disparate figures."

Ultimately, though, the combination of style and narrative which, by now, after two books, has become a personal signature, was Ellis's creation, based on what he felt would be the most proper method of relaying the story of his psychologically drifting teenagers. In both novels, he says, "there is a lot of aimlessness and wandering around, and there just doesn't seem to be any room for plot. Imposing a narrative on these books seems to make everything else you're trying to do invalid. My least favorite section of *Less Than Zero* is the last quarter, where it does get this plot and semi-storyline. The same with *The Rules of Attraction.* I guess it just kind of ends up that way, when a book comes to an ending, just by the nature of the form."

Today, the publication of *Less Than Zero* is almost the stuff of legends in publishing circles. While a freshman student at Bennington College, Bret Easton Ellis took a junior-senior–level writing course taught by Joe McGinniss, author of the best-selling *Fatal Vision.* To be considered for admission into McGinniss's workshop, students were required to submit writing samples, and

Ellis turned in some of his high-school nonfiction writings. Not only was he admitted to the class, but he became one of McGinniss's star pupils. Ellis's writing so impressed McGinniss that he sent a sampling to Morgan Entrekin, then an editor at Simon and Schuster. Like McGinniss, Entrekin felt the work was noteworthy. He and Ellis met in New York, and Entrekin told the young writer to look him up if he ever got around to writing a novel.

"That all happened the fall of '82," Ellis remembers. "Then, between December and March, Bennington has what's called a 'nonresident term,' when you're not at school. School's closed and you go out and get a job that corresponds with your major. I was going to be a Lit major, so I decided to take that time to write the first draft of *Less Than Zero*. The book took a very short period to write—literally, I think, a period of eight weeks—but it also took two and a half to three years to rewrite, edit, and cut down."

That process, in many respects, was accomplished by "committee"—an irony which doesn't escape Ellis, who claims he chose writing over careers in music and film because he doesn't like to work in collaborative adventures. McGinniss (to whom the book is dedicated) and Entrekin took active interest in the novel's progress, but much of the supervision in the book's revision and cutting became the responsibility of Robert Asahina, a recently hired editor at Simon and Schuster. Prior to his job with the publishing house, Asahina had acted as an arts editor at *Harper's* magazine, where McGinniss had sent him some of Ellis's class assignments for review. Asahina and Ellis stayed in touch: Ellis sent him a copy of the *Less Than Zero* manuscript at the same time that Morgan Entrekin was getting a copy from Ellis's agent. Asahina and Entrekin co-sponsored the book at Simon and Schuster, and Asahina was assigned the editing tasks.

The book wound up being cut and revised substantially—including a change of voice, from third person to first person. (In an interview conducted by Joann David of *Publishers Weekly*, Asahina praised Ellis's professionalism during this reworking, calling him "as talented a rewriter as he is a writer.") Ellis credits Asahina and Entrekin for much of the help he received during the early stages of *Less Than Zero*, but he reserves his highest praise for McGinniss, who he says was "inordinately helpful" as a teacher, advisor, and friend.

"It's great having a guy like that as a teacher," says Ellis, "especially when you're first starting out, getting your foot in the door. You run into a lot of erudite, pseudosophisticated professors who speak with slight British accents they've picked up somewhere, but he's not like that. He's a nice, jovial kind of guy who's not really a part of the whole literati scene. Because of that, I could be more open with him."

Ellis laughs when he recalls one of their major disagreements, a running argument about the book's title, which Ellis had lifted from an early Elvis Costello song. "He hated the title, and he tried to persuade me for months to change it—even when the book was in galleys," Ellis says, adding that other people at his publishing house agreed with McGinniss. (Ironically, it's a title that Jay McInerney, now a friend of Ellis's, once considered for *Bright Lights, Big City*.)

The book, published in May 1985, was a critical and popular surprise. Despite a glut of unfavorable reviews, *Less Than Zero* received support from *The Village Voice*, as well as from Michiko Kakutani of *The New York Times*, who wrote that *Less Than Zero* "possesses an unnerving air of documentary reality." Penguin paid $99,000 for the book's paperback rights, and its movie option was purchased by Twentieth Century-Fox. Ellis was on his way.

"The whole *Less Than Zero* experience cemented my total faith in fate," Ellis says in understatement. "This one amazed me, it was so fortunate."

Less than twelve months prior to writing the first draft of *Less Than Zero*, Bret Easton Ellis debated whether he should attend college at all. He had just completed high school at the Buckley School, a private school in Sherman Oaks, California, where, he claims, he failed to wow his educators with his grade point average and SAT scores. He had applied to a number of liberal arts colleges, including Bennington, Sarah Lawrence, and Boston College but, even though he had been accepted at a handful of schools, the prospects of his attending any of them grew dimmer as the summer between his high-school graduation and the first semester of college progressed. He knew he wanted to write, but he had recently joined a rock band, and the latter career seemed attractive.

"It was a garage band in L.A.," he explains. "We were going to try to get a record deal or something like that. I'd already been accepted at Bennington, but I thought, 'Well, I'll just blow it off and not go.' I really hated high school—the whole process—and I had this idea that college would be four more years of the same sort of institutionalized blandness. I went to a very strict private high school, where we had uniforms and haircut regulations, and I thought college would just be an extension of that."

While in high school, he had considered careers in writing, film, and music, but the nature of the work in filmmaking and music turned his head toward writing. "Growing up in Los Angeles around the film industry, you notice a lot more quickly than, say, the students at NYU, that filmmaking is a collaborative art, and I wanted to control what I was creating. I'm a big control freak. And I've always wanted to be a musician—I'd much rather be in a band than be a writer—but that's a collaborative process because even if you write the songs and do all the riffs, you're still working with other people who are playing other instruments, getting together, and having schedules."

Ellis is quick to point out, however, that writing was far from a last-ditch career choice. He had written two novels in high school, and he traces his early writing efforts back to kindergarten or first grade. "Every other kid would be painting or doing music or stuff like that; for some reason, I was always really interested in writing. Reading had a lot to do with my wanting to be a writer. I was an avid reader and, as a child, reading a lot makes you want to write. You want to mimic the book and duplicate the things that entertain you so much. I *seriously* started to write in seventh or eighth grade."

Whether it was fate or just a matter of his coming to his senses,

Ellis is glad he eventually decided to attend Bennington and study writing. The garage band, he recalls with amusement, broke up a few months after he left Los Angeles. ("I never felt like the fifth Beatle or anybody," he chuckles.) In less time than it takes the average college student to decide on a major, Ellis had written the first draft of a book that would build his career.

~~~~~~~~~~

Looking back, Ellis believes that he was very fortunate to have still been a college student when *Less Than Zero* hit the best-seller lists. As the newest, youngest member of the "literary youth movement," Ellis found himself the focus of a media storm. His still being in college insulated him from many of the sudden demands being placed on his time.

"It saved me," he says. "The timing couldn't have been better. I was really in the middle of Nowhere, Vermont, away from the publicity and the whole press machine. Bennington is small, and you end up knowing everyone. It's like a family, so [the success of *Less Than Zero*] was no big deal at all. I got the same looks walking to classes as I did before."

His introductory course to the publishing world went smoothly, as well. Every day was another test—or, perhaps more accurately, a pop quiz—on his abilities to handle his reviews and publicity, the comparisons with other writers, and, to some degree, his notoriety. He learned very quickly that there could be a vast difference between how he originally conceived the publishing business to be, and how it really was.

"Before *Less Than Zero* came out, I thought I would pore over every review I got, but after the first couple of reviews, they really didn't matter that much. I viewed them passively and from a distance, which I didn't expect. A bad review was not going to ruin my day, and a good review wasn't going to make it. I hate sounding this blasé, but it's not important for me to be accepted by reviewers or by people writing about my books. In the end, it becomes a very closed thing for me: If I'm happy and satisfied with this book that I've worked on for a couple of years, if I feel there have been artistic and emotional gains, the publishing aspect is really sort of secondary. I'm not writing for prestige or praise."

Handling publicity, he continues, is more complicated. Because of his youth and the subject matter of *Less Than Zero*, he was initially in great demand as a guest on television talk shows, or as a subject of newspaper or magazine profiles—situations Ellis claims he is only marginally comfortable with. And, whether he likes it or not, his name almost always pops up in conversations or articles about America's hot young talents, most often in connection with a trinity made up of Ellis, Jay McInerney, and Tama Janowitz. Perhaps the attention, as has been noted by a number of writers who feel exploited by the press, is part of a media blitz, but Ellis will never be accused of being a recluse; he has appeared in too many highly visible places—including photo layouts in *Interview* and *Vanity Fair* magazines—to cry "foul" too loudly.

Ellis asserts that publicity is a question of making the right choices, of trying to properly promote a book while maintaining artistic integrity. "I don't know," he shrugs, "I'm really *not* a big self-promoter, and I sort of go along with it. In a way, you owe your publisher because they *are* publishing your book and putting a lot of money into it, and you want to help them recoup their investment. I was very hesitant to do all the publicity the company wanted me to do for *Less Than Zero*, and I did draw a line. I've turned down ads. I won't do Scotch ads or male clothing ads, and I've turned down a couple of modeling jobs because I don't think that's how I want to be perceived. If it *was* me, I'd do it in a minute. Tama can do it because it's part of her persona, but it's not part of mine. I feel very, very uncomfortable in it."

As his name and image gained currency in the publishing industry, Ellis also found himself facing another publicity-related aspect of the book business: the prospect of blurbing books. All of a sudden, at twenty-one, he was considered a literary authority, at least by publishers trying to hawk their books—a "name" whose endorsement was worth a dollar figure.

Ellis kept his distance and continues to do so. "It's insane how they sometimes send you the wrong books. A lot of it isn't in my field, and my name on the book would misrepresent it and lead the wrong people to it. It would be ridiculous if I gave a blurb to a lot of the books I'm sent, though I'd gladly give a nice blurb to a great first novel if my name would make any difference at all, and if the book needed a lot of push, but I haven't been faced with a lot of that."

Ellis, along with Janowitz and McInerney, may be in the position—enjoyed by only a small number of serious literary writers—of knowing that their books have a certain guaranteed audience, no matter how the books are received critically. Considering the idea, Ellis says, "I never really thought about that. In some perverse way, I guess you have to be grateful for it. That's a weird feeling."

Attending Bennington, the country's most expensive university, afforded Ellis the opportunity to consider what might happen when the affluent young subculture, chronicled in *Less Than Zero*, grew a few years older and relocated its designer clothing, expensive sports cars, and credit cards to the East Coast. If anything, the young adults in *The Rules of Attraction*, Ellis's account of this, are more frightening than their teenaged counterparts in *Less Than Zero*: At this juncture in life, some consideration is usually given to the future, but the future to Ellis's college students rarely extends beyond midnight—if, in fact, their ambitions and memories are capable of lasting that long. Presented in a mosaic of individual voices, *The Rules of Attraction* is still another book about a generation destroyed by madness, the book's characters being so desultory that a reader might think that this was the condition required for admission to the college. Two decades ago, this group might have used its prodigious energy to protest the Vietnam War; today, it lacks a unifying force, other than a taste, which pulls it like a dowsing rod, for a party. Education is beside the point.

Sean, the novel's most compelling character, is a Rimbaud-like figure whose outward cynicism and recklessness mask an inner awareness of his academic and social failures. He has as little use for his inheritance—a successful business which he associates with an equally contemptible Yuppie older brother—as he has for any solutions the ambiguity of college may have to offer.

The book's other major characters are just as unsettled. Paul, who has a crush on Sean, is a student whose bisexuality seems to be more the result of confusion than choice, while Lauren, the novel's main female character, still pining over the loss of a boyfriend, is the object of Sean's pursuit, a young woman who uses sex as a means of filling a void. Both entertain marginally romantic notions about relationships, but neither seems capable of aligning those attitudes, presumably formed over a period of years, with the fast, disposable mores of college life and their day-to-day urges.

When discussing this book, Ellis makes a special point of remarking about these characters' being representative of only a small segment of the college students at Bennington. The characters, he remarks, are composites of students, and their actions are exaggerated. And—again—he hopes his readers, many of whom he assumes have read *Less Than Zero*, will be able to see that he does not endorse the actions of his characters, even if he doesn't place judgment on them.

Two years before the publication of *The Rules of Attraction*, and shortly after the publication of *Less Than Zero*, Ellis wrote a long essay, "Down and Out at Bennington College," for *Rolling Stone*. The essay not only foreshadowed the major theme of *The Rules of Attraction*, but it also made quite clear some of the disillusionment Ellis felt toward the aimless, noncommittal elements of the campus scene:

> I've talked to students at other colleges, especially politically outspoken ones such as Columbia and Oberlin and Berkeley and UCLA, and they agree that student activism has taken on a strange, pervasive party atmosphere. A keg in the name of nuclear disarmament or a keg in the name of antiapartheid or a keg for the starving masses of Ethiopia

or for the prochoice movement. The one topic you'd think college students, especially males, would have protested against would have been the Solomon Amendment, which said that federal aid to students would be cut if they didn't register for the draft. But then, you think, who didn't register? And you have the answer. In reality, the only activists left on most college campuses are the teachers who were activists in the Sixties, who can't instill those values in a generation of students so party-close-minded.

"I lost a lot of freshman friends at Bennington because of that piece," Ellis jokes, adding that the campus's reaction to *The Rules of Attraction* was slow in coming from Bennington. ("But I don't know if I'm going to get the newsletters anymore," he cracks.)

The novel, he says, was a challenge. "It was a hard book to write, and it took a long time to write because, in this book, what you're essentially writing, a lot of the time, is *nonprose*. You're putting your characters' thought processes into words, and that's hard to write because no one thinks in prose. That's why there are a lot of one- and two-word sentences, and a lot of very long paragraphs that aren't grammatically correct. A lot of those sections aren't smooth reads. But, to me, it seemed like the most honest and accurate way to describe a person. You might think, 'Well, this sentence sounds so much better,' but then you'd go, 'But no one thinks that way,' so you would have to chop the sentence sometimes and make the transitions seem a little clumsier than usual. I felt this approach was necessary."

As he did in *Less Than Zero*, Ellis weaved song lyrics, movie titles, brand names, and elements of pop culture into *The Rules of Attraction*. At times, the book reads like a catalog of disposable culture, mid-1980s style: Today's megahit will be tomorrow's trivia question or golden oldie, the same way a gruesome campus suicide today will be forgotten tomorrow (or worse if, as in *The Rules of Attraction*, it's seen as a disruption or inconvenience). Though he has been sneered at for such pop-culture inclusions, Ellis defends its liberal use in his books.

"I consciously worked at it," he says. "A lot of people put songs into certain scenes in their books because they love the songs. I don't really like most of the music in my books—that's plain— but it seemed authentic that these songs be playing and the characters be listening to them. In *Less Than Zero*, it would have been hard to write about that group of people and not mention the film community. It wasn't a *choice* to be made. Plus, the idea of images—conceptual images and movies and TV screens—was important to me."

The little touches, Ellis insists, make a great deal of difference to him, even if they irritate his detractors. As an example, he points to the way *The Rules of Attraction* opens and closes in midsentence—a point of style which drew fire from a number of reviewers. "I always wanted to do that," he says. "I would have loved to have done it with *Less Than Zero*. With such little effort, it says a lot, I think, about the tone of the book."

The addition of Clay, the protagonist of *Less Than Zero*, in *The Rules of Attraction* was another of the book's last-minute adjustments which Ellis believes "made a little bit of a difference." Ellis included Clay in the manuscript for *The Rules of Attraction*, but when the film company making *Less Than Zero* objected to the use of the character in the new book, Ellis had to rename the character, only to change it back between the galleys and the published book after a legal struggle allowed him to do so. In the final, published version, Clay's voice appears in one segment. This kind of effort can be seen in some of the other changes made between galleys and the final product—efforts which are usually overlooked by those who claim Ellis's books are hastily or shabbily written.

"They were important choices to me," Ellis says. "Sometimes you go through your books and see choices you wish you hadn't made—or choices you wish you *had* made—that aren't in the texts, and those are sharp, painful moments. Overall, I think the reworking here made a big difference, even if the reader going through it wouldn't notice it that much."

A few weeks after the publication of *The Rules of Attraction*, Ellis walked into a large Fifth Avenue bookstore, where he hoped to kill time before meeting a friend for lunch. It wound up being a very short visit. A huge spiral display of *The Rules of Attraction* had been set up, and Ellis found himself face-to-face with the mass marketing of his own novel. "I had an anxiety attack," he remembers, "and I had to leave. I was very embarrassed."

Success has given him a lot at an early age. Money is no problem. He is a recognizable literary figure. He has a reputation in a business that ignores the vast majority of people who labor all their lives to become known. His books are prominently reviewed. This sort of attention has gone to the heads of writers twice Ellis's age, but it doesn't seem to have affected him too much. If anything, he is still coming to terms with the fact that he is an established, as opposed to being an aspiring, writer, and he admits that it makes him a little uneasy at times.

"In a lot of ways, I hate thinking, even to myself, that I'm an artist. I really feel uncomfortable using that term, but in a literal sense, it's true. I've always felt undeserved to be mentioned in these reviews, to be compared with some of these other writers. I felt out of place, mostly, I guess, because of my age, though it does make it a little easier that there are a lot of young writers getting published at the same time.

"I'm very self-conscious about the whole thing. In a figurative sense, I *write*, but I'm not a writer, in the sense that it's very easy to get snooty and erudite and highfalutin about it, and that bugs me. Writing may be interesting to talk about, but so are sports, so are movies. But then everyone thinks you're the reverse snob, a reverse intellectual who's being sort of slummy, when you're not, when these are the things that give you pleasure. There's so much more to life than reading and writing—well, not a lot. . . ."

He laughs. He is still adapting to fame and success, finding himself confronting aspects of the writing life that he never considered before. He is still surprised by the scope of it, by the ways lives interconnect when author reaches reader. Even his mail serves as a reminder.

"When I first started, I said I was going to answer all my mail," Ellis says. "I answered the first letter I got, and that person ended up sending me three manuscripts, which he wanted me to read and send to publishers—and I still haven't gotten rid of the guy. I mean, I've got my own life. You know?

"Then I got a letter from someone in Italy. I couldn't read a single word of it and I didn't know what I was going to do with it." The thought strikes him funny, even though he intends for his books to strike a universal chord.

"How do you translate 'dude' into Italian?" he wonders.

R. Estell

LORRIE MOORE

Lorrie Moore settles back in her chair and considers a question that has been posed to her. As a writer and as someone who has done a fair amount of book reviewing, she knows the value of a well-placed word, as well as the damage that can be caused by a misused one. Now she has been asked to address questions about her own work, and she realizes the inherent dangers of the task: If you are too serious in your self-analysis, you wind up looking as if you believe that every word you produce is precious; if you are too glib or self-effacing, you come off sounding as if you don't take to heart the commitment to writing serious fiction.

As an individual, part of Moore's charm is the fact that she is both self-effacing *and* serious about herself and her work. One moment, she will protest the way her work—especially her novel—has been handled by critics, and in the next, she will wave off a sentence from her work as being either very good or very bad, as if she really doesn't know.

"I wanted to write stories that you weren't supposed to write," she finally says, as a means of characterizing her short fiction. "I wanted to write things that broke the rules a little bit."

She has done just that. The stories in *Self-Help*, her first book, focus on the individual's ways of coping with assorted personal crises, many of the stories being written in a second-person, present tense narrative characteristic of the style used in popular self-help manuals. *Anagrams*, Moore's second book, an exploration into the nonlinear novel, considers the ways people's lives can be changed by rearrangement of circumstance, and rather than give her readers one story, Moore has given them five, all essentially involving the same set of characters who behave or misbehave according to the different situations in which they are placed.

In terms of style, Moore's stories and novel may break the rules a little bit, but her greatest risks may be taken in the way she aligns her style with her point of view. Most of her characters internalize their feelings about the problems that plague them, and for many writers such introspection lends itself to long passages of intricately detailed prose which borders the precious; instead of taking this safe approach, Moore writes in a stripped-back prose which leaves emotions essentially bare and vulnerable. Internal feelings, if simply stated, risk looking ludicrous or overstated; Moore counters with humor, or by allowing her characters to slip into fantasy.

This writing has elicited some interesting, if conflicting, critical response. Writing for *Commentary*, critic Carol Iannone compared Moore's work to that of David Leavitt, complaining that while both writers are perceptive of "the terms of our liberated culture" and choose to address these terms in their fiction, neither seems to directly challenge the deficiencies of these cultural aspects:

> Accepting these terms as given—even at times celebrating them—they devote themselves instead to spare, taut chronicles that are the byproducts of personal and cultural expansion. The tension between the complacent perception of such expansion and the unhappiness occasioned by it can shape both the form and the content of their work. . . .

Dissatisfied with the way Moore's characters address the issues of their lives—particularly in the case of Benna Carpenter, the protagonist of *Anagrams*—Iannone concluded that "Miss Moore's remedy for the turmoil of such a life is fantasy."

Ironically, in reviewing *Anagrams* for *The New York Times Book Review*, novelist Carol Hill also focused on the ways that fantasy shapes Benna's methods of surviving the harshness of her world, but instead of criticizing this aspect of the book, Hill praised it. "[*Anagrams*] is a powerful example of how imagination can save us with temporary pleasures," Hill wrote.

But Moore herself probably summarized the most important theme of her first two books when she wrote in her short story "To Fill": "You live if you dance to the voice that ails you."

There is no question that Moore's characters are dancing to their own inner music, to songs that are, however, far from upbeat. The stories in *Self-Help*, written mostly as a Master's thesis when Moore was studying at Cornell, focus on suicide, death, divorce, madness, and infidelity.

Today, dividing her time between a half-year spent teaching in Madison, Wisconsin, and a half-year's residence in New York, Moore confesses a feeling of removal from much of that early work. She has traveled a great distance, she says, from the obsessions of her days as a creative writing student.

"A journalist came to my office at the University of Wisconsin, sat down and said, 'You know, don't you, that *Self-Help* is the work of a clinically depressed person.'" Moore laughs, as if to refute the recent memory. She pauses momentarily to sip from a mug of coffee, and then continues. "As it's said, you don't *choose* your obsessions—they come out and you shape them and play with them. I was writing something that I would have been interested in reading. I couldn't write that book now because every book is a metaphorical document of a certain period in your life. It doesn't stand for what you did, but it stands for what was on your mind.

"I used to be a little more panicked about certain things. In *Anagrams*, there's this recurrent concern about childlessness and in not having children—a concern about what replaces the child in a man or woman's life. I'm not so concerned about those things anymore."

Moore's obsessions are often on the minds of serious writers, young or otherwise, but what distinguishes her early work from the fiction of other contemporaries covering similar territory is her deadpan writing style, delivered with the timing and sense of irony present in comedic stand-up routines. Her wit slices to the heart of her subject matter, her characters dance for their lives.

In "How to Be an Other Woman," the protagonist, a compulsive compiler of lists, defines the sources of her unhappiness with her love affair as such:

1. This affair is demeaning.
2. Violates decency. Am I just a scampish tart, some tartish scamp?
3. No emotional support here.
4. Why do you never say "I love you" or "Stay in my arms forever my little tadpole" or "Your eyes set me on fire, my sweet nubkin"?

Then, in her following passage, she answers the reader's question about why her character would stay with a married man if the relationship made her so unhappy:

> The next time he phones, he says, "I was having a dream about you and suddenly I woke up with a jerk and felt very uneasy."
> Say: "Yeah, I hate to wake up with jerks."
> He laughs, smooth, beautiful, and tenor, making you feel warm inside your bones. And it hits you, maybe it all boils down to this: people will do anything, anything, for a really nice laugh.

Like a comic, Moore assumes that her audience is familiar with the material she is covering, that her readers' prior knowledge of and opinions about her stories' themes will aid her in her development of irony.

"I don't consciously imagine any particular reader," she says, "but I suppose I am writing, unconsciously or subconsciously, for a roomful of people who are my friends. My readers would know what a friend of mine would know. There's an assumption of a kind of friendship between author and reader, but that's also the project of the fiction or the story, to bring about this particular friendship."

In her fiction, Moore would like to replicate what she calls the "wedding between the humorous and the profound" present in the work of writers such as Kurt Vonnegut or Joseph Heller, but she is not intent on making humor her signature. Despite the humor in her work, she does not depict herself as a humorist. For Moore, humor and irony are tools, not objectives. If a crisis is the music Moore's characters hear in their hearts, humor is a dance step.

"It would be difficult to make a lifetime of writing funny stories," she says, "but there are certain times in your life when writing funny things is what you want to do, and what you have to do. You have the energy and sensibility for it."

Many of the stories in *Self-Help*, such as "How to Be an Other

Woman" and "How to Become a Writer," depend on humor for their structure: Moore's short "takes"—and many of the stories are more "takes" or "bits" than traditionally structured short stories—depend on the density of language and wordplay, packed into a few pages. In *Anagrams*, Moore moved away from a strong reliance on humor needed to contrast and heighten serious points. The longer structure of the novel afforded her the luxury of using humor less directly and, as a result, she was able to use a greater variety of humorous devices (the pun, the one-liner, sarcasm, the inside joke) than she was able to integrate into her stories. Humor was used to accent the text.

It also allowed her to employ a lot more wordplay, one of her favorite devices, into her fiction. Moore's use of wordplay has been compared to that of Tom Robbins, and though Moore is hesitant to call Robbins a literary influence, she does admit his effect on her in terms of inspiration.

"There's something about reading his books that gives me tremendous joy and courage," she says, "because he just takes such chances. Sometimes he falls on his face and it's an embarrassment, but other times it's this wigged-out genius that makes you laugh out loud."

In her role as a creative writing teacher, Lorrie Moore encourages her students to take chances. She wants them to take risks in their fiction although, she says, the results are often predictably unpredictable.

"Risk is sometimes a different thing to students," she points out. "Sometimes you have to get students to really write about the stories they know—and they know some wonderful stories—when, so often, what they want to write about is, say, sharks: Sharks are a big thing in Wisconsin. Students are obsessed with sharks and love to write shark stories. So you have to say 'No, no, no—no sharks. C'mon, you've never even seen a shark.' They've been to the movies and they want to participate in some pop-cultural theme or fiction out there. So, for them, taking a risk is telling what they really do know. At the undergraduate level, that can be risky. At any age, I suppose, it is."

Moore recalls her own undergraduate days, when she took

creative writing classes from Joe David Bellamy at St. Lawrence University. Bellamy was editing *Fiction International*, and he assigned his students a number of experimental short stories as readings. Moore's interest in this kind of writing, along with Bellamy's encouragement, strongly influenced her decision to pursue writing seriously.

"I was very receptive to whatever positive reinforcement came my way," she says of those early writing days. "On the surface, I think I resisted or protested, but deep down I was easily encouraged. If someone said something smart or enthusiastic about my work, I went home and thought about it all week."

She had little trouble finding subjects to write about. "Go Like This," the first story written for *Self-Help*, was started in 1980, when Moore was twenty-three. An account of a woman who gathers her friends and family around her to plan and discuss her pending suicide, "Go Like This" was Moore's outraged reaction to an actual occurrence, a news item which deeply disturbed her.

"It was a response to something I'd seen on television," she remarks. "A woman in New York, a sculptor, had cancer and was going to kill herself, and she videotaped the gathering with all her friends and family. The people in her life were very calm, and there was a panel discussion afterward. *Everyone* seemed to be calm about it—except me. I was horrified. No one seemed to see how torn this woman was. So I wrote a story about a woman who does something similar, but who's completely torn. You see the mess that she is inside, and the discrepancy between that and what she's calmly choosing to do. Finally, everyone is monstrous in the story: She's monstrous for asking her friends to endorse her and participate in her death, and they're monstrous for agreeing to do it. It becomes a story about rescue—and the failure of anyone to rescue anyone else. To some extent, that is what all the stories in the collection are about."

The story, Moore continues, has elicited strong reader response, and she is encouraged that her readers react with the same emotions that she felt when she saw the original story on television. "I wanted to write stories that moved me," she explains, "stories that I'd read and cry over when I finished them.

I still do sometimes, but I no longer trust that as evidence of good writing."

One of the most touching stories in *Self-Help* is also one of the collection's most experimental works: In "How to Talk to Your Mother," Moore narrates her story in reverse chronology, moving backward from a woman's adulthood to the moment of her birth. Throughout the story, Moore uses the historical development of the heart transplant as a major symbol, yet unlike the case with "Go Like This," where a news event formed the foundation of the story, Moore feels that this later story suffers from its being written *before* a major news event occurred. The story might have been better, Moore reasons, if she had been able to include the artificial heart as part of her symbolism.

"When Barney Clark died, I felt very, very upset," she says. "The papers were following it, and the whole thing was uncomfortable from the start. It was the same way with William Schroeder. I wrote the story in '83, before those particular manifestations of artificial hearts, and I'm wondering what would have happened if I had written it later. The story, of course, is about coming to terms with the mother inside of one and the mother outside of one, and of the heartfulness and heartlessness of living."

As an exercise in experimental writing, it was a demanding story. Rather than write it the easy way—composing it in straight, chronological order and reversing it when the story was completed—Moore disciplined herself to write the story backward. This decision may seem minor to readers, but Moore believes that the discipline enabled her to write a better, more moving story.

"In the writing, the compelling thing for *me* was the birth at the end of the story, that first moment between mother and child. I wanted to move the story back *to* there, through a course marked with children and mothers, and the relationships between mothers and children. If I hadn't aimed at that moment, nothing would have propelled it, so moving backward in *time* was actually moving forward in the *story*."

The tactic was effective: The tenderness of a first moment between mother and child offers a sharp contrast to the ensuing detailing of the rocky relationship between the protagonist and her mother which, predictably, began with great hope.

⁂

In January 1977, *Seventeen* magazine published a story entitled "Raspberries," written by a teenaged writer named Lorrie Moore, as the winning entry in its annual short story contest. For many aspiring writers, early national publication of this nature would have signaled the beginning of and commitment to a promising literary career, but Lorrie Moore insists that this was not a determining factor in her decision to pursue a writing career. Nor, she adds, was she similar to the student protagonist of "How to Become a Writer," who wanders into the wrong college classroom, attends a creative writing class, and goes on to become a writer.

"I didn't drift in completely by accident," she says, "but I didn't at first have any real calling or guidance, either. I took seriously the courses I had with Joe Bellamy. At that point, I was becoming more serious about my studies, and writing came to me via this particular academic world. It came to me as a course I wanted to excel at. It didn't initially come out of anything more romantic than that.

"I mean, I was seventeen or eighteen years old. To a certain extent, I have a feeling that if anyone had come along and said, 'Ah, you play the piano so well,' I would have tried to become a concert pianist. When I was writing, I had the sense that I was doing something vital and exciting and dangerous—and getting college credits. What a deal! It was a fiction-writing drug that I was on: I'd walk around the campus in a haze of first drafts."

For Moore, the experience represented growth, a coming of age from her childhood days in upstate New York. Born in 1957, in Glens Falls, New York, a small city near the Vermont border, Lorrie Moore was her parents' first daughter, and the second of their four children. Children were important to her parents, who took in a number of foster children over the years, and the family unit is a continuing concern to Moore, who has written about it in her fiction.

As a child, Moore studied piano and took ballet lessons, and she has warm memories of what she calls "probably a typical small-town childhood, though who really knows what that means." She jokes that her early fears centered on her being tall and thin. "I was afraid of falling into places I couldn't possibly fall into," she cracks. "I was suspicious of the gratings in the street and of certain public toilets. I suppose I was afraid of being swallowed up somehow."

Moore's sharp memories of her childhood have led to some very poignant writing about the world as seen through the eyes of a child. In *Anagrams*, Benna Carpenter's six-year-old daughter, Georgianne, affords Moore the opportunity to explore the mother-daughter relationship to a greater depth than she could in her stories. Drawing upon her own childhood memories, Moore recreates tiny scenes of domesticity which add dimension to her adult characters:

> George smiles and I lean over and give her a *puffle*, something my mother used to do with us: press mother's mouth against child's neck and blow out air. It's warm and wet and tickles. George tenses, shoulders up by her ears in anticipation, her whole body in a scrinch—then she giggles and relaxes. "Do it again," she says, and I do it twice more.

This scene is so seemingly trivial that it would be considered filler in another novel, but when the reader sees Benna Carpenter, the mother, pitted against a childless Benna Carpenter in another section of the book, Moore's commentary on the effects children have on adults (and vice versa) becomes unmistakable.

"The Kid's Guide to Divorce," a story in *Self-Help*, finds Moore presenting the entire narrative through the consciousness of a young child spending an evening watching television with his divorced mother. The domestic scenes give Moore the opportunity to be both subtle and poignant:

When the popcorn is all gone, yawn. Say: I'm going to bed now.

Your mother will look disappointed, but she'll say, okay, honey. She'll turn the tv off. By the way, she'll ask hesitantly like she always does. How did the last three days go?

Leave out the part about the lady and the part about the beer. Tell her they went all right, that he's got a new silver dartboard and that you went out to dinner and this guy named Hudson told a pretty funny story about peeing in the hamper. Ask for a 7-Up.

Bringing such elements of childhood to serious adult fiction is one of the major contributions of the best of today's young female writers, though the matter of gender and age is an area about which both young male and young female writers appear to be very touchy, if not ambiguous. In an article written for *Gentlemen's Quarterly*, Tad Friend theorized that in the absence of war as a larger-than-life subject to focus a generation's interests, "familial strife has become the writer's battleground. It is here that one group of writers have cleared their throats—young women writers."

The best of these women writers are writing not about confused loners but about families, considered over the course of generations—women seem to know where they've been and thus have a better sense of where they're going.

There may be some truth to this, and there is no denying that, in terms of sheer numbers, more young women writers are concerning themselves with the "family theme" than their male counterparts. Lorrie Moore, whose writings on the family issues have been considered in a number of critical articles, has mixed feelings about all this. She is delighted to find so many women finally being published and marketed, yet she is also concerned about the problem of stereotyping when writers are being examined in terms of gender.

One particular published piece brought this into focus. In

"Publishing's New Starlets," a roundup article appearing in *U.S. News and World Report* in December 1986, Julia Reed portrayed a number of young women writers in a sort of demographic common to roundups looking for common denominators: In turns, women writers were young, attractive, trendy, single, childless, minimalist, graduates of writing programs, and recipients of "a lot of incestuous connections" in the publishing world. Near the end of the article, Reed mentioned that Jayne Anne Phillips and Louise Erdrich have been deemed to possess "more lasting voices" than the rest of their contemporaries, adding, not so subtly, that both authors "have families and live in New England" (and, presumably, away from the glitz and distractions of New York City, where so many of the authors reside). In a photo caption, Phillips is portrayed as an "earth mother."

Despite the merits of her female contemporaries, Lorrie Moore resents the elements of sexism present in reviews and articles about their work. Writing for *Mademoiselle*, Moore expressed some of her vexation:

> There is a built-in obsolescence to these new literary tags, and behind them lurks a bitter synthesis of ageism, careerism, amnesia and, particularly, sexism. This last is especially dismaying. When a certain group of young writers happens to be female, it gets slapped with the phrase "young women writers." When the group of authors is male, however, it inherits the category "the new young writers." No one, it seems, ever says, "young men writers."

Moore still bristles at the mention of the *U.S. News* article, and while she makes it quite clear that she does not wish to become a spokesperson in a debate of the literary merits of writers categorized by gender or age lines, she does offer a few parting shots.

"That article seemed to suggest that the *serious* writers were not the single ones—that, in fact, if you were married, with children, you acquired literary seriousness. That was so completely offensive. Erdrich and Phillips are terrific writers, and it has nothing to do with their being married and living in New England."

⌣⌣⌣⌣⌣⌣⌣⌣⌣⌣

If Lorrie Moore dislikes the categorizations typical of journalists or critics seeking common denominators, she may have discovered the ultimate way of addressing the issue in *Anagrams*, her 1986 novel which devours sterotypes and takes on dualistic or linear thinking in a fashion that is part Lewis Carroll, part William S. Burroughs, and part Richard Brautigan—all caught in a perspective which defies simple classification. With only the sketchiest of plots, *Anagrams*, for its readers, can be slippery and difficult to get a handle on, and even its reviewers struggled mightily to pin down what the book was about. Writing for *Mademoiselle*, Joyce Maynard concluded that in *Anagrams*

> Moore conveys rootlessness as subtly and as well as any writer around. But there is a dispiriting centerlessness here. When it's all over, a reader may find herself asking (as I did) what the point was. Maybe it's that there isn't any.

Novelist Hilma Wolitzer, in her review for *Ms.* magazine, highly praised the novel for its themes and humor, though she admitted that "when anyone asked me what the book was *about*, in terms of story or plot, I was hard-pressed to say."

The reviews reminded one of the story of the person who wandered into the surrealist room of a modern art museum. Standing in front of a Salvador Dali painting, slightly nodding his head in appreciation, the man is asked by his companion what he sees in the painting. "I'm not sure I know," he answers, "but I know I like it."

In explaining the structure of her novel, Lorrie Moore calls *Anagrams* "a kind of cubistic experiment with a vaudevillean strain—language on tilt."

"I began by starting the 'Nun of That' section first. Because it was about the relationship of reality to imagination—or art, if you will—I became acutely aware not only of the transmutation of real-life information that I was making in order to create a fiction, but I was also aware of the transmutations the trans-mutation itself was inclined toward. It was as if a dream you'd concocted began to have a dream life of its own. And the rela-tionship of dream to life, of the dream of the thing to the thing itself, I discovered, is roughly anagrammatic. Dreams are wild and reckless rearrangements of stored information, done in an attempt to edify and amuse—to create something new from a limited supply of component parts. Biological life is built on this idea as well. There are only four basic building blocks in DNA, but the arrangement is played with endlessly. It's rearrangement that generates new life forms. And so I allowed my novel the structure it now had: a short novel prefaced by the rearrangements that sprang simultaneously out of it during the writing."

The four prefatory stories are an interesting experiment. Each stands independently, like a sliver filed from the novel, bearing significant details about the characters the reader will meet in the main body of the novel. There are three epigraphs to the four-story section, each providing clues to what Moore will be doing with her book: We will be dealing with alternate realities, in the possibilities we encounter in mythology or dreams, or in choosing one path over another—and these possibilities can be haunting. In "Strings Too Short to Use," one of the stories in this section, Benna Carpenter, talking to her closest friend about the across-the-hall living arrangements she shares with Gerard, her lover, offers another clue when she says the arrangement is like living in "parallel universes . . . like living in twin beds."

There are parallel universes in Benna Carpenter's life—the corporal and the spiritual, the dream worlds and the real world, the struggle between who one is and who one wants to be:

> In nature certain species, in order not to be eaten, will take
> on the characteristics of something that is an unpleasant
> meal. The viceroy, for instance, as a caterpillar looks so

much like a bird dropping, and as an adult so much like the ill-tasting monarch, that birds, as agents of natural selection, as Darwinian loser-zappers, leave the viceroy alone. Similarly, the ant-mimicking spider is avoided because it appears to have the fierce mandibles of an ant, though it's really only a dressed-up spider making pretend. The function of disguise is to convince the world you're not there, or that if you are, you should not be eaten. You camouflage yourself as imperious teacher, as imperious lover, as imperious bitch, simply to hang out and survive.

Suffering from loneliness and the struggles of day-to-day life, Benna allows her fantasy life to fill in the blanks, each fantasy being as realistic to her as her own life, if only circumstances were rearranged. In one section of the book, Benna has a child, a daughter who seems to give her life a different but important meaning; in another section, a cynical Benna has an abortion. She spins through a series of jobs which find her being a nightclub singer, a college teacher, an aerobics instructor. Even her relationship with Gerard changes according to her circumstance. Throughout the book, the only consistencies are Benna's feelings of rootlessness.

The novel reminds one of Burroughs's experiments in folding and cutting: Snippets of one reality, pasted alongside fragments of another reality, create a different consciousness. Instead of dealing with visual stimulus, as Burroughs did in the best of his cut-ups, Moore superimposes the subconscious upon the conscious, lending her work a sense of Lewis Carroll surreality. Benna uses humor—wise-cracking word games and puns—to stitch the two together:

> Gerard also leans over and kisses me, apologizes for the birthday card, reminds me not to drink too much I have to teach tomorrow, says, jokingly, "You're almost as drunk as I am," and soon Gerard and I are up and doing Motown Shakespeare. Verrie has requested it. "As you from crimes would pardoned be/Let your indulgence set me free why

don't you babe." We do footwork and spins like the Temptations.
All the world's a stage we're going through.

In creating a character which defies classification, Lorrie Moore
may have created an archetypical symbol of the American woman
in the late twentieth century: In turns, Benna Carpenter is a
career woman, single, a mother, married, widowed, independent, dependent, happy, depressed. . . . At once, she battles and
accommodates the social programming of her youth, all in the
context of her adult needs and realities, and the result is a complex, enduring character who embodies a spiritual growth es-
poused by feminists and lived out by countless women who dance
daily to the voices that ail them.

Unlike many writers who can move freely from writing short
fiction to writing novels, Lorrie Moore finds the transition difficult. She began *Anagrams* almost as soon as she had completed
Self-Help, and while she has written a handful of stories, as well
as part of another novel since the publication of *Anagrams*, the
going has not been easy.

"The story is such a strange, delicate form that if you get out
of the habit of it, it's hard to go back to it," she says. "I suppose
it's like working on doll houses and then, all of a sudden, building
entire cities. The doll house is less generous and forgiving; you
have to be completely committed to the detail of it all. A novel
can be sort of sprawling and messy, and it can embrace all sorts
of things. *Anagrams* is a strange book, structurally, and it's hard
to go from that to writing stories.

"I used to collect notes for a story, and suddenly the notes
would come together in a sort of spontaneous combustion, and
I would stay up all night and write the story. I'd be a third of the
way through the story and I'd see exactly how it would end, and
I'd just blaze my way through to the end. There would be this
wonderful, incredible feeling in writing a story. I'm not writing

that way anymore." Laughing, she points out that maybe it's a matter of aging, that "maybe your body chemistry changes and you're not capable of that sort of energy."

More likely, the difference in Moore's case can be spelled out in terms of the difference in focus and psychological commitment to the two forms. This difference applies to all writers, but it seems especially accute in the case of someone like Moore, whose writing style can be typified by spare sentences dependent upon a dense, accumulative overall effect.

"My prose is rooted somewhat in poetry," Moore says of her writing style. "Part of it comes from an interest I have in language—which every writer, I think, has to have—and part of it may come from me, from my feeling that the English language is still mysterious and interesting."

This interest in language, she says, is what keeps her working with the anagrammatic possibilities of arranging and rearranging words into sentences, stories, and novels.

"I love to come at it and play with it and see what it can do," she says.

NANCY LEMANN

"My career? I don't want to set the world on fire. I just want to start a flame in your heart," Claude said, quoting the Ink Spots.

—from *Lives of the Saints*

"He's off in his own world," I said, referring to George, one day at the trial, to the courtroom philosopher.
"He certainly is."
"I admire that. People who are off in their own world."
"Don't worry. You're on a fast train there."

—from *The Ritz of the Bayou*

Imagine Blanche DuBois with Dorothy Parker's intelligence and wit, give her a typewriter and a ream of paper, and ask that she write about saints and sinners.

We're not interested in finding someone to write accounts of heroic actions and dirty deeds (although, Lord knows, there will be plenty of both in this author's books); instead, we seek the accounting of the human spirit, the elusive "heart of the matter" borne from the choices that determine the lives of the saints and the demise of sinners.

This writer would have to possess great tolerance—no, make that *empathy*—for the foibles that plague the human race, yet this same writer would have to be astute enough to know that these quirks also help define it (and therefore are to be celebrated). This writer would have a motto such as "Nuts made life worth living"—and she would labor tirelessly to prove it.

That writer would be someone like Nancy Lemann.

Regardless of the material she is covering, whether it be in a fictional account of the lives of a zesty family of New Orleanian eccentrics (*Lives of the Saints*) or a true-life story of the corruption trial of a Louisiana governor (*The Ritz of the Bayou*), Nancy Lemann is doing her level best to make the word *nutty* a full-fledged term of endearment. Her work, described by one reviewer as being "like walking around a big crowd on a city sidewalk trying to peer through to see what everyone is looking at," focuses on actions taking place in clear view, but with implications that seem to be flitting about near the edges of one consciousness. The off-center characters that populate her books are reminiscent of the types of people you meet in the novels of Thomas Berger or William Kotzwinkle, or in the screenplays of the late Paddy Chayefsky.

This is not an especially safe stance for the serious writer, especially when Intellectualism, that keeper of the literary mansion, frowns upon guests who don't keep their neuroses in strict control or, at the very least, check them at the door. The compassionate intellectual may examine the eccentric, but always from a slightly superior posture, with the payoffs of such examinations being pity or oblique understanding; to actually celebrate the eccentric is considered to be something else—at best, an ugly admission of some sort.

Nancy Lemann disagrees. "There's nothing like a good eccentric," she says, "and maybe there are a few more of them than usual in New Orleans, but humanity is the same all over. I get my love of eccentrics from my father. My father is an incredible eccentric, and that's what I was raised on."

She says this lovingly, almost reverently, explaining that the character of Saint Louis Collier, the father figure in *Lives of the Saints*, is "the only character who is really quite closely based on someone real." Amidst all the book's crazy goings-on, comic or tragic, Collier remains a bastion of kindness and gentility, a figure whose spirit cannot be eroded by fate or circumstance. In Nancy Lemann's world, eccentrics not only survive—they lead by example. They are romantics, served with a twist: "The sorrows of the world," Lemann writes, "are such that only a screwball can surmount them, even in his innocence."

On a larger scale, New Orleans represents to Lemann the ultimate study of eccentricity. She views her native city as a place of contradictions where, on any given day, one witnesses the best and worst of civilization vying for the upper hand in a location that lends itself to the brand of romanticism which Lemann finds so attractive. New Orleans, she offers, has an aura of timelessness which seems to encourage quirky behavior.

"It's not like any American city," she believes. "It's a beloved, drowntrodden place. As I kept saying in *The Ritz of the Bayou*, my heart goes back in business whenever I go there. The people there have unusual hearts. They have good values. It's a sort of grandiose society where people are very elegant and genteel—off in their own world. During the carnival, they literally think there are kings and queens.

"But, of course, there's a dark side. It's a crumbling, down-trodden place. Economic depression is no stranger to New Orleans. In fact, it's only known three brief moments of prosperity, and those were due to the steamboat, cotton, and oil. Other than that, it's always been in economic depression, which is why our architecture escaped the wrecker's ball: There is such depression and lethargy everywhere that they didn't even have urban renewal. So there's this startling juxtaposition between a state of intrinsic depression and corruption but beauty. And this is the human condition."

This juxtaposition has appealed to a large number of American writers, including novelists such as Walker Percy and William Faulkner, as well as to playwright Tennessee Williams, who set one of his most memorable plays (A *Streetcar Named Desire*) in the city. In New Orleans, people are constantly on the verge of Falling Apart (such capitalization being one of Lemann's stylistic quirks), yet they somehow manage to maintain their sense of dignity or decorum. It is a haven for the offbeat, but its people, as fictional characters, remain enduring, if not endearing.

"I think you get to a point where, if you're *that* eccentric, you sort of get beyond criticism," Lemann theorizes. "You know, if someone's that 'out there,' you can't really criticize him. This is, to me, what Tristram Shandy is, for instance. Off in his own world, cultivating his own garden. Like my father grading the oysters."

The characters in *Lives of the Saints* are nothing if not "out there." Caught in the slow, languid, day-to-day life in New Orleans, where liquor is used as a cool shield against the tropic weather, Lemann's characters become distinct for their eccentricities. One character howls endearments at the top of his lungs ("BECAUSE I LOVE YOU, GODDAMNIT!"), while another has a fixation on hats, which she'll discuss at the most inopportune times. Characters are caught in a dervish of bizarre behavior, and these traits, more than their actions, make them memorable. In this regard, *Lives of the Saints* is as much a personality pastiche as it is a novel.

The book's reviewers took special notice of the way Lemann made character and location mirror images of one another. Writing for *The New Republic*, novelist Anne Tyler notes that "words are slung about recklessly, piled in staggering heaps, and what emerges from this is an almost hypnotic portrait of unforgettable people in a strange and magnificent city." The key, Tyler writes, is the novel's location: "Maybe the scenes in *Lives of the Saints* could have happened meplace else, but it's difficult to think where."

The one uniting factor in the book is the sense of yearning its characters share but cannot adequately express. Lemann would like you to believe that this failure to define—and, therefore, satisfy—yearnings is a result of the effects of a combination of climate and aspects of New Orleans's more squalid history, and even those who temporarily escape New Orleans in the book are still doomed to a type of psychologically magnetic pull.

"You know, Louise, you and Claude are always yearning after vague things," Claude's mother tells the book's narrator.

> You cherish illusions. I met someone the other day who was just like you—he yearned after vague things. You could tell, when you asked him about his job, that what he really liked to do was just yearn after vague things. You're all living in a dream world.

This dream world, explored in undulating, repetitious prose in *Lives of the Saints*, affords the book a surreal edge which, in turn, highlights eccentric behavior. People's hearts may be breaking, but sad people keep on their carnival faces: "Only the truly gallant, so it is said, are lighthearted in adversity."

⁓⁓⁓⁓⁓⁓⁓⁓⁓⁓

Kindness—which, in much of Lemann's writing, may be translated to mean gentility—is another major character determination in Lemann's two books. Her best characters possess a kindness which overshadows or overwhelms their glaring character flaws. (Or, perhaps, it's better said that the character flaws seem—or must be—more glaring in light of human kindness and decency.) In *Lives of the Saints*, Claude Collier is the novel's most gentle and kind character, yet his decadence makes him an enigma to the reader. Edwin Edwards, the former governor of Louisiana, alternated between being contemptible and charming in *The Ritz of the Bayou*. What makes Lemann's characters so compelling is a reader's inability to easily embrace or dismiss them: You'll tolerate their flaws because they possess character.

There is a touching scene, in *Lives of the Saints*, in which Louis Collier imparts upon his son his personal code of behavior:

> "Take things with a brave face. Never pity yourself. Three-fourths of all sorrow is self-pity. You must realize the inconsequence of your sorrows in the perspective of time.
>
> "Secondly, you must pursue a course to its end. If you do, you'll succeed in it, I don't care what it is. This is what distinguishes a strong soul from a weak one, to persevere.
>
> "Thirdly, put others above yourself. I've always told you to be kind. People will rely on you in life and you must protect them. Sometimes you must lie—to shield them. It is only a white lie. It's what is known as a white lie. . . .
>
> "The last thing I want to tell you is open your heart, open your heart. 'The great secret of morals is love.' "

Asked if she ever received similar words of advice from her own father, Lemann shakes her head and smiles. "I made it up," she says. "Angels were in my head."

"The people in the South *are* more kind," she continues. "People can't say anything without prefacing it with 'Precious' or 'Sugar' or 'Sweetheart,' and these endearments are not the shallow thing that Yankees often take them for. They *mean* it. I mean, if your plumber will come over and says, 'How are you doing, Precious Heart,' he means it. This is a small thing. But in a larger view, it is to me a less corrupted world."

The terms of endearment and tiny kindnesses have an accumulative effect in Lemann's books. The humanity of eccentrics becomes exemplary, as if a reader can lift those traits from a character while discarding the more unsavory character flaws as well. One winds up searching for a moral order.

This suits Lemann just fine. "Literature should teach you how to act, and it should give you hope," she says. "It's like religion or ethics. I wouldn't want to write about a bunch of depressed people who are living life wrong, and to some extent I'm actually out to provide a certain amount of lighthearted, escapist entertainment. My aim is to provide a world that you would want to dwell in while you're reading the book—a world you wish you could dwell in when you close the book. My aim is to give hope and consolation."

The Ritz of the Bayou is as much a nonfiction *novel* as any of its so-labeled predecessors. In terms of style, the book is a literary tour de force, a series of impressionistic sketches which, taken in composite, offer a sweeping portrait not only of a trial, but of the manners of the South. Lemann uses all the local color she has mixed on her palette, and her creation is almost as impressive for its technical achievement as it is for its story.

"Sometimes I think style overrides substance with me, and that's not good," she admits, adding a soft-spoken adjoinder, "but style is very important to me.

"I'm a novelist at heart, and when I was writing *The Ritz of the Bayou*, I constantly felt like a novelist trapped in politics. In *Lives of the Saints*, the theory was to portray people who I thought were saints, in order to show a way to behave. The characters in the book were people you could look up to—people who give hope. It was a sort of innocent stance, but that was the artistic stance that I chose. *The Ritz of the Bayou* may as well be called *Lives of the Sinners*, for these were real people, not saints, and that was the picture. I had to play with the cards I was dealt, much as I might wish it were otherwise, much as corruption's not my ordinary turf. I take writing to be, as Walker Percy said, an enterprise mounted in hope—I look for a hopeful sign."

Not an easy job when you're covering a widely reported corruption trial involving a state's highest elected official. Not only was Lemann forced to play with the cards she was dealt, but she had to do so with a lot of reporters looking over her shoulders.

"At first I felt uncomfortable with reporters, because they're not allowed to just write what they want; they have to write boring news stories. But newspaper reporters, they fascinate me, and I doubt that I'd have been able to fulfill what they had to fulfill. We novelists are lucky: We get to sit here and analyze our very feelings and emotions. We just analyze the human heart. What could be more interesting?"

⎯⎯⎯⎯⎯⎯⎯⎯

If the human heart is the novelist's turf, Nancy Lemann had to use all of her novelist's abilities, as well as her native knowledge of New Orleans, to find the story behind the story of the trial. She found it in courtroom corridors and backrooms, in cramped elevators, on the streets outside the courthouse and in local bars. Her appreciation of the offbeat led her to some interesting conclusions:

> Boredom was, to Louisianians, or must be, much worse than corruption, and so again [I] felt that the real theme of this trial was not written in the indictment. The real theme is the personality, the recklessness, of the Governor. For better or worse, some like it, some don't, those personal traits would be hard to separate from the Governor's interpretation of the letter of the law.

This theme afforded Lemann the chance to apply her skills as a fiction writer to real events. She could juxtapose the coldly rational and the eccentric, and let the chips fall where they would. This was essential, Lemann says, because she had no desire to be a political reporter.

"I have no interest in politics," she says. "I actually pride myself in having written something that doesn't have one line about politics in it, although it took place in a political arena, with politicians. It is not politics that interests me. Politics is not my beat. I was looking at it as a tragedy, the downfall of a man by his own flaws. It's called the human condition. I saw the dark side, but also the atmosphere, the characters, the very South, sangfroid, grace in adversity and in defeat. The Governor, needless to say, is unconstant. He may be the dark side, but he has his points, and it is not for me to be his judge.

"I came across something that is much more a mystery to me. Whereas honor is a thing that I can understand, because of the climate I grew in, with my brother. . . . The veil is not rent from the temple for me on a man like the Governor, though it is my opinion that you can't blame one man for the intrinsic troubles of the state, as things are not that black and white to me.

"In a courtroom, there is a lot of human condition floating around—the big things, good and evil, innocence and corruption, right and wrong—so who is to say? There is a deeper morality than the standard one—such as the judge in *All the King's Men*, who perjured himself to cover an old friend—in a courtroom, things are larger than life. The Governor is larger than life, and that is why he is so dramatic. I saw corruption, betrayal, weakness, and worse, but I also saw a great deal of life, and I saw a hopeful sign. There were great men, such as Camille Gravel, the Governor's lawyer. In this case on the whole, the truth was stranger than fiction. This *[Ritz]* is a hybrid genre. It's nonfiction, but it reads like a novel, I think."

To accomplish this effect, Lemann avoided the type of analytical writing characteristic of book-length reportage of crime or courtroom drama. Instead of presenting hard facts in strict chronological order, she layered detail, often in short, irreverantly humorous anecdotes and "pops," which begged not for the author's analysis but for reader association and empathy. In *Lives of the Saints*, there is a brief passage which explains this method:

The weather had turned fine. Dark fell. I looked into the glittering night. Suddenly, a parade came out of nowhere and passed through the unsuspecting street, heralded by African drumbeats in the distance vaguely, the approach of jazz, the smell of sweet olive, ambrosia, the sense of impending spectacle. Then it passed in its fleeting beauty, this glittering dirge, and, as suddenly as it came, I was left, rather stunned, in its wake.

It is this passing parade which I chronicle.

There are risks in taking this approach, the least of which being, in the case of the trial, the glorification of unsavory characters by making them less black and white, but more human. How, for example, can the reader feel a modicum of compassion for an arrogant public official accused of using his office and position for financial gain? What are the dangers of feeling anything but contempt for such an individual?

But even more risky, perhaps, was Lemann's faith that her readers would understand (and accept) a regional underlay essential to her story. If the reader were to accept Lemann's premise that there was beauty amidst corruption, he or she had to embrace the notion that the rules, legal or moral, are different in the South (and particularly Louisiana) than they are in the North. Style had to be viewed as being as important as substance or the bottom line: *How* something was done was as valid as *what* was being done. Sinners may not have a lot of virtue, but they could have style and, in a region still stinging from the defeats suffered over a century ago, where prominent politicians continue to rise from the masses, style is the mask worn by the wounded. It can be a falsehood lending further endurance to the human spirit.

"I have what is known as a love of the underdog," Lemann admits. "The South is the underdog, humanity corrupted and undisguised, even if they attempt to disguise it with levity or desperate gaity. What it comes down to is human frailty, the dark side."

But will it play in Cleveland? Or, for that matter, in Chicago, where political corruption is standard fare (but where politicians are confrontationists with all the style of a man wearing a bowling shirt and wing-tipped shoes to a garden party)?

In its review of *The Ritz of the Bayou*, *The Chicago Tribune* provided an answer: yes *and* no. Douglas Seibold, the book's reviewer, acknowledged that

> The theme of the defense as Lemann sees it is a "psychotic jollity," an irrepressible attitude of winking good humor that makes out the defendants' alleged miscreancy little more than back-room hijinks—essentially, business as usual in Louisiana state politics.

The reviewer, however, went on to write that he couldn't help but wonder if "the whole episode could possibly have been as much a gas as Lemann makes it out to be."

A perfectionist, Lemann isn't at all certain she was totally on the mark in making all her points in *The Ritz of the Bayou*. In terms of style, the book was a success, but was it good nonfiction? She mentions that she was originally dispatched to New Orleans to cover the trial by a magazine that eventually rejected her reportage. (*Esquire* and *The New Republic* did wind up publishing excerpts of the book.) When she's in a self-critical mood, Lemann can be as hard on herself as any of her critics.

"In *The Ritz of the Bayou*, I may not have gotten my point across," she says. "Maybe, in this case, saying too little may have been not saying enough."

She was not, however, out of form. In *Lives of the Saints*, she had told a story with only the most threadbare of plots and, as was the case with *The Ritz of the Bayou*, she instead focused more on mood and symbolism and, perhaps most significant, ideas. All serious writers toil to present polished (and usually not-so-obvious) ideas in their work, but taken in the context of the work, the ideas are presented in a peaks-and-valleys effect, with much prose devoted to the development of a "peak" idea. In Lemann's work, each brief passage is an idea, sometimes disguised in a symbol, often veiled in humor. Writing along these lines is much simpler in fiction, where the author can manipulate material, but this type of writing is difficult to employ effectively in nonfiction.

Lemann's "beauty amidst corruption" theme was accorded its larger-than-life symbol in an Alexandria hotel which is given piecemeal description on a number of occasions throughout the book. Two brief passages illustrate the way Lemann layers her individual ideas to achieve her "passing parade" effect:

> In Alexandria, there is an old hotel where the pols have always gathered when campaigning in northern Louisiana. A splendiferous, gigantic, megalomaniac hotel also known as the Ritz of the Bayou. . . .

Having established her symbol's grandeur, Lemann, eleven pages later, makes her juxtaposition:

> Situated in its lonely splendor, in a small crumbling town, the green humble South. Gigantic architectural friezes, domes, columns, and potted plants populate the lobby, which is of course deserted. Been down and out myself. I've been there. . . .

Molding ideas this way, Lemann says, is hard work—almost a matter of playing percentages. Although her books are short, the finished products represent only a fragment of the work that has gone into them.

"It's a question of perseverance," she says, "but, to me, application is genius. You can have all the talent in the world, but only in perseverance or application can you succeed. It is a huge, concerted effort, and the more time you bring to it, the better. The odds are against you. If you write a hundred pages, you get maybe ten good ones. Therefore, a huge concerted effort is required. Perseverance is the only answer, and in the face of repeated doubt."

Two of her models, she continues, offer exemplary work which she admires but cannot really emulate. She enjoys the political satire of Evelyn Waugh, and she tried to employ elements of his biting satire in *The Ritz of the Bayou*, and while there are also elements of Walker Percy in that book and in *Lives of the Saints*, Lemann claims his genius is so distinct that she could never cover the South the way he does.

"Walker is the living writer I admire. It was he who ever made me see a way to write. He has a marriage of style and substance in his writing that is unique. He is a true original and a true modern. He has a profound solicitude, which is what makes him dear to me. The generosity of the man, to look outward instead of in. I'm an introspective type myself, of course, and that's the only way that I can find the universal, to find it within myself; but Walker has the genius to sit in his office in a small Southern town and see the universe and dream it up out of his head. I went to the Governor's trial and followed the Governor to get material, because I couldn't always dream things up out of my head, and I had to see more of the world because I did not know it in my heart. Walker's stance is: *Something is wrong—what is it?* He relates this to the individual as well as to the century—both the specific and the general. This is what I mean by his profound solicitude. He is the great man I have known."

Very few living writers have had this effect on Lemann. Beside Percy, Lemann lists J. D. Salinger and Graham Greene as authors she reads and admires, but she is quick to add that she generally avoids reading contemporaries or living writers, mainly in deference to writers whose work has already withstood, to some degree, a test of time. Pressed for names, she mentions that she has always appreciated the work of Balzac and Tolstoi and, among the moderns, Hemingway and Fitzgerald.

"And then I always felt a love for Dostoyevski," she says as an afterthought, "because he covers the self-loathing beat. I feel close to that."

When asked about her background, Nancy Lemann hesitates, hedges, and, in general, displays a reluctance to provide detailed information about anything from her age ("It's a woman's pre-rogative never to tell her age") to her childhood experiences. One senses, however, that this is due not to the type of mythmaking which rises out of secrecy but to the notion that an author tells you all you need to know about her in her work. A good part of her can be found in Louise, the heroine of *Lives of the Saints*, or in her very personal observations in *The Ritz of the Bayou*. She is not, she'll tell you, much of a public person. She attends or gives readings only when she has to, and she leaves you with the impression that she views the high-visibility literary parties and gatherings as dog and pony shows which distract her from the work at hand.

The "big story," she goes on, is the fact that it took her eight years to find a publisher for *Lives of the Saints*. Lemann attended Brown University from 1974 to 1978, majoring in English lit-erature, and she wrote *Lives of the Saints* in a three-month span when she was twenty. But no publisher seemed interested in bringing out a quirky, tragicomic novel written by a young woman from New Orleans.

Upon graduation from college, Lemann moved back to New Orleans, where she took a job as a secretary for a law firm. After a brief stint there, she worked for Pelican Publishers, where, she jokes, she had occasion to look at "many fascinating books, such as *Mississippi Governors, Mississippi Wildflowers, You Can Be President of Your Own Life*—stuff like that." For an aspiring novelist who was getting an increasing number of suggestions that she might try abandoning pursuit of a publisher for *Lives of the Saints*, these were less than ideal times.

Four years passed. Lemann was working at still another job (for the Preservation Society: "my one burning cause," she ex-plains) when Susan Minot, a college acquaintance and aspiring novelist with whom she had been corresponding, urged her to come to New York. "She kept trying to convince me to move to New York, with great generosity on her part, her customary generosity," says Lemann of Minot. Lemann resisted the idea, but Minot insisted. "Ultimately, she *made* me move to New

York," Lemann recalls. "Wild horses had to drag me away from New Orleans. But it was the right thing.

"New Orleans is a hard town to leave. The place you are from is a hard place to leave. Yankees don't often have to, i.e., people from the vicinity of New York and Boston, who stay here, and it is normal and they don't have a big wound in their hearts for the place that they left. New Orleans is my heart. It is itself a character, like Paris is in Balzac. But there is the spurious allure of the North—or not so spurious, ambition-wise."

She moved to New York in 1982 and enrolled in Columbia University's writing program. Even though she wanted to write, her going back to school was not a case of careful career planning, and even now Lemann is skeptical about how much university writing programs can teach students. Their main contribution to the writer, she says, focuses more on the business, as opposed to the creative, aspects of writing.

"They can't teach you how to write," she says. "No one can. What New York and writing school did for me was give me the chance to see who the editors and publishers were. I could see the different people and what they were like. Finally, after about three years, I saw Gordon Lish. He gave a lecture. I said, 'He's a nut; that's the man for me. That's the only man who's going to take a chance on me.' I believe I was right.

"Unfortunately, I think that if I had remained in New Orleans, sending out my unsolicited manuscript, I might not have been able to find a publisher. That's a very sorry statement, but I think it might be true."

Gordon Lish had his own reputation of eccentric behavior. Lemann appreciated that, as she also admired Lish's commitment to championing the underdog. Lish treated fiction writing as a vocation, not just another job (or, even, another profession), and his encouragement gave Lemann a sense of legitimacy as a writer.

"He certainly changed my life," she says of the man who became her editor at Knopf, and to whom *The Ritz of the Bayou* is dedicated. "He took a chance on me and gave me the key to my life, and I can never forget a kindness."

Nancy Lemann is currently at work on a new novel ("Some people will be glad to know that it does not take place in New Orleans or in the South," she cracks) and, like most serious novelists self-sentenced to the creation of art, she realizes that what imprisons her is also what gives her her greatest freedom. She remembers the time when she was unpublished—"a laughingstock," as she says, perhaps in overstatement—when writing was a career overwhelmed by the necessity for her to work a nine-to-five job.

"It sounds corny, but I am daily grateful," she says of the turn of events which have changed her life in recent years. "I just thank my stars. Elizabeth Hardwick once said to me, 'Honey, what else would you rather be doing?' and that actually does sum it up. She certainly has a way of penetrating to the heart of the matter. This is the thing I would most rather be doing."

Kelly Wise

GORDON LISH

In the world of contemporary fiction, Gordon Lish is a true Renaissance man: He teaches fiction, edits it, and writes it, in that order of his stated personal preference. To Lish, fiction isn't an entertainment—it's a consciousness, a never-abating drive to create work which is, by his estimation, "universal in its purchase on the human heart." Fiction is a passion that Lish intends to pass on to his students and readers.

"I think each of us should have the opportunity to reduce to objectivity that object of our hearts, the cornice that we see in the summer that we are alive, and the way the light played upon that cornice. As a writer, one has the opportunity to get down onto the page that which is his quiddity, so that he can feel that he has entered himself and given himself away utterly before he's gone to his death."

Lish gives no quarter in his pursuit of excellence. His fiction workshops are infamous for their being exacting tests of endurance in which he challenges his students to put their mental toughness on the line. Survivors of these sessions tell a seemingly endless series of "Lish stories," some of which depict him as a genius, others which offer less-charitable assessments. One of the more interesting reports had a potential literary giant of the future placing thumbtacks, points up, on Lish's chair.

Lish couldn't care less whether he is loved or hated, as long as he can act as a catalyst in the development of important artists. Nicknamed "Captain Fiction," he possesses a literary track record meritorious of his reputation of being one of the world's premier discoverers of fiction writers. Among those he has taught or edited are Raymond Carver, Barry Hannah, Bette Howland, Mary Robison, Anderson Ferrell, Amy Hempel, Yannick Murphy, and Nancy Lemann—and this list doesn't include the writers whose careers he jump-started or helped along during his eight years' tenure as fiction editor at *Esquire*, or the expanding list of newcomers that he is presently developing at Knopf.

Despite the impressive list of discoveries, Lish insists that he is not a talent scout.

"I'm not interested in talent," he says. "I'm not even convinced that talent exists in any kind of degree that would make it a palpable object. My position is that maybe one has talent at playing a musical instrument or at doing mathmatics or in science, but writing is like speaking, and I think we all have a talent for that once we're liberated to speak in certain kinds of ways. What counts is perseverance, concentration, bravery, courage, and will. Talent is really beside the point."

Today, he continues to teach his workshops and edit books for Knopf, though his latest project, editing *The Quarterly*, a literary magazine published by Vintage and devoted almost exclusively to new or unknown writers, may be his most ambitious task to date. In stating his goals for the magazine, he speaks with the characteristic candor that has endeared him to his followers and infuriated his detractors.

"I have the highest ambitions for this magazine. I have the objectives to see it understood as the place where one is going to see the liveliest writing in America, writing that is as free of pretention and bullshit as I can find, and writing that is as universal in its purchase on the human heart as I can find. I hope that the publication of such writing will impact the literary establishment and shape editorial practices elsewhere."

I have an underdog's way of perceiving America. I mean, I'm not saying that right. I come from a time when it was characteristic of the American Spirit to favor the underdog. I can't think of a time, when I went to a prize fight or baseball game or football game when I was a kid, when my father wasn't rooting for the underdog. Everybody was. It was the American Way.

When I came, as innocently as I did, into publishing, I carried forward that general stance. When I went to *Esquire*, it virtually delighted me to set aside the regular practice of publishing "name" writers, and paying them large fees, in favor of publishing writers who were not known. You could buy more of them: You could have, say, ten of their stories for what you paid for one John Updike or Philip Roth or Saul Bellow and so on. As I've remarked before, if I had a story by X and a story by Y, and X was already from the established national consciousness and Y was not, and if I thought both stories were equivalent in force, I would publish Y. That, to me, seems to be utterly in keeping with everything decent, since X has had his day in the sun. Y deserves it. Everybody should be invited to the table and should have a chair at the table. Nobody should be left out.

I have a complaint—a very, very considered complaint—that a lot of the literary magazines are not really fulfilling their mandates to publish the new and untried. They're mainly looking around for the castoffs of the national magazines, and I think that's worse than regrettable—it's scandalous. Back in the Fifties and Sixties, literary magazines weren't quite so "name conscious" as they are now.

I'm interested in doing what I can to encourage people to be developing artists, to be people who own their lives and wills. I'm not interested in getting people published. If they want to grow, I'll do what I can to get them into print and knock down anybody who gets in the way. I have a very combative relation with the national literature and those persons who I figure run it. Once I have a writer like Yannick Murphy or Amy Hempel or Mark Richard, they're like clubs to me: I want to pick them up and make a mace with them. I think what they have to offer us is vital. They aren't simply additives or advantageous—they're *essential*. These people are telling us their truths; they're not there simply to smear their vanity on the page and get paid for it and get their names in print and so on. So I feel that the work I do, as an editor and teacher, has a dire necessity about it, and I feel that my energy for it, and my impatience with those who do not honor the same object, grows out of my feeling that the writers whom I publish are in the prospect of saving people's lives. Art can do that for us.

I can remember how I felt myself virtually saved by a copy of *Discovery* or *New World Writing*. I felt that these were magazines that were reaching out to me and talking to me in my loneliness and in the life I lived, which had nothing to do with literary matters. I came from a home where the only books we had were a set we had in the living room, and they just sort of went with the carpet my mother had in there. They were to look at, they weren't books to read. I didn't really read a book until I was fifteen.

So I can recall when I did begin caring about books, and how I cared about them. First, I cared about them as places to find dirty words in, and then as places to whack off in. Then I cared about them because I found I could get girls with books. If I had the right kinds of books, I could get girls that I couldn't get otherwise. So books became a kind of talisman in that way.

In that period, when I was sort of finding my way, reading more and more esoteric stuff—because the more esoteric the work, the more esoteric the girl you got *(laughs)*—I began reading *Discovery* and *New World Writing*, and they became very important objects. You'd wait for the next number to come out because you really began to care about it. It began to persuade you that there was something that had pertinence to your own life.

I am inclined to take a very concerned stance with respect to the people I publish. I feel concern to convey, to those persons, a set of standards, a respect for literature that will inure to their favor for the rest of their artistic careers. I'm concerned about every facet of their presentation of themselves to the national literature. That would mean that I would be concerned with what kind of books they review, if they were asked to review, and where they publish first serial, and so on. I can't imagine any editor who would be of any value to a writer if he were not so concerned. I mean, what one is hoping to do, when he has a writer for whom he has the highest ambitions and respect, is to do what can be done to insert that writer into the national literature in a way that is consistent with the writer's best interests, and that sometimes requires offering up counsel which may not go directly to the text itself.

I had a call from one of my students, who said, "Gordon, I have two literary magazines that are eager to acquire a certain story. One magazine pays more than the other. Which magazine should I give the story to?" I was quick to say that, in this case, it would be the magazine that paid hardly any fee because, in my judgment, it is more in keeping with that writer's best interests and how he should be perceived to be. I'm glad he thought to put the question before me, and I would hope to have that kind of sway with my writers, such as they would believe my counsel would be valuable to have. I would be much chagrined if one of my writers would publish a piece of fiction, for whatever fee, in a magazine I thought would be inimical to how that writer was perceived, and I've had that happen again and again and again. This is intrusive in the writer's affairs, and I'm willing to be intrusive in a writer's affairs.

These questions do come up, and one has to propose a way of being in the world as desirable, so the writer is protected from local distraction. Envy among writers is a local distraction. I think the best models in this respect are writers like Don DeLillo, Cynthia Ozick, and Harold Brodkey—especially DeLillo, who keeps himself really apart from local distraction. You'll never find DeLillo taking himself off into the bathroom to compare the size of his pecker with somebody else's pecker. That's just not De-Lillo's style. He's not concerned with what advance you're getting, what magazines you're publishing in, who took your author's photograph, and so on. I think a lot of writers are so concerned, and that always runs contrary to the concerns of the text and how that writer will configure in history.

Writers tend to find themselves distracted by fame, power, notoriety, and other kinds of appeals that are made to them, and it's easy to exhaust oneself as a writer because there's really only so much speech in one. Then it becomes very tempting to avoid confrontation with one's diminishing powers by simply becoming a figure, as many writers are: going around and doing readings, only publishing anthologies, just appearing at writers conferences or being judges—but not doing their work.

One way or another, we have the lives we want. I don't really have to persuade any of the persons I was talking about to live a certain way. No one has to talk Brodkey into being exacting to such extremes that Brodkey's idea of perfection is much more extravagant than somebody else's. We have the lives we want, and if someone capitulates in midlife, or if someone sees himself turned into a creature of the times or his readership, then that's what he really proposed for himself. I'm inclined to be skeptical about the naysaying of such persons. I think they want to have their cake and eat it too: They want to pretend to turn to the sort of high-minded way of being in the world but, in fact, they like to party.

Marion Ettlinger

DAVID LEAVITT

Walking down Columbus Avenue, heading in the direction of one of his favorite coffee shops, David Leavitt steps into an intersection and the path of an oncoming car. He pulls up short, listens to the angry driver lean on his horn. Shrugging it off, Leavitt mentions that he is so rarely in town that he is sometimes absentminded about these things.

Summer heat has driven a lot of people from the city. Leavitt, who has lived on Long Island for two years, spends as little time in Manhattan as possible, though he sublets an apartment on the Upper West Side. New York, he says, has a way of sapping his energy; he'd much prefer having his friends visit him at his home in East Hampton. The heat is as good a reason as any for his acquaintances to get away.

A different kind of heat necessitated his own move to the country. He found New York's publishing community, with its gossip and parties and readings and focus on just about anything but the actual work at hand, suffocating. He was a visible figure in a visible community, one of the youngest of the rising stars on the literary horizon, a precocious voice in the clamoring halls. His talents were prodigious. He had published a short story in *The New Yorker* when he was twenty and still attending Yale; his first book, *Family Dancing*, published two years later, had been greeted by universal critical acclaim; his opinions and essays were widely sought. In many ways, he was symbolic of how *good* the literary youth movement could be.

And, since this was the case, he got to wear the thorny crown reserved for such symbols. One heard rumblings that Leavitt was talented at writing about one or two things—mainly, the family and homosexuality. Magazines and newspapers seemed more interested in fitting him into the "young writers" framework than they were in his writings. There was even talk that his new book, a novel, was a disappointment—a rumor that kicked into overdrive when Leavitt left Knopf, publisher of his first two books, and shopped the novel around at a number of other houses. (Conversely, another rumor had it that the novel was so good that Leavitt's agent was testing its market value.)

As is usually the case, none of the talk mattered very much —at least, not where it really *counted*—but it all served as a means to further convince Leavitt that the city was not the place for him.

"I had to get out," he says. "It was very draining."

~~~~~~~~~~

This is not to imply that David Leavitt cannot face the opposition; indeed, over the course of several hours' conversation, he can be charming or disarmingly candid, and he addresses all questions, however pointed, directed toward him. He describes himself as a sort of throwback, a writer with very little interest in all the attention being paid to America's young writers. He has work to do and, in too many cases, the demands made on his time have little to do with the real work. As an example, he recalls a telephone call he received from a nationally distributed weekly gossip magazine. "They asked if I would pose in a fashion layout. It was so annoying to me that I didn't even return the call."

He labels the national interest in young writers a "media invention, a fad."

"It was an outcropping of the fascination with Yuppies, with these young, unbelievably ambitious, well-dressed, rich bankers and things. Clearly, youth sold magazines; articles about young achievers sold magazines. There were a few books published that actually had a lot of success, and the next thing you knew, the media vipers sort of jumped on it. The stories weren't written by people who cared about literature; they were written by people who cared about gossip and selling. It's created problems because it's annoyed the writers so intensely."

He concedes, however, that some merit has come from all the attention. "There is more interest in books by younger writers than there had been before. It isn't like there are more books by young writers—they're just being noticed instead of being ignored."

In this respect, Leavitt has actively participated in the promotion of the writers he considers to be worthy young talents. "New Voices and Old Values," a long essay published in *The New York Times Book Review* in May 1985, discussed the work of Meg Wolitzer, Marian Thurm, Elizabeth Tallent, Peter Cameron, and Amy Hempel—all writers, Leavitt felt, who were part of "a new generation of writers who are recording through their fiction the changes in the way young people think about family, marriage, love and loyalty," his conclusion being that "home may be the most dangerous place of all, this new generation of writers suggests, but it is also the only chance we have." Leavitt was a logical choice to write on this topic, since *Family Dancing* had addressed these themes, but the essay was also a thinly disguised plug for the works of five young writers whose talents were yet to be fully appreciated.

That essay, along with "The New Lost Generation," a lengthy piece published by *Esquire* the same month the former appeared in the *Times*, more or less established Leavitt as the voice of his generation, making him not unlike Norman Mailer or James Baldwin two or three decades earlier. Today, despite the fact that he recently served as guest editor of an issue of *The Mississippi Review* entitled "These Young People Today" (featuring the short stories by Leavitt cronies such as Hempel, Cameron, Thurm, Gary Glickman, and Anderson Ferrell, among others), Leavitt is not so sure he is at all comfortable with the idea of being any generation's spokesperson.

"At this point, I'm more interested in writing about literature than I am in being a spokesman for my generation," he explains, pointing out that his recent book reviews and critical essays have focused more on older, more-established writers than on his contemporaries. The *Esquire* essay, he adds, "put me in a 'call me a spokesman for my generation' context, and that's not something I want to be. I was interested in it at that point, but that's not what I'm interested in anymore."

In a review of Alice McDermott's novel *That Night*, Leavitt addressed the issue of the place for suburbia in American literature. The suburbs, he maintained, were somehow seen by literature to be representative of "the decay of civilization," places where "high culture is being most visibly strangled by the overwhelming encroachment of television shows, junk food restaurants, rock videos, video games." Unimpressed with the tone of most of the fiction set in suburbia (though he praised Mc-Dermott's novel, along with the short stories of John Cheever), Leavitt argued that "much of this literature has been brilliant, cutting and important, but it is nonetheless written from a defensive position, as if the chronicler must necessarily cultivate an anti-intellectual style, must wave the labels of his Franco-American Spaghettios can in conscious defiance of high culture's urban disapproval."

This is a telling stance for Leavitt to have taken, because even though his heart is in the suburbs, away from some of the more stifling aspects of urban intellectualism, he is, in fact, in his writings and in real life, more a part of the insulated, upper-class (or upper-middle-class) 'burbs, which have as much in common with the working-stiff suburbs as an opera singer has in common with an interior lineman for the Los Angeles Raiders. One just can't imagine Leavitt standing in his next-door neighbor's backyard on a Sunday afternoon, half-listening to a baseball game while he trades dirty jokes with the boys, turning barbecue chicken on the grill, talking shop in a voice that is always a few decibels too loud for the occasion. Still, Leavitt has an understanding and sympathy for these people that is reflected in some of the stories in *Family Dancing* (even if his characters own built-in pools, as opposed to the tinny, aboveground models more common in the suburbs), and he makes a valid, important point about the defensive posture of much of the literature of the suburbs. There is no reason, he feels, for literature set in the suburbs not to have a grace and style reflective of intellectual fiction *and* the best interests of the people populating the fiction.

"Suburbia has never been allowed any dignity," he says. "What was so wonderful about Alice McDermott's book was that she gave suburbia a feeling of dignity and importance. She romanticized it, but she did so in the *real* way: She showed how it was beautiful and, in doing so, she showed how it was important. This is *the* only book so far that tells what it was really like to live in those new suburbs of the Sixties, which were a very important cultural phenomenon.

"Raymond Carver and Richard Ford brought working-class America into the literary world," he continues, "and I think the suburbs are the next barricade to knock down. In a sense, working-class life has always been respected by high-culture snobs because it's the real thing—it's bad and it's dangerous. But suburbia is considered to be stupid." Leavitt believes that writing about the suburbs is not that much different from writing about more well-set environs. "The story of a rich family and the story of a poor or middle-class family are finally going to be the same kind of story. It's all in the telling," he says.

The stories in *Family Dancing* attest to that. Each of the volume's nine stories involves a test of a family's internal strength, the test brought about by outside forces beyond the family's control. In "Counting Months," a single mother dying from cancer worries about what will happen to her children when she's gone. The title character in "Danny in Transit" is an only child, living with cousins after his father leaves the family for a gay lover and his mother cracks from the strain; Danny's perfect existence is in an imaginary television show which he acts out alone in the woods. In "Family Dancing," a graduation party finds children, mother, father, and stepfather "dancing" for the rightful positions in each other's lives, their jockeying about clumsy, when the embittered daughter remembers her father's telling her, when she was a little girl, that they would someday dance under the stars. The different crises in the stories are familiar, and all take place in the home, which *should* be a familiar, comfortable setting. Madness, injury, sadness, illness, and death—all drive wedges into family unity and test the strength and endurance of family love. Taken as a whole, *Family Dancing* is a sad but hopeful book which underscores Leavitt's observation, made in his *Times* essay, that the home, for all its danger, is still "the only chance we have."

Published when Leavitt was twenty-three years old and fresh out of Yale, *Family Dancing* gains much of its wisdom from the ways its author marries perception and style. The family theme, for which Leavitt is probably best known, is a natural choice for a youthful writer, but unlike many of his colleagues, who chose to write short stories in minimalist style, or in fresh, hip prose reflective of their rock 'n' roll influences, Leavitt stayed closer to a more traditional style. He may have been very young when *Family Dancing* was published, but from a point of style he more resembled John Updike than Jay McInerney, with whom Leavitt is often compared. (Ironically, *Family Dancing* and *Bright Lights, Big City* were published on the same day—a point of trivia which only encourages further those feature writers who like to lump the two writers into the "young, hot author" category.) Leavitt's style, along with the issues being addressed in his stories, afforded him a sense of maturation that, rightfully or otherwise, set him apart from his peers.

Leavitt is comfortable with the distinction. "Anyone who puts me in this group, or links me with somebody like Jay McInerney, has got my life all wrong. I'm a total anachronism. I live here in this little house in East Hampton, and I never go to the city. I don't reflect the lifestyle of my contemporaries because I don't live it—at least, not now. I'm not a misanthrope, but I think my social life is fairly anachronistic at this point, and I say this rather proudly because I feel happy to have escaped all that."

There was a time when it was different. Born in 1961 in Pittsburgh, Leavitt was the youngest of his parents' three children. His father moved the family to Stanford, where he taught organizational behavior at the university, when David was four. It was a significant move. The Sixties, with their years of Flower Power and Vietnam War protests, were in full bloom, and Leavitt got an early, firsthand view of one generation's commitment to ideological causes—a commitment he would later effectively contrast with his own generation's sense of aimlessness.

"My brother and sister are much older than me," Leavitt says, "and they were both sort of hippies—or radicals, at least. They both went to Stanford, and when I was a kid, I was always wandering over to the leftist communal house where my sister lived. She made me little hippie clothes and I had long hair. I had a guitar and I wrote songs and played them at the dining hall. I wanted to be Joni Mitchell—I still do." He laughs, but then adds, seriously, "That's why the heroine of my new novel is a singer."

In "The New Lost Generation," Leavitt complained about being caught between generations:

> By the time I was old enough to take part in any real way, disillusion had set in, people had given up, cocaine was the drug of choice. Tail end. We have always been the tail end—of the Sixties, of the baby boom. We hit our stride in an age of burned-out, restless, ironic disillusion. With all our much-touted youthful energy boiling inside us, where were we supposed to go? What were we supposed to do?

Though he didn't know the answer to those questions, Leavitt believed a change in locale might help. An aspiring writer, he romanticized the East—particularly New York—as symbolic of stable tradition, a type of cultural and literary center, the next best thing to living in Europe. "I felt way out of place as an adolescent in California," he remembers. "I wanted someplace with a sense of history and that, to me, meant East."

And Yale. At the university, Leavitt took a creative writing class from Gordon Lish, who was teaching there at the time. As a teacher, Lish had less impact on Leavitt than he did with Amy Hempel and Nancy Lemann, both friends of Leavitt's today, and Leavitt is less reverent in his assessment of his former teacher. "He's a genius as a teacher, in certain ways, but he's erratic. You have to take the good with the bad with him, because the two are so inextricably joined. If you can't deal with his craziness, you're never going to learn anything from him; if you *are* able to cope with him, he can teach you more than anyone in the world. I think I benefitted enormously from having him as a teacher, but he's like any true genius: He's a mass of contradictory tendencies."

Leavitt's college years also found him developing his literary tastes. He focused on Renaissance literature; his senior essay was on Spenser. His original plan was to continue on to graduate school, but *The New Yorker's* publication of "'Territories" altered his direction. He decided to go to New York and write fiction instead.

＿＿＿＿＿＿＿

Leavitt expresses surprise when it is mentioned that his brief writing career is rather similar to the early years of James Baldwin's career, at least in terms of the ways both authors chose to write and publish their work. Baldwin's early writings also included a novel and a collection of short stories, as well as essays and literary criticism. Baldwin's *Go Tell It on the Mountain* and Leavitt's *The Lost Language of Cranes*, both first novels, employed the family setting—and the tense, ambiguous relationships between father and son—as the backdrop to the struggle of the young protagonist to break away and establish a separate identity. Even more telling may be the comparison of the importance of Baldwin's novel *Giovanni's Room* and Leavitt's *The Lost Language of Cranes*: Both books were unflinching looks at gay lifestyles, and while nearly three decades separated the publication of the two books, both were significant arrivals on the scene of the national literature, Baldwin's because its frank depiction of a gay love affair was virtually unparalleled in his time, Leavitt's because it arrived at a time when serious literature dealing with the subject, intended for mainstream distribution, was seriously threatened by the country's concern over and reaction to AIDS.

And, like Baldwin, Leavitt appears to have begun his career on the cusp of a major movement. Baldwin's early writings can be characterized by their forceful and eloquent (and angry) persuasions that racial issues had to be addressed in the context of the *human* condition, and Leavitt, though nowhere near as overtly political as Baldwin, seems to be urging the same terms relative to the gay lifestyle and society. Leavitt may not want to be a spokesman, but he is not afraid to speak his mind on the topic.

Gay fiction, he says, is "problematic," not so much by definition as it is in terms of its being published and received. "You have to contend with a whole level of responses *before* you get down to the responses of whether people like a book," he says. "First of all, you have to contend with people being horrified by what you're writing about—and it's not just gay fiction, it's any fiction about any lifestyle that is controversial or unpopular. My first experience with vicious homophobia was with the publication of *The Lost Language of Cranes*. It made me understand why gay writers have disguised it in their work for so many years: It's very hard to take, this sense of being 'ghetto-ized' literarily. When I published the book, I wanted it to be received in the world, and for every effort I made to push it out, there were ten sets of hands trying to push it back. They were saying, 'This is a *gay* book, and that's all it is.' "

The critical reaction is noteworthy when placed in the context of any discussion of *Family Dancing*. Of the nine stories in that book, five included gay characters or references to homosexuality. "Territory," the collection's first story, focuses on a mother's coming to terms with her son's gay lifestyle, which includes a lover he brings home for her to meet. Despite all this, the national press generally refrained from any discussion that tied Leavitt to the gay themes in his stories.

Leavitt has his own theory about why issues of sexuality were ignored in *Family Dancing* but criticized in *The Lost Language of Cranes*. "It was always part of a larger spectrum," he says of the gay themes in his first book. "I've discovered that I can write about homosexuality and be accepted in the mainstream world if I do it that way, but when it comes to the forefront, the way it did in *The Lost Language of Cranes*, it sort of sparks people into saying 'Enough is enough.' Darrell Pinkney, a bright young critic who writes for *The New York Review of Books*, said something about my first book in a big review: He said that my 'trick' was to make homosexuality just one more card in the family deck—sort of by mixing it in with everything else. I've found that as long as I do that, I can win over any hearts.

"What infuriates me is the idea that somehow that's the only way you're supposed to write about homosexuality—if you don't want to get shit from the world. So the question, then, is: Do you write about it anyway? Or: How can you help but be affected by that kind of pressure? It's made me think a lot of Forster, and it's made me think about Proust."

AIDS, it's suggested to Leavitt, may be a greater factor in the problems of publishing and marketing gay fiction than the homosexual lifestyle itself. There is no question that the national focus on AIDS has resulted in the discovery of another common denominator among Americans, and it is an ugly one. Traditionally, it has been difficult to market gay fiction to a mainstream readership, and the task will be nearly impossible as long as the public blames the homosexual for the AIDS epidemic.

Leavitt realizes this, but he argues that this line of thinking is misguided. "The most dangerous thing you can say is that if you are writing about gay men's lives, you have to write about AIDS, because it simply strengthens the association between AIDS and homosexuality that much more. Certainly, I don't think you can write about AIDS without dealing with homosexuality, but I don't think it's a two-way street. It seems to me that there's every reason to write about the gay world without even mentioning AIDS. This is a disease that is above and beyond homosexuality."

So far, he continues, he has been disappointed in fiction addressing the topic of AIDS, though he praises Susan Sontag's story "The Way We Live Now," originally published in *The New Yorker* in 1986 and already anthologized, as "one of the most important things that has been written in a long time." The story, which deals with a man dying of AIDS (though the disease is never mentioned by name), gains its impetus by its being told from the viewpoints of scores of people who know the victim: A chain of humanity, exclusive of sexual preference, is formed, with Sontag ultimately showing that the disease confronts all people, regardless of sexual preference.

Leavitt reserves some of his strongest criticism for the way network television has dealt with the issue. Although AIDS is still linked with the homosexual lifestyle, he says, "television is incapable of dealing with AIDS in gay people." Citing a newspaper article by *New York Times* television critic John O'Connor, Leavitt points out that not since *An Early Frost*, the ground-breaking television movie, has network television presented a fictionalized account of a gay man suffering from AIDS. "Every special they do is about someone who gets AIDS from a blood transfusion. That's what's so interesting to me: Finally, people are having to admit that this is a disease with many, many facets—it's not just a gay disease—and when there finally is some public sympathy, it always goes to the straight man. It's unbelievable."

AIDS was absent in *The Lost Language of Cranes*—intentionally so, despite the book's explicit detailing of the sexual behavior taking place in the gay porn theaters—and while this led to some criticism of the book, Leavitt reiterates that he wanted to present a story about gay lifestyles without necessarily linking homosexuality to AIDS. He has, however, recently written a short story about the fear of AIDS.

"It's the first thing I've done about it, and I'm sort of following Susan Sontag's lead: I don't mention it by name. What this brings me to, as a writer, is thinking about how the disease is changing our notions about what experience and innocence mean. I keep coming back to those two words: *innocence* and *experience*. When I was growing up in the Sixties, experience was everything. You *lived* to experience. You lived to experience drugs and sex, and now, suddenly, it's as if this 'great chain of connection,' as Susan Sontag calls it, is turning into a chain of death. How do you cope with that? In my story, the narrator is a woman who is sexually inexperienced and, after feeling sort of left out for years, suddenly begins to wonder if she's not the lucky one after her best friend, who's a gay man and very sexually experienced, becomes obsessed with the fear of AIDS."

Our conversation turns to the new novel which, Leavitt jokes, is "all the same" in terms of its having gay themes and characters. "It has a lot of similarities to *Family Dancing*, in terms of what it's about. I think it's the novel people expected me to write after *Family Dancing*, but the writing is totally different. It's much more complex than *Family Dancing*, but it covers a lot of the same territory and subjects. See, I think its subject matter is irrelevant—it's all *how* you say it. . . ."

~~~~~~~~~~

That certainly was the case with *The Lost Language of Cranes*, at least in terms of the importance of *how* a subject matter is addressed: Rarely does a first novelist take on a subject with as many built-in pitfalls. Leavitt readily admits that it was a challenge—and that that was precisely why he decided to write the book.

The novel is the story of a father and son, both gay, both coming out at the same time. Owen Benjamin, the father, is an admissions officer at a prep school; his son, Philip, is a twenty-five-year-old editor for a publishing house specializing in romance novels. Owen has lived with his secret his entire adult life, mostly, one presumes because of the societal conditions he had to endure in his youth; Philip, a member of a more open generation, is simply trying to find a gentle way to admit his sexual preference to his parents. Owen, a pragmatist, has all but given up on any chance of any involvement other than sex; Philip yearns for romance and a solid relationship. As symbols, they display changes in attitudes spanning a quarter of a century, changes which "straight" America might term sweeping, yet changes which have yet to totally address the urges and needs of the human heart.

The novel's chief ambition is not so much in its subject as in the way it is treated. The gay father/gay son theme has the potential for bathetic scenes or—as seems to be the case with much youthful writing today—scenes tinted with a sort of knowing, sneering cynicism. Either way, the novel would have lost its punch or credibility (or both), but Leavitt attacks his subject with such ferocious sincerity and in such a polished style that his readers are willing to give him the benefit of the doubt on those occasions when a scene seems overwrought.

The sincerity was the response to a genuine fear of the author's. "The book grew out of the prospect of finding out my father was gay, which I found so alarming that I decided to write a book about it," Leavitt says. "I wanted to write something fairly unflinching, and I also wanted to do something inter-generational about gay men, describing how attitudes and times have changed."

The book's catalyst, as well as its main heterosexual symbol, is Rose Benjamin, Owen's wife and Philip's mother, upon whom Leavitt heaps the responsibility of sifting through the complex issues at hand. She is the book's strongest character; she is so completely grounded in reality that her reactions to her husband's and son's confessions create an edge which keeps the book from slipping into the stuff of soap operas. Even her disbelief and initial reluctance to accept the direction her life is taking rings true: "I don't believe that just because something's a secret it therefore by definition has to be revealed. Keeping certain secrets secret is important to—the general balance of life, the common utility."

The family issues of *The Lost Language of Cranes* are not so different from themes raised in *Family Dancing*. Leavitt is deeply concerned—to the point of obsession at times—with the forces that hold together or destroy the nuclear family, with the need to communicate love pitted against the necessities to keep secrets. In *The Lost Language of Cranes*, the need to divulge important secrets brings the novel's emotional pitch to its limit.

Leavitt acknowledges the inherent hazards of the gay father/gay son theme. "I was worried that it would seem extreme, that people would be saying 'My God, everyone in the book is gay!' In the new book, I have a gay brother and gay sister, but it isn't nearly as disturbing."

The book drew a mixed reaction from gay readers, but Leavitt feels it was generally favorable. "I got some flak from within the gay community, but not very much. By and large, the response of gay men—especially younger gay men—has been enthusiastic. I think they felt that it told their story."

There were also positive responses from gay father/gay son family members, though Leavitt characterizes these relationships as being different from the one he presented in his book. "By and large, the fathers were more 'together' about their sexuality than Owen," he says.

Leavitt almost dismisses the publication of *Family Dancing* ("I mean, it was kind of exciting, but it happened in a completely ordinary way"), but there is little doubting that the book's success reinforced his belief in the *way* he told his stories. And when it comes down to analyzing today's fiction by other writers, Leavitt is not without a strong opinion or two.

"In my own reading, I'm moving increasingly toward writers who are perceived as intellectual writers. I'm reading Cynthia Ozick and Alice Munro—who I'm always reading—and Stanislaw Lem. It seems that so much of the fiction I was obsessed with, over the last couple of years, didn't have enough ideas. Or the ideas were there, but there was some kind of resistance toward expressing them. There was the whole 'minimalist' thing, and I still love a lot of that fiction, but I've found that, for me, it has reached a point where people have done everything with it that they can. It's one of those terms which has been so misused and abused and kicked around and misapplied that it now means nothing in relation to writing. I'm trying to be more intellectual. I'm more willing to write ideas—to put in these kind of Proustian, extended metaphors—than I used to be. I want a little more 'messiness.' "

To illustrate his point, he lauds a recent novella, "The Age of Grief," by Jane Smiley, a piece that originally appeared in *The Quarterly* and since has become the title story of Smiley's collection of stories.

"It was so full of ideas that when you finished it, you felt like saying 'This woman knows everything about life. She knows all about marriage and raising children and being in a family and growing older.' I was so moved. I cried and cried when I read that story because I was so touched and thrilled by the depth of knowledge that I felt. As a reader, I like to come away from a book with the idea that I've learned something. I want more than just people, a place, and events. That's something that I'm craving and, to some extent, trying to do in my own work now."

He typifies his own writing process as "sheer torture," filled with insecurities and self-doubts which only get worked out through the actual writing. Such insecurity, he says, is not harmful to the work; instead, it keeps him from growing complacent or vain. "Anyone who loves his or her work is someone to watch out for," he says, only half-joking.

For the past few years, he has lived with Gary Glickman, a graduate of the Iowa Writers' Workshop, a teacher, and author of the novel *Years from Now*. Two writers living under one roof presents its own special problems, Leavitt admits, but he is very comfortable with the relationship. Unlike many of his contemporaries, who express cynicism toward lasting, modern relationships, Leavitt exudes optimism.

"I have enormous faith in relationships. *Family Dancing* has a lot of broken relationships, but it certainly has a lot of faith in them, anyway. *The Lost Language of Cranes* is ultimately about the redemptive power of love and how everybody wants to love. My next book is really about marriage—about the sort of unavoidability of marriage. I suppose that makes me a bit 'retro' or something, but I find this chic rootlessness extremely boring. I read all this fiction and nonfiction about young people who go around screwing each other, one after the other, but they can't attach, they can't commit, and it doesn't seem true to me. It seems to be some kind of big egotistical invention.

"Everyone I know *desperately* wants love, and it's hard to find, and you do all this shit when you're finding it, but it's the same old story. My experience isn't the only one in the world, but I think young people have convinced themselves not to believe in relationships. It's a self-delusion. It's a *pose*. It's like saying 'This is our way of being modern,' and I just don't believe it. If there's anything that's universal with human beings, it's the absolute, uncontrollable lust for love. It's always been the strongest thing in my life, and it's certainly what my fiction comes down to."

TOM JENKS

Tom Jenks lives on New York's Upper West Side with his wife and two children. Like most successful editors, he has bookshelves lined with books and magazines that he edited, and the collection is especially noteworthy when you consider that a decade ago Jenks was working a construction job and had yet to attain so much as an undergraduate degree. Since then he has: graduated from the University of Virginia; completed graduate work in the M.F.A. writing program at Columbia; worked for two publishers, as editor for one and in the public relations department for another; edited fiction for *The Paris Review* and *Esquire*. During his tenure as editor at Scribner's, Jenks edited Ernest Hemingway's novel *The Garden of Eden* and he compiled, with Raymond Carver, the anthology *American Short Story Masterpieces* for Delacorte Press. He also assembled *Soldiers and Civilians*, an anthology of short stories examining the various influences of war on our lives. His magazine pieces have appeared in a number of national publications, and he is writing a novel, *Our Happiness*, to be published by Bantam Books in 1989. He teaches a private class in fiction writing and is the editor of the Writer Nights reading series at the Lincoln Center in New York, as well as the literary editor of *GQ* magazine.

Working in these different disciplines not only appreciated Jenks's love for contemporary fiction, but it also afforded him a practical education on how publishing works. A hard-nosed realist, Jenks is skeptical of literary gimmickry, an attitude that becomes quite apparent when he discusses the large number of young authors being published today. It's one thing to market quality fiction aggressively, he says, but it's entirely a different matter to market *any* fiction just because it has been written by youthful authors.

"I'd like to see a retrenchment or pulling back from all the hype," he says. "I'd like to see more understatement—books going out without any blurbs on them, book advertising without all the incredible copy.

"Right now, there's a young man directing the Lincoln Center Theater. He's directing a theater that had been dark for about five years. Before, he had worked out of Chicago and had done rather exceptional things there, and he came to New York to take over two theaters: a very large theater of about one thousand seats and a smaller one of about three hundred. Everyone expected him to come in and open the big theater right away, but he opened the small theater instead. It was an understated and quiet beginning that produced a lot of good work and soon prompted audience demand that would support the larger stage. Everything he touches, he touches very lightly, and when it works, it's that much more pleasing. He really does let the work rise or fall on its own without pressuring the players, audience, or critics. There is a grace in that I quite admire."

⸺⸺⸺

This has really been a good time for contemporary American fiction.

I can't imagine that there is any neglected contemporary fiction at this point. A lot that has been reprinted and packaged just is not as meritorious as it could be. I think you've got to believe that if the work is good, it'll surface. When you're innocent and starting out, you believe that and, after you get older and jaded, you have to continue to believe that. The good stuff will surface, if only because there are five thousand new titles and new editions of fiction published in the United States every year. The bigger houses are doing anywhere from one hundred to, in some cases, three or four hundred titles a year. I don't think there's a lot that slips through the cracks.

You've read *What Is Art?* by Tolstoy? He estimates that there were thirty thousand painters in Paris, and maybe that many musicians and writers, so you had perhaps one hundred thousand artists in Paris, and probably equal numbers in England, in Germany, and in Russia, Italy, and the smaller states combined. Suppose each of those artists produced three works in a year's time. How many works of art do we have? About a million—all in a year's time. And of course all of the novels are divided into chapters; all of them describe love, contain effective situations, and correctly describe the details of life. But among them all, Tolstoy says, there may be one not only somewhat better than the rest, but different from them as a diamond differs from paste. The one is priceless; the others not only have no value but are worse than valueless, for they deceive and pervert taste. Tolstoy noted this decadence at the end of the nineteenth century. We are witnessing similar pressures, attenuation, and affectation, the hasty urge to make things seem greater and more significant than they are, at the end of the twentieth century.

How do you account for what's going on today? Fiction is selling better than ever.

A market phenomenon. The idea that there's a Short Story Renaissance today is a fallacy. But there *is* a good market, a vogue, for short stories; book publishers are bringing out more collections than ever, and there are even some signs of the return of another short form, the novella. So, there's more fiction available than there was in the recent past, more noise being made about it, but there's not a great deal more good fiction around. By good fiction, I mean work that will last after all the noise dies down, work that will inspire works of genius, the way Chekov's influence can be traced to two short story writers as different from each other as Raymond Carver and Peter Taylor.

When the vogue for fiction passes, publishers will promote new fashions. Front-list publishing runs on novelty—new books, new kinds of books, new designs each season.

Hype is the state of the world, and for the artist that means being patronized. An artist can overcome hype by making art out of it, or at the other extreme can refuse to take part in publishing except by writing books. I admire Cormac McCarthy, Don DeLillo, and others who keep out of sight and let the books speak for themselves. When we talk about today's young writers and the interview and publicity circuit, what we're talking about is artistic absolutes being dictated by "Good Morning America" or "Today." What kind of ruler is that? There are never that many readers or patrons for what's really good. Popularity is no more of an indication of literary worth than the Pulitzer or other prizes and awards. Art may be but is not necessarily democratic. Mass media are naturally more sensitive and responsive to what's topical than what's substantial. Politics and random fate play perennial roles in the making of reputations.

If you're a writer, you can be both an artist and businessman, but you're going to come out on the business end of it much better if you have a fair idea of division between the two. Business is business, and art is art. Now, you will find young editors and young agents using phrases like "You have to understand how publishing works today," and what they're talking about is an understanding and acceptance that publishing is about money and fast marketing. In the past few years, most of publishing has been taken over by conglomerates and big corporations, and there has been a corresponding change in values.

Almost no one in American business can afford to look at products or people or business as something to be developed over a long period of time. Bottom-line performance and stock prices, as viewed on a daily to quarterly basis, have become an imperative, so marketing has been stepped up incredibly.

Jay McInerney's *Bright Lights, Big City* is an interesting study. It coalesced with a cultural tide: The book was published and it blitzkrieged Columbus Avenue and through downtown with the cocaine trade. It was followed by Bret Easton Ellis's *Less Than Zero*, which was marketed behind an extremely sophisticated awareness that McInerney's urban paperback success could be co-opted for Ellis, dressed in hardcover, and sold at shopping malls to a younger audience that really didn't know what the experience was and, for the most part, couldn't appreciate irony or satire directed against it but rather began to *identify* with the upscale decadence that was getting so much press. That is, until "Black Monday." Now, a popular literary and cultural backlash has become a mini-fad of its own. And why? Because "end of the Yuppie" articles and disparaging reviews of McInerney et al make headlines that will sell magazines, quite apart from any serious consideration of the meanings of any of these phenomena. And the effect of the backlash is to heighten reputation—that is, the high public profile of the personalities involved. For the sake of marketing, it scarcely matters whether the reputation is good or bad, just so long as it's hot, contemporary—*now*.

⁃⁃⁃⁃⁃⁃⁃⁃⁃⁃

We had all the experimentation of the Sixties and Seventies —or what was *called* experimentation. I would say now that it turns out to have been formalism. But what it produced in writers of Debra Spark's and David Leavitt's generation is exceptional stylistic accomplishment. The 1980s have been more about style than substance. We have all of these young writers—just as we have young bankers and young advertising agents—who are enormously successful and have established a well-recognized style of life. This whole young generation has had all this success, but what are they going to do with it? And what does it mean to them?

In earlier generations—let's say, Mailer's generation—you had writers coming of age in their late twenties, after their war experiences. You had Robert Stone's generation coming of age much later, in their mid-thirties, after the Sixties. Now, suddenly, you have a generation coming of age at twenty-one or twenty-two—coming of age in terms of success, meaning popular recognition for a certain style. My hope is that these writers, bankers, and lawyers will find that this sort of success isn't satisfying. In other words, what are these writers, with all this style, writing about? Most of them don't know yet. Most of them never will know. Only a few will find a long path. In the Sixties and Seventies, many writers, readers, and editors began to view fiction as a vehicle for communicating a feeling rather than as a vehicle for communicating an idea. Fiction was no longer to be a medium for meanings. Tone, mood, atmosphere, color, and form were to be the principal elements in a piece. But now, fiction is moving more toward coherence and a weighing of values in life and literature, not necessarily values moral or redemptive in the churchy sense, but certainly positive and negative values that can be measured in a world of meaning. To the extent that any fiction is authentic, it is *felt*. I look for that, as well as for coherence, narrative, and meaning as it relates to a world beyond the confines of the story or its author.

I like editing and I like writing, but it's hard to do both, not just because it's hard to find enough hours in the day, or to change hats, or to do one without depleting energy for the other, or be responsible to other writers while caring about your own writing, but also because it is hard to find the right situation within the literary publishing world that will allow you to operate in a very freehanded manner, which you have to do. There have not been many editors who have been writers. Gordon Lish is one, and Toni Morrison is another. Ed Doctorow is another and, to some extent, so is Chip McGrath. By far extension we could look at Richard Yates. And we can notice a number of things: Within the writing itself, there are very clear marks in the energy of the work, in the style of the work, that can be traced back to the editorial occupation. Gordon's first stories are very interesting in terms of an editor's reading, absorbing, and presenting what he absorbed, say, from Barry Hannah or from Roth, Salinger, and Elkin. In Richard Yates's case, you can feel the tinge or elision that occurred for him in his copywriting career. And McGrath has shaped himself to the charms, correctness, and quirks of *The New Yorker*. Most editors who write wind up leaving publishing. You hope you can go out through the top, having had a successful editorial career. Toni Morrison left. Doctorow's idea of success is getting up in the morning and having writing be the first thing he turns to.

You know, no matter what you're writing, you find ways to write that fit the life you're living. Let's say you're living a seven-in-the-morning to seven-at-night workaday job and you've got an hour and a half here, or two hours there, or four hours every other day, to write. You figure out how to use it. Harold Brodkey composed his first stories on the subway while riding forty-five minutes out to a school on Staten Island to teach a class. He would get a story in mind on the subway, out and back, and when he got home, he'd write it. The sentences and paragraphs in his stories from that time are as long and rushing and jangling as the trains on which they were composed. Time and circumstance can lend themselves to the discovery of form.

Elizabeth Hardwick, who's so very sharp, once told me: "You think it's going to be easier when your first book is published, but it's not. It only gets harder." That's certainly true. There's the illusion that success makes things easier; and when we live with difficulty we may grow accustomed to it and be strengthened by it, so that at times life and work do seem easier. From the young writer's point of view, there is the idea that once you attain a certain stage, everything gets easier. From the older writer's point of view, there can be a sense that struggle itself is worthwhile, the hope that nothing tragic—failure, betrayal, injury, disregard—will occur, and that when it does, faith will survive and the work will go on. Struggle, tragedy, and success will be conveyed, understood, and redeemed through the telling of stories. That's what you must believe.

Thomas Victor

MONA SIMPSON

" **I** was writing about an American mythology," Mona Simpson says, discussing her first novel, *Anywhere But Here*. "I think all real literature considers the same question—how to live—and one form that question takes is whether to stay in the place you started, to accept what life gives you and make the most of where you're born, or to move, go somewhere else and look for something different."

The question is one Mona Simpson eloquently addresses in

her novel, a rolling tour de force which became one of 1987's success stories almost as soon as it was published. Within two months, the book was in its sixth printing and Disney Studios had purchased its film option. Rumor circulated that Meryl Streep was interested in playing Adele August, the book's enigmatic heroine.

An account of powerful yearnings, *Anywhere But Here* gives us a mother and a daughter on a quest for fulfillment. Twice divorced and trapped in what she calls a "dead-end town," Adele August packs her daughter, Ann, into a "borrowed" Lincoln Continental and, with virtually nothing but the clothes on their backs, takes off for the West. "We were going to California," Ann tells us at the novel's opening, "so I could be a child star while I was still a child." Adele promises, in whispered confidences, that her mission is to get Ann on a TV series in Hollywood, but the reader begins to suspect Adele's kinship with the traveler in the book's epigraph from Emerson, who says "anywhere but here."

The book pits Adele's lofty ambitions against the harsh and sometimes cruel realities of day-to-day existence. Nor surprisingly, Adele's dreams are about the only possessions that are not taken from her, but she and Ann are hard-nosed and resilient, and while their lives may be characterized by a string of personal setbacks and very few victories, neither will be defeated. Ultimately, the novel supports Norman Mailer's theory that we have to keep changing or else pay the price for staying the same.

Mona Simpson lived in each of the places she wrote about in *Anywhere But Here.* After her childhood in Wisconsin, she lived in California's Bay Area through young adulthood, and she now lives in New York City. Like Adele, Simpson spent many of her first thirty years moving not only temporally, but spacially as well, and wondering whether she was better off where she was or where she had been before or could be next.

"For personal reasons, I wanted to write about that basic question," she says. "I also wanted to explore the ideas of changing social class, the yearning toward betterment, money, the trek West, the struggle for glamor—from the point of view of a young woman, a mother. A lot has been written about these American myths, both their glory—in the romantic Horatio Alger stories —and their underside. Sam Shepard writes about these men. We have Jay Gatsby, Dreiser's heroes, and Willy Loman. They are all men. I wanted to write about these same wishes embodied in a woman."

Adele and Ann August are only two of the female sensibilities present in *Anywhere But Here*. Running counterpoint to Adele and Ann's voices-in-flight are the voices of Adele's mother and sister—the people who stayed behind, the symbols of Midwestern tradition and stability. That lifestyle has its own mythology, and the success of the novel depends on Ann's—and the reader's— measuring the merits of the two lives and making a choice.

These choices aren't always easy to make. Simpson talks of a recent visit to Green Bay, where she grew up as Mona Jandali, daughter of a Syrian college professor father and speech therapist mother. Green Bay is a quiet Wisconsin community, especially during football's off-season, and Simpson's trip to her old home-town brought her novel's dilemma into focus for her.

"There's something about the Midwest that's so good," she says. "It's very hard to put your finger on what you love. It's not flashy, and many people who live there have always lived there and have always known. It owns the power of safety and solidity, a continuity of values. I think of Nick Carraway at the end of *The Great Gatsby*. . . ."

She retrieves a copy of the book, searches for a passage, and reads the passage that illustrates her point:

> One of my most vivid memories is of coming back West from college at Christmas time. Those who went farther than Chicago would gather in the old dim Union Station at six o'clock of a December evening, with a few Chicago friends, already caught up into their own holiday gaieties, to bid them a hasty good-bye. I remember the fur coats of

the girls returning from Miss This-or-That's and the chatter of frozen breath and hands waving overhead as we caught sight of our old acquaintances, and the matchings of invitations: "Are you going to the Ordways? the Herseys? the Schultzes?" and the long green tickets we clasped tight in our gloved hands. And last the murky yellow cars of the Chicago, Milwaukee and St. Paul railroad looking cheerful as Christmas itself on the tracks beside the gate.

When we pulled out into the winter night and the real snow, our snow, began to stretch out beside us and twinkle against the windows, and the dim lights of small Wisconsin stations moved by, a sharp wild brace came suddenly into the air. We drew in deep breaths of it as we walked back from dinner through the cold vestibules, unutterably aware of our identity with this country for one strange hour, before we melted indistinguishably into it again.

That's my Middle West—not the wheat or the prairies or the lost Swede towns, but the thrilling returning trains of my youth, and the street lamps and sleigh bells in the frosty dark and the shadows of holly wreaths thrown by lighted windows on the snow. I am part of that, a little solemn with the feel of those long winters, a little complacent from growing up in the Carraway house in a city where dwellings are still called through decades by a family's name.

"The Midwest is Fitzgerald country, William Maxwell country, Lincoln country," Simpson adds. "Even Alice Munro's part of Canada seems essentially the same.

"When I was in Green Bay recently, my first-grade teacher, a nun in retirement who lives and works in the convent library, came to see me. I went back to the convent, too, to visit her. But she found me at Saint Catherine's Bookstore, a place I went as a child after school until four o'clock, when my mother picked me up. My mother always worked. A woman named Mary Lou Ziga runs the bookstore. I've always known her. She is not a nun but she never married. Her house is always open. She lives upstairs from the bookstore and there are a few extra bedrooms, decorated with papier-mâché flowers and prepared for guests. A woman who had just returned from the Peace Corps in Africa was staying there, and a Franciscan priest, who had just walked barefoot through Italy with no money, had just left. There are always scented candles burning, chimes over the doorjambs, tea brewing in the sunny kitchen. To me, this is the Midwest, all these people Westerners."

Although she was pleased to see many of her childhood friends attend her bookstore signing, she was also reminded of some of the reasons she left the city.

"On the street where I grew up, kids' mothers stayed home and kids' fathers were carpenters or milkmen or mailmen—something like that. One worked for the Electric Company—public service. We always said, 'Well, Guy works for the public service.' Of all those kids I played with—years of kick-the-can, fort-building, games we made up with no names—not one of them went to college. It's all so rigged. I believed, at first, that the kids I'd meet at Berkeley or at Columbia or *The Paris Review* or Princeton would be different, more brilliant, quicker, funnier, more stylish. They are more stylish, but not even that, really. You know a person's mind pretty well after a decade of playing with them. A few of them were true originals, fast as flint. But they're all right. Most of them have worn the years amazingly well. The boys across the road grew up tall and dark and handsome. And funny. They can always make me laugh a night away.

"I have a second cousin, to whom I'm pretty close. She just came to visit me in New York. You would be very impressed by her. She's sixteen years old and she grew up just outside Green Bay—'in the boonies,' as she would say—along Route 1. But she held her own in New York City. I'd take her out to dinner with three other New Yorkers and she proved to be a sophisticated conversationalist—still the Wisconsin girl, wide-cheeked, easy to enthusiasm, polite, but also smart, with an air around herself. She goes to Prebble High, a school that's not particularly geared to college. If I hadn't gone over her curriculum, she wouldn't have been eligible for the University of Wisconsin because the guidance counselor failed to tell her that you need to take three years of language. That kind of thing. The school is almost *not* geared for college. She already works for the Ponderosa Steak House nights. I hope she'll go to college, but most of her friends won't. They'll get jobs in town at the mall and they'll share apartments. . . ."

Simpson's description of her Green Bay visit brings back a line from *Anywhere But Here*, a sentence which not only summed up one major theme of the novel but also pinpointed the Midwestern city that inspired it: "I guess when you go away, you want it to be the same, but when you stay, you want it to change."

Time has eroded the traditions established by family, church, and society. Holidays, for example, are often days to endure more than occasions to celebrate. Pop culture has rendered history into a disposable state, undermining tradition and altering perception of how a single moment fits into a grand scheme. Traditions become ambiguous, present in American consciousness but not necessarily honored the way they once were. It's an idea that Simpson finds compelling.

"You can't ignore holidays if you're writing about the family in the twentieth century, or about people's yearnings and the forms they take," she points out. "People have yearnings for spirituality and connection and they are expressed in schmaltzy ways—in all the commercial faces of Christmas and Valentine's Day—and in disappointments. I like the extravagance of American culture. I like schmaltz."

When asked about today's trend of inserting a lot of pop culture into serious fiction, Simpson says, "It depends. It depends on the purpose it serves in the fiction. A writer is always on a sort of tightrope: You want to write about eternal questions, but you want to do that in the context of your own time."

Adele and Ann August may sleep in Travelodge Hotels and eat at Hobo Joe's, but Simpson's use of product names has a way of telling you something about her characters that you might not otherwise pick up. Adele drives a Lincoln Continental which, paid for or not, has its own connotations for most readers, but Simpson also uses this status symbol ironically: The car is the only place where Adele and Ann feel their sense of being a family. The car is home.

━━━━━━━━━━

When Simpson was a child, she spent her time on visual art. "I was always drawing. I started out a shy, frightened student, then I was one of those girls that's always jumping out of their seat, talking too much in class, and the only thing that kept me from being a constant troublemaker in school was drawing. I drew on the sides of my papers, on my wooden desktop, everywhere. I always had ink drawings on the inside of my hands. I was known as someone who could draw drum sets and flowers. A friend would ask me to draw a rose on her hand and she would hold her arm still while I did it.

"Then, in high school, I spent four years working in clay. I took regular classes, but I lived in the ceramics room. It was 1971 when I started high school, and I had long, hippie hair and I wore Oshkosh overalls everyday which, by noon, were covered with slip and clay. I had an amazing teacher, a true artist, named John Riddle. He ran classes with about fifty people in them but, in a way, he led a congregation, formed a community. He could cure our spirits by his comments on how we held the clay at the wheel. He taught us to do everything, to make glazes, to fire, to learn to make bats, and to clean up. He wanted us to do everything from start to finish, to understand the clay in every transformation. He let us work in the room at night and he showed us how to put paper in the lock of the door so we could come in on the weekend. He'd learned that trick from reading detective novels. He taught us to keep the room clean, in a gentle way.

"He had been in Vietnam. He told us about waking up one New Year's morning in a ditch, covered with his own vomit and piss, and seeing an Asian woman already up, sweeping her porch. He told us this in the days before New Year's. After that bad morning of his, he always spent the days before New Year's cleaning his house and washing his clothes. He ate vegetables and went to bed early New Year's Eve. He asked us to clean the room for the new year. We all did. We all wanted to please him. "I remember washing out a big bucket. Later, he called me across the room. 'This bucket clean, Simpson?' It was clean, but I shrugged. I was such a nervous kid. I always expected the world's standards to be impossibly high. 'Could I eat out of it?' 'Not the outside,' I said. 'That's all right,' he told me. 'I don't eat off of the outside.' He was like that."

Even with all that time in ceramics, Simpson did start writing poetry in high school. "I think it was something I just came to on my own," she says. "My mother bought me a little yellow and white typewriter and I taught myself to type with two fingers. I tried taking a typing course and I couldn't bear it, but I'd stay up late at night, typing these poems and stories. I never showed them to anybody. But I kept them very carefully and took them with me to college. I had a sense that they were precious. It—writing—had nothing to do with school or other people. It was just mine.

"I started reading in a serious way, almost by chance. It wasn't from school. School seemed to give us the wrong books at the wrong time. But I fell in love, sort of, with a boy two years older than me, who was a true hippie and very silent. He was first in his class and also a dope dealer, he had long hair, and all through high school he wore a red-plaid lumberjacket that came from the Peoples' Republic of China. Anyway, he told me his favorite writer was Yeats. So I went to the local bookstore and looked for Yates, because I thought Yeats would have been pronounced like Keats. So I bought *Revolutionary Road*, by Richard Yates. Later, in college, when I learned my mistake, I believed I was destined to study Yeats. I took a senior thesis course my first semester of my freshman year, and from then on I've read Yeats almost every day."

Simpson attended college at Berkeley, where she witnessed the awkward cooling-down period from the intensity and theatrics of the politically active Sixties. The University of California at Berkeley had been one of the mainstays of political activism during that decade, and despite the heated debates and demonstrations and student confrontations with symbols of government, time—in the Bay Area, as well as throughout the rest of the country—continued on without the arrival of the predicted apocalypse.

There is an infrastructure of that feeling in *Anywhere But Here*, a sense that the human spirit endures regardless of time and circumstance. The novel values passions of the moment and seems to place them as part of a larger picture, a greater plot.

"I don't think of plot as anything but time—time on one axis, character on the other," Simpson explains. "Plot is the line they make. One of the most amazing things for me about growing up is coming to believe in the kind of extravagant, old-fashioned plots that always gave me pleasure in books. But believing in plot from the inside, believing in the rises and falls of empires and fortunes, in missing identities, in long-lost family members—that all these things truly happen in a life—took time.

"I had little time for food. I had little time for most things. I'd drive with one hand, eating, to San Jose, where I went four nights a week, for months, doing research for a long article I was writing on incest and incest treatment. I sat in and watched therapy groups, listened to fathers who'd molested their daughters tell their confessions to each other. I was always a slow journalist. One person would talk to me for a long time and almost always, at the end, he'd say, 'There's something going on in Alameda, a group with all the family together, who you might want to go see.' Stories grew and grew. I spent months on most of the long stories I did. They became lives for me. I'd make friends. I had teenage girls sleeping on my living-room floor.

"I couldn't make a living on journalism. I was too slow. Seven or eight months on the incest story, three months on a story on the indigent hospital. I applied for jobs. The closest I came to a social life those days was walking with a bean bow down Clement Street and seeing my old boyfriend folding clothes inside the laundromat; I'd knock on the window and say, 'Hey, those are my socks.' In the spring of 1981, I applied for a reporting job *and* graduate school at Columbia. I came close, but I didn't get the job, so I moved. The paper folded after I left, so I was lucky."

She enrolled in the M.F.A. program at Columbia and moved

to New York. "It was a big move," she remembers. "I had no family, no money, and I didn't know anyone east of the Mississippi. I went to visit the spring before I moved for good in fall. I'd applied to Columbia two years earlier, right out of college, and I'd received a big scholarship. At the last minute, I fell in love and canceled. I called them up and told them I'd fallen in love. So, this time around, they wanted to see me before they committed themselves. While I visited, I signed up for Columbia housing. They gave me an apartment that looked out on a brick wall. It had no oven—just a hotplate on the floor. I had to turn on the overhead light in the morning. There was lots of room to move up. But I worked hard. I'd moved to New York for fiction, and I built my life around that certainty. Ideas that make people move, dreams that buy passage across oceans, change us forever. We value the ideas we acted on."

At Columbia, she studied under Elizabeth Hardwick, Chip McGrath, and Edmund White. They were each, she says, very helpful, profoundly inspiring in the best way. "Each one of them truly impressed me as a person. In some way, they taught character—the deepest things, the hardest things. They fooled with commas, too, but that was only the surface. The real lessons were much more far-reaching. I remember the last workshop, the last day of my last semester at Columbia. Chip McGrath was the workshop leader. Nancy Lemann, Susan Minot, and I each had turned in stories or chapters of our novels. Nancy's was the last; it was the beautiful first chapter to *Lives of the Saints*. Most everybody liked the piece, and we talked about it and a few people began to say that the end of the chapter needed something more, something more dramatic, perhaps more violent. And Nancy burst out and said that she'd had exactly that, that a bride had said horrible, unforgivable things, drunk, but that she'd cut it out because it was just too cruel. And then the class spun up.

"We talked seriously and for a long time about cruelty. I remember Susan's saying, 'If it's true.' Finally, Chip McGrath said something like, 'Well, maybe this is a good place to end things. If you really want to be writers, you're going to have hard lives. You're going to work alone for years, with little recognition, no money, no health insurance. It's a hard, hard life. And if you want to be a writer, somewhere along the line, you're gonna have to hurt somebody. And when that time comes, you go ahead and do it. And if you can't or don't want to tell that truth, you may as well stop now and save yourself a lot of hardship and pain.' "

During Simpson's early years in New York, she also did some journalism, quite a few book reviews for *The New York Times Book Review*, and some longer author interviews. She was also employed as an Urban Corps (a form of work study) assistant at *The Paris Review*. After graduation from Columbia, the magazine hired her on staff, where she rose from assistant to associate and, finally, senior editor. "I never liked that title," she says today. "I used to say, 'I'm too young to be a senior anything.' "

She did like the job. "I sat in an overstuffed chair in the corner, with my feet propped up, reading manuscripts all day," she remembers. "The snow would fall outside and we would be suspended. I was able to find some stories, in the piles and piles of mail, which meant a lot to me—stories I learned from and was able to see them into print in the magazine. That was a pleasure. And then there were the extracurricular amusements of office life. Issue Eighty-eight, I remember, was our true issue. Two of us were breaking up with long, important boyfriends at that time, and all we did was read Mallarme and look ruefully out at the sky. We felt so adult, so suddenly. We were twenty-five, twenty-six. The other person had lived with a man for a while and they often fought. The mornings after these fights, she would bring in a draft of a letter and she let me rewrite them; we'd spend the whole day tinkering. I had a year-old correspondence with this man I nodded to on the streets. I'm sure he never knew. But Issue Eighty-eight ended both our affairs. We put it all into the magazine, into a beautiful new translation of a sad Eluard poem and a Lydia Davis story called 'Break It Down.' My interview with Raymond Carver was in that issue, as was one of his stories. It was, in every way, an issue about endings, about regret."

If the first words to *Anywhere But Here* were written years earlier, in California, the novel as a whole began to take form the summer of 1982, when Simpson went to Yaddo, the artists colony that has bred several generations of serious writers, including Philip Roth, John Cheever, Allan Gurganus, and Jay McInerney. Richard Price, one of Simpson's teachers at Columbia, suggested that his students apply. Simpson did, and she was accepted for her first summer in New York.

"I took a train which runs alongside the Hudson," she recalls. "I had two big suitcases—one with my typewriter and enough paper and ribbons for the whole summer, and the other with books and a pair of jeans and sneakers. I walked onto the platform of what looked like a summer dacha: a small train station, trees all around, birch and elm. Upstate New York is pretty in such an understated way. The low hills and coloration of the sky reminded me of the Midwest—the modest scale, the pure summer values in the colors. I was there for nine or ten weeks. I knew I'd be going back to classes and work in fall, so I just wrote all the time. I had a wonderful, simple energy. I was completely at ease, writing and lining my pages up. I wrote a whole draft that summer."

From that draft, she later found and honed several excerpts which were published in *The North American Review*, *Ploughshares*, and *The Paris Review*. "Approximations," an excerpt which was expanded and appeared in the novel under the title "Las Vegas, Disneyland, Egypt," was published in the anthology *20 Under 30*. Although Simpson also writes short stories today, very few were completed during the writing of *Anywhere But Here*; one, called "Lawns," was published in 1985 in *The Iowa Review* and found its way into the *Best American Short Stories of 1986* and *The Pushcart Prize: Best of the Small Presses XI* anthologies.

The first draft of the novel may have been written in ten weeks, but Simpson spent over three years revising it. "Writing a novel may take years, but it's also something you do every day," she says. "It's a commitment, like a commitment to a person. And what gives a marriage or childrearing or teaching or religious practice or any other sustained project its real substance are the repetitions of effort, every day, over a long period of time. I don't know if it's *hard* work; it is serious work. With most jobs I've had, there are days when one chats on the phone, balances one's checkbook. It's a rare office where everybody is working with real concentration all the time. But writing is a discipline. It's a way of life, a practice, a kind of devotion. Every minute you're really writing counts and adds up, gives to the book.

"I worked on my novel for a long time. Sometimes I feel I grew up writing that novel. In a way, I learned what my opinions were, what I loved in the world, what I did and did not want to do with my life. I started writing the book in earnest the summer I was twenty-four. Nothing good had happened to me in my life yet. I'd come to New York, partly to go to graduate school at Columbia, mostly to be a writer.

"Sometimes I lied. I said I'd started a novel, even before I had. Later on, when I was on page fifty, I'd say I was on page seventy. I think that was partly because I was ashamed to be spending as many hours as I was and leaving normal life as much as I was and producing so little, and I think it was partly to make me stay up later and work harder.

"This novel was the first thing in my life that I cared about desperately and knew I cared about, before it was too late. I gave everything I knew, everything I had, to it. My grandmother died in 1979 and left me three thousand dollars which came from a gas station she owned. I remember the third year on my novel, living in New York, making little money at part-time jobs—I spent that money. I felt that it was the last security I had in the world—all my family was in California, poor themselves and a million miles away—and it felt good to be giving the book everything."

These efforts weren't unnoticed when *Anywhere But Here* appeared. Its dust jacket carried eight blurbs by critically acclaimed writers, including Alice Munro, John Ashberry, and Louise Erdrich. Mary Robison endorsed the book as "necessary," while Walker Percy lauded it as "a stunning first novel—a real big, burgeoning talent." Good reviews poured in and *Anywhere But Here* was being touted as one of the most impressive debuts of the year.

––––––––––

Mona Simpson was born in 1957, the year Jack Kerouac's *On The Road* was published; thirty years later, *Anywhere But Here* studied many of the same themes, but with a twist. Kerouac's vehicle was a silver Hudson and a frenetic protagonist in search of the elusive "IT"; Kerouac's writing style moved like a speeding car, rambling at breakneck speed until all time and event blurred like road signs viewed from a passenger's window. Motion became the point. Dean Moriarty was "fastestmanalive" (as Ken Kesey would call him a quarter of a century later), a symbol of perennial youthful restlessness.

Simpson's protagonist is also on a quest, and while what Adele August searches for is every bit as elusive as the indefinable "IT" of the Kerouac novel, she and her daughter, with their traditional Midwestern roots, are less willing to totally discard their pasts in favor of an uncertain future. Ann and Adele packed up and left, but not without trepidation, as is evident in the following passage describing the mixed feelings Ann felt when she boarded a plane to fly back to Wisconsin for a relative's funeral:

> It wasn't the falling that scared me, but the slow band of time as you're beginning to go, when you can still see the world in clear patterns, the web of lawns, and your fingernails cut into the soft nicked wood and everything in your body screams Stop. But you're moving. . . .

Both novels are distinctly American, not only in their westward movement, but in their dealing with time and place, their spacial relations. In the twentieth century, the highway has become *the* symbol of the American spirit, and both Kerouac and Simpson considered it the ultimate American cultural icon—the vast expanse of land itself which, like the individual, has limitless potential yet definable limitations and boundaries. Ironically, both novels' characters were misinterpreted by some reviewers as being the voices of alienation when, in fact, if a reader were to look closely, he or she would see that the protagonists of *On The Road* and *Anywhere But Here*, while being far from pleased with the status quo, were American Dreamers in the classical sense. To call them alienated is to deny them the faith that motivates them.

Simpson is currently in the middle of a new novel, with a working title of *A Regular Guy*, and from the way she describes it, the novel continues her exploration of some of the themes examined in *Anywhere But Here*.

"It's about a ficticious town in the West," she explains. "It's the history of that town for a couple of generations, but it's particularly about that period of time in people's lives, in their twenties and thirties and forties, when they come to terms with their ideals."

The success of *Anywhere But Here* has put Simpson in demand as a lecturer, book reviewer, and potential fiction contributor to highly respected magazines, but her life, she says, is "simple and focused," which is another way of saying that her work is still the core of nearly everything she does. She shrugs when asked about her ambitions.

"I want to be a writer," she says.

Paige Powell

TAMA JANOWITZ

". . . I realized that I wanted a fame of my own, something to make me into a real person, a human being. If I was famous, I would know I existed, a fact I was not absolutely positive of right now." —from *American Dad*

⌃ May ⌃

A trendy Italian restaurant in SoHo, early Sunday afternoon: People are just beginning to air out their hangovers from the night before. Some of the customers sip Bloody Marys and watch a soccer game being played out on a huge screen suspended over the doorway; others huddle at tables along the wall and listen to the mood music, which now happens to be Tom Waits yowling something about Union Square in a tone that sounds like a circular saw cutting through a quarter-inch strip of sheet metal. A few daring souls even go as far as to order something to eat.

Outside, a cab pulls up to the curb and Tama Janowitz steps out. She is wearing all-black, a sort of personal trademark, and her hair flies in all directions, as if being whipped around by a wind machine. She enters the restaurant and, for an instant, while she pauses in front of the glass door and allows her eyes to adjust to the dim interior of the building, she is framed like a shadow figure projected onto a white sheet.

The past twelve months or so have been very good to her. Her collection of short stories, *Slaves of New York*, established her as the literary counterpart to her friend the late Andy Warhol, an image she enhanced when she and her book became subjects of the first MTV literary video. Her first book, *American Dad*, a critically acclaimed novel long out of print, was being reissued in trade paperback by Crown. Her new novel, *A Cannibal in Manhattan*, was forthcoming. Appearances on "Late Night with David Letterman," "Good Morning America," and "The Today Show" afforded her a visibility she'd only been able to dream about a couple of years earlier. She was a cover story for *New York* magazine, and she was being featured in magazine ads for Amaretto and Roses Lime. For a writer—even one who admittedly enjoys the spotlight—this was high visibility.

Too much, in fact. The visibility had become so intense that she welcomed the opportunity to get away from the city—a chance that came around when Princeton University officials asked her to be a writer-in-residence during the 1986–87 school year. Today, she mentions, as she sits down at the table, she is in the city to participate in a PEN Club reading and to scout out new living quarters. She'll be back in Manhattan as soon as the school term ends.

The break from New York, she says, was beneficial. The success of *Slaves of New York*, along with the very public way in which she promoted the book, had cut into her work time. Public persona was getting in the way of the work that put her there in the first place. "The last year I was here was difficult," she says, "because I had spent so much time in New York without the phone ringing, going out very rarely, not meeting people, and all of a sudden the phone was ringing, virtually thirty to fifty times a day, and people were calling, left and right, saying 'Come out and do this or do that,' and naturally I'd rather do anything but write, so I had a great time. But I found it hard to work. This year, I've been in Princeton, in an extremely isolated environment, writing like mad. I feel that now I've found some sort of order: I had my year of total fun, and now I've once again gone back to the sort of isolated and secluded life and am at a point where I've found a balance."

Her words come at you like a spray of bullets. It's no wonder she is popular on the interview and talk-show circuit: She lacks nothing in the self-confidence department, yet she punctuates her conversations with enough smatterings of humorous self-deprecation that she avoids sounding overbearing or cocky. So many writers, when being interviewed, hem and haw and grope for words or apologize for sounding dry or boring; Janowitz may be afraid of a few things, but a microphone isn't one of them. She doesn't just get to the point—she pounces on it, and from there she embellishes until she's given you both the story and the color.

Still, as Tama Janowitz herself might say, *it's like this*: If you want to be considered a serious literary presence, you damn well better recognize a few rules. For one thing, you have to look and act serious, which means you don't promote your book on MTV, drop your makeup artist's name next to the jacket photo on one of your books, or in any way give any indication that a writing career is any less excruciating than delivering triplets while trying to negotiate your car through the Lincoln Tunnel during a Friday-night rush hour. It's also helpful to be sullen. (In fact, being sullen may be the primary prerequisite to being taken seriously as a young, literary presence.) Finally, never, *ever* give your book a title like *Slaves of New York*; it sounds too much like a movie they'd play on Times Square.

Janowitz has broken these and other rules. She clearly enjoys promoting her work, and for this she's had to contend with accusations that her work is more packaging than substance, that she is more concerned with her public persona than with her private art. Janowitz has heard more than her fill of these complaints, and they bother her not one bit. The media attention, she insists, has only helped her put her books in front of the public.

"It's really thrilling for me," she says of the attention she's been getting. "I could care less what they decide my image is. When you've spent years and years of your life struggling to write, learning how to write, being absolutely broke, you want your book to sell. I spent years trying to write, doing the best job I could at that particular time. I was proud of the work. The other part—selling it—has nothing to do with the agony I went through with my work. I'll be damned if, after spending that much time, I wouldn't want somebody to read it. I mean, when *American Dad* was published, it got a number of very good reviews but nobody bought the book, and that's pretty much standard fare for a first novel. Now, if I have the chance to make the damn thing sell, I want to go for it."

As for the substance of her work, she points out that her publishing history is diverse enough to keep her from being packaged as a writer appealing to only one type of audience. "It was always important to me not to be slotted into one particular type of group, and I was pleased, by the time *Slaves* came out, that the stories had been appearing in places as wide-ranging as these little East Village magazines like *Between C and D* and *Bomb* to national magazines like *The New Yorker* and *Harper's* to literary reviews like the *Mississippi Review* and *The Paris Review*. It made me feel great to know that I was stylistically diverse enough to appeal to different types of circles, that I ended up in all those places."

Maybe, it's pointed out, the objections stem not so much from the idea of promoting a serious work as by the way it's being promoted. The author photograph on *Slaves of New York*, for example, a glamour shot depicting Janowitz, in silk pajamas, reclining on a bed, was the most provocative portrait of its kind since Truman Capote's picture on *Other Voices, Other Rooms*, and it's no secret that Capote spent a good portion of his life either trying to live the photograph down or trying to live up to its strange promise. And, as flamboyant as he was, even Capote never made a video designed to run after the latest rock 'n' roll ode to technology.

On this last count, Janowitz was the first. However, making an MTV video was hardly an act of whimsy. It was, Janowitz says, a calculated attempt to reach what her publisher perceived to be a solid audience, a troop of potential readers who enjoy the energy and artistry in rock videos, and who might like the same in a book. People who read the Style section of the newspaper before they turn to the Book Review pages—if they even bother with the latter at all.

The problem, Janowitz asserts, is no one knows how to find books in the glut of new novels and story collections published each year. The video was a way to really reach them. "I think that's why Crown was so brilliant, because publishing is so notoriously a gentlemen's profession. It's fifty years behind the times. Meanwhile, you've got banks advertising their services—everyone's advertising their services—and publishing's like, 'We don't do that. Oh, yes, we'll take out an ad in the *Times*, because that's standard, but we wouldn't do something else.' I mean, you wouldn't even go into a grocery store and buy a new variety of cat food without having seen it advertised someplace."

The video project, Janowitz continues, was a marketing experiment in which she was "the test guinea pig." An independent production company had approached Crown Publishers with the idea of putting together a literary video, and Janowitz seemed to be a likely subject. "I seemed to lend myself to it for a couple of reasons," Janowitz says. "I have a certain look—I 'look' New York—and the stories themselves take place in a very dramatic or theatrical nature. We knew we could show some settings, like the nightclub or my walking on the streets of New York, and get the whole feeling to the book, so there were a couple of days of shooting—it wasn't scripted, it was just me talking—and it was a big production. It was a lot of fun. I felt like George Plimpton pretending to be a football player: Here I was, in a rock 'n' roll video. I'm not sure, truly, if there's any way to do a follow-up on how many copies of the book would have sold had they not done this, but it helped my book get attention."

As unorthodox as this approach may seem, it pales in comparison to one of Janowitz's efforts to gain attention for her book of stories. Shortly after the book was published, Janowitz and two friends loaded booklets of *Slaves* excerpts into the back of a cab, and the three spent an afternoon cruising around midtown Manhattan, handing out the pamphlets to anyone who would take them. They checked into—and were excused from—places such as The Four Seasons and the Oyster Bar, where their outrageous fashion drew stares from astonished patrons. It was the kind of spectacle you might expect to see in the East Village on a Sunday afternoon, but hardly the norm for a district known for multi-martini lunches and business power deals.

Nearly lost in all this hype and glitz is the fact that Janowitz *can* write. Her lean prose is tinged with humor and more than just a small dash of pathos; as a storyteller, she can hold her own with any of her contemporaries. The characters in her story collection are slaves to their hungers. They're broke, destitute, unhappy, and living on the edge, and while all of these conditions could be partially attributed to the fact that most of them are artists of one sort or another, these characters nevertheless are more concerned with corporal comfort than spiritual fulfillment. They'd gladly trade in any long-shot chances to be the world's next Jackson Pollack for three squares a day, a decent relationship, and a roof that doesn't leak every time a renegade rain cloud opens over their apartments. But such a trade isn't in the offering, so Janowitz presents her stories' desperate characters with a sympathy similar to the sentiments one of her characters expressed when trying to explain why he couldn't kill cockroaches:

> "It's obvious they're running for their lives," he said. "To kill something that wants to live so desperately is in direct contradiction to any kind of philosophy, religion, belief system that I hold. Long after the bomb falls and your good deeds are gone, cockroaches will still be here, prowling the streets like armored cars."

Janowitz's interests in people living outside the margins are both literary and personal. She lists Dostoyevski, Chekhov, Nabokov, Henry Miller, and Saul Bellow as her favorite authors, and she is considering the idea of teaching a course, which she calls "The Outsider in Society," when she does her occasional college lecturing.

"This course would deal with books that have always been my favorites, from Kafka to Beckett," she says. "George Orwell's *Down and Out in London*. Joyce Carey's *The Horse's Mouth*. Maybe one of Henry Miller's books. These books are about the outsiders in society who, for one reason or another, are starving to death. They're alcoholics or drug addicts or people who circle society as kind of desperate figures. I mean, I read anything, and I admire, let's say, Raymond Carver or Ann Beattie, but for my own work, I look for the energy in somebody who can't stop himself, who's going on in a most intense, insane, *extreme* fashion."

Slaves of New York, Janowitz's contribution to this tradition, is nothing if not intense, insane, and extreme. The word "quirky" pops up quite often in reviews of Janowitz's writing, but the adjective seems a little light when it's weighed against the deeper intentions of the author's fiction. For instance, the lethargic pimp in "Modern Saint #271" may seem "quirky" because he likes to lounge around his garbage-strewn apartment and read Kant, or when he brings his prostitute/girlfriend flowers and pastrami sandwiches when she's confined to a hospital bed after being beaten up by a john, but neither he nor any of the other characters in *Slaves* are used purely for humor's sake. Janowitz uses humor and irony like a surgeon uses a scalpel: Only when you're healing do you realize that you've been cut and hurt.

Janowitz, who once wrote that she wanted to be "a sort of modern Jane Austen," finds New York the perfect environment for her study of social mores. She enjoys the constant motion in the city and the diversity of its people and experiences. "It's all coming at you, and that's when I feel alive. You can be sitting at the typewriter and nothing's happening, and then you go to the window and look out, and there's a man chasing a woman down the street, and she's in pajamas, and she's screaming and people are calling the police and all this stuff is going on. It's all around, and if you can't transmit that, in some way, to the printed page. . . ."

She pauses, as if the notion is unspeakable to her: How could anyone not observe the spectacle of New York and *not* find a way to write about it? Her stories, she wrote in a statement about *Slaves of New York*, are really fictionalized eyewitness reports:

> . . . I wrote down what I saw. And this involved the action on the street, which most of the time was violent. And the interaction between people, which was also pretty violent. Because there are a lot of people being stepped on by those people who want power, and this means there are a lot of people who are trying to get someplace. Where they're trying to get, I don't know. But to me, this was pretty funny—in a black way.

In the best of her stories, Janowitz superimposes humor on the violence in a fashion that disarms even her detractors. ("Janowitz has a catchy style and achieves her satiric effects with a sly Valley Girl delivery," wrote R. Z. Sheppard of *Time* in an otherwise unfavorable profile of what the magazine termed "Yuppie Lit.") Still, there is an air of detachment about the work which has disturbed some reviewers.

Like other fiction writers who take a quasi-journalistic approach to their writing, Janowitz argues that taking a stand on what she was writing about was not her duty as a short story writer or journalist. "I don't feel that it was my job to be in any kind of moral position of passing judgment on what I was witnessing," she says. "I simply was there as a reporter, to say that this is how it is to live in this particular time and place. My interest was to take my notebook and pen and write down little snatches of overheard conversation. Or, if three or four different women called me up and each was having the same type of trouble in her relationship, I would think maybe there was some kind of pattern going on, and that made a jumping-off point for another story about a woman having a similar type of trouble. But I never felt like I wanted to say 'Look at the crummy, shallow, superficial world of New York' or 'Look at the great world of New York, with all this energy and creativity and excitement and enthusiasm.' It wasn't my job to do either. My job was to write down what I was seeing, and to be as true and honest to it as I could."

For much of her life, Tama Janowitz has been an outsider or observer, a position she attributes to her moving thirty-eight times in her first thirty years. Her father was in the Army when she was born, and she was quite young when he was transferred from San Francisco to the East Coast. After some bouncing around in New Jersey and New York, the Janowitz family settled in Amherst, Massachusetts, where Tama's father took a position in the mental health department at the University of Massachusetts. Her parents divorced when she was ten, and Tama and her brother, David, were raised by their mother, a poet, who made ends meet through poetry grants. In 1968, the three of them went to Israel for a year, where they spent a lot of time "traveling around." By the time she reached high school, Tama was not only well-traveled, but as a constant outsider, she had a sharp eye for observing details of the ways in which people behaved. She also found herself facing the dilemma of whether to struggle to fit in, or work to stand out, in a crowd. It is a dilemma, she now believes, that all writers face.

"I think there's a little of both in everybody," she says. "One part of being a writer is to want desperately to be liked, while at the same time you want to rebel against society, to just throw everything up into the air and watch where the pieces fall. I think that's natural."

Because of all the moving around, she says, she had an unusual formal education. "By the time I got to college, I didn't have much of a background. I'd been to private schools some of the time, and some years I went to experimental schools, so I didn't have a standard upbringing. I couldn't add or subtract numbers —and I still can't. I graduated from school a year early, and even though I didn't have good SAT scores, I was accepted to Barnard

College. My fear was that if I had to take regular undergraduate courses, I would be 'discovered': I knew I could never write a paper on Cervantes, so I majored in writing, which you could do in the Arts program. I never thought I would be a writer, but I knew they couldn't flunk you out—they could just say they didn't like your stories when you handed them in."

The combination of New York City and the writing program acted as a catalyst in Janowitz's early writings. Though she claims her teachers were "shocked and horrified" by her stories, her writing was noticed elsewhere. She won a scholarship to the Breadloaf Writers' Conference when she was a sophomore; she won the Elizabeth Janeway Prize and spent much of her junior year in England; and the following year she won three other prestigious awards, including the *Mademoiselle* Guest Editor award. Despite the recognition, Janowitz still insists that writing was "a dumb thing to have majored in as an undergraduate."

She goes on to explain that her college background did little to prepare her for postcollege employment. She wanted to go into advertising as a copywriter. "I liked advertising," she explains. "It wasn't hypocritical. It wasn't pretending to be doing good deeds for the world. They were doing the same things that everyone else was doing: selling their products. You'd make money and have this one job of writing copy. With a background in creative writing, it seemed like a smart thing to do."

Instead of taking a job as a copywriter, she moved to Boston and accepted a position of assistant art director for an advertising agency. It was a miserable, short-lived stint. ("I couldn't use a T square, and I couldn't draw anything representational, do paste-up, layout, or mechanicals. I could just draw these weird little figures that were half-men and half-animal.") She lasted six months before she was laid off.

Wanting to try her hand at writing a novel, she applied and won a fellowship to Hollins College; at the very least, she says, she would have graduated with a Masters degree. As had been the case at Barnard, she found herself successful as a writer.

"I *did* write a novel that year, and the following year I sold it.

I thought, 'This is a cinch: You write your book and you sell your book and then you have enough money to live on for a year while you're writing another book.' "

Janowitz was twenty-four when that first novel, *American Dad,* was published by Putnam's. Written in the first person, from the viewpoint of Earl Przepasniak, son of a psychiatrist father and poet mother, *American Dad* is a coming-of-age novel which finds Janowitz taking heavily autobiographical detail and twisting it with her own particular brand of humor. From a standpoint of style, the book is much more traditional than her later works, which may account for its being ignored by those wishing to label Janowitz a strictly "trendy" writer.

Writing the book, Janowitz says, was really a process of discovery. "When I sat down, I had no idea of how to write a novel or what to do. But I did know that they say to write from experience, and my experience was growing up in the country in rural Massachusetts. When I began to write that beginning section, I thought, 'Well, here I am back in rural Massachusetts, but this writing from experience is so boring. Why not change the *me* to a male?' As soon as I did that, it became fiction. The events and incidents were no longer the same. I was just delighted to put myself in a different character's head."

Writing from the male perspective is something Janowitz likes to do. *American Dad* and *A Cannibal in Manhattan* are both narrated by male characters and, in the case of her first book, Janowitz even marketed an excerpt to *The Paris Review* under the pseudonym of Tom A. Janowitz.

Earl's parents, the two other major characters of *American Dad,* were roughly modeled after Janowitz's own parents (to whom *American Dad* is dedicated), and some of the novel's funniest moments are the results of her exaggerations of her father's love of sculpting and nature, and her mother's love for poetry. Neither of her parents, Janowitz says, is nearly as wacky as the ones portrayed in the book.

"The mother in the book is in a dream state of ineffectuality. After my parents split up, my mother went back to school, became a poet, and is now a professor at Cornell. All this is a second career because when she got married, women didn't have careers—they got married and had kids. So she's been a real role model for me. My father sculpts and is extremely physical, and I feel that I got so much from him on that side. Both have been supportive of me, my father in a more distant way, my mother as a mother and fellow writer saying 'Yes, it's tough, but if this is what you want to do, keep doing it.' "

These were strong words of advice because, as Janowitz learned, writing wasn't the "cinch" she initially made it out to be. With her *American Dad* advance, Janowitz enrolled at the Yale School of Drama, where she found the collaborative process of play production unsuitable to her notion of the creative process. A new novel went nowhere. She dropped out of Yale and attended the Fine Arts Center in Provincetown on a fellowship. She wrote another novel that failed to generate any interest among publishers.

The only thing that kept her going, she remembers, were the occasional awards. There was a $12,500 award from the National Endowment for the Arts—money she used to relocate to New York City. Within a year, that money was gone and she was again faced with the prospect of finding a nine-to-five job. "I knew that would have been the end of my writing career, because I never had that much physical energy," she says. "I could never be one of these people who get up at six in the morning, write for two hours, and then go to a job. But each time I thought I'd have to go out and get a job, I'd win another prize. Little things would happen to keep me going for six more months. I got a CAPS grant, which is a New York State grant, and I won the CCLM General Electric Foundation Award. At that point, I'd switched over to writing short stories. I had sort of given up on writing novels for the time being, because I thought that if nobody wanted to publish a story, it only took a few weeks or months to write, where with a novel it was a year. Then I sold a story to *The New Yorker*, and that was the break that really changed things around."

This hard apprenticeship period gave Janowitz a greater appreciation of the business aspects of creative writing—an appreciation which led to her awareness of the idea of self-marketing. She hung out with artists who were going through similar trials and, in recalling the period in *Slaves of New York*, she stripped away the romanticism associated with the starving artist concept, her characters motivated by factors that were less than aesthetic.

"When I came to New York," she explains, "I hung out with painters and artists. That was a whole interesting, fascinating scene. If you had ten painters who were out to dinner, nobody discussed the aesthetics of painting. Nobody discussed composition or great works of art. They discussed: 'Did you hear So-and-So switched galleries?' or 'So-and-So is now selling his paintings for twenty thousand dollars.' I found the art world of New York at this time—in the early Eighties—like the rock 'n' roll scene of the Sixties and Seventies, and I was just fascinated by it. It gave me a sort of jumping-off point to start writing about this whole world that I didn't see anybody else writing about."

An editor at Crown had seen some of those stories and offered to publish a collection of short stories. Janowitz, then studying under Elizabeth Hardwick in Columbia University's M.F.A. program, went through "a huge box of stories" and began compiling the collection that became *Slaves of New York*. She had the work; all she had to do was figure a way to get it in front of the public.

⁻ September ⁻

A bagel shop on Manhattan's Upper West Side, a short walking distance from Tama Janowitz's new (and, she hopes, long-term) apartment. It's late morning, and Janowitz sips coffee and looks over a new issue of *The Village Voice* before getting down to the business of discussing her new book.

The last few months have been hectic, culminating in her finding new living quarters and launching a new book. She is just returning from a short promotional jaunt to Minneapolis, and she now has to look forward to a national tour which will take her to ten cities and their inevitable barrage of talk shows, book signings, and public appearances. The early reception of *A Cannibal in Manhattan* all but assured her a continuation of the rather schizophrenic literary experiences to which she has become accustomed: Critics were panning her book, and readers were eager to buy it.

She says she's feeling "feisty" about the way the book has been received by critics, and she's anxious to hit the road and address her readers—the people she's really writing for. Despite the attitude of defiance, however, it's clear that she's been hurt by some of the criticism, especially the articles that poke fun at her personally and ignore her work. She suggests that too much work has gone into the work for it to be ignored or quickly dismissed in favor of glib discussions and caricatures of the way she looks.

A Cannibal in Manhattan, she explains, is a special book to her. "I always wanted to see this book published. I felt like this was my child: I just love this man, and the only thing I wanted to do was see him published."

The novel, one of the earlier books that Janowitz couldn't publish, was actually referred to in *Slaves of New York*, in a story titled "Snowball":

> Years ago, in his artist days, he had written a book. B.B., Before Bomb. The book was called *Mgungu*, it had little text. His wild English friends, decked in sixties' sequins and satins, arrived in Manhattan and posed for a series of pictures: staggering out of a studio-set jungle, indulging in birdlike mating rituals. The book was a spoof. Once he had been an outsider, a marginal figure, capable of making fun. Now he saw things were too serious for that. . . .

A Cannibal in Manhattan was overhauled and rewritten after the publication of *Slaves of New York*. In many respects, the book's subject was custom-made for Janowitz: Instead of lampooning one segment of New York society, why not write a satirical overview of an entire city, from its street people to its social climbers, as seen through the eyes of an innocent? Her main character, Mgungu Yabba Mgunga, is a calm, polygamous former cannibal from a fictitious South Seas island, a leader of a dying tribe. A rich socialite sees him in *National Geographic* magazine and, after joining the Peace Corps, tracks him down and offers to bring him to New York, where he will be featured in a museum's international dance festival. They marry and after a series of mishaps—all allowing Janowitz the opportunity to comment on life in New York—she is murdered by underworld figures who persuade the oblivious Mgungu to eat the evidence as part of his first American barbecue. From there, life is all downhill, Mgungu finding himself facing survival situations more brutal than anything he had to deal with as a "savage."

The noble savage idea is hardly new to fiction, but Janowitz's version is the result of a combination of fond childhood memories and her adult sense of satiric possibilities. "I think I saw some little, tiny article about a man who had come from another country to buy brassieres for his wife, and that sort of set the whole thing off," she says. "That was the germ. For about two months, I researched New Guinea and other South Pacific islands, and when it came time to write, I made up my own island. It's a fantasy island, and it's not entirely logical—there are certain things that really couldn't be—but it's coming from this childhood love of books about the explorers. Books that stayed with me, like *Robinson Crusoe*. The books I read during childhood were the most vivid because I had no critical ability as a child: You read books and you fall into them. It was better than going to the movies. You'd just enter into that world without question, without doubt."

Much the same way Mgungu entered the "fantasy" world of New York. His observations about civilization, Janowitz says, stem from her watching television documentaries and wondering how we would feel if such a documentary were filmed about contemporary life in New York. "Turn on the TV and there's constantly a *National Geographic* special on about some primitive tribe," she points out. "I would always laugh to myself because if an anthropologist, say, from another planet were to come here and do a TV show, we'd be laughing our heads off about the way we were portrayed. So that was about what we consider civilized versus what we consider primitive. The primitive man may not be civilized, but he may not be quite as primitive as we think, compared to how primitive this place is."

For a novel, A *Cannibal in Manhattan* was not a low-budget production. To heighten its comic effect, as well as to recreate the type of book Janowitz enjoyed so much as a child, endpaper maps of New Burnt Norton were created, photographs representing the action in the book were taken, and specially designed lettering was used to open each new section of narrative. Janowitz oversaw all of these aspects of production, and while they did occasionally cause delays in the book's publication processes, she is very satisfied with the way they turned out.

"For me, the aesthetics of the bound book were extremely important. I love books, and I wanted a beautiful book. I mean, look at some of the old books from, let's say, the Twenties: They're just set up so beautifully. The text on the page *looks* good, and the books *feel* good. The little drawings and endpaper maps came from my wanting to recapture that. I wanted that sort of magic quality, where you'd read the book and then you'd go back and look at the maps and trace their passage through the mountains and the river. It took a long time for us to come to the quality that those little drawings should have. We decided they couldn't be jokes unto themselves, that they had to complement the text and not be little cartoon scenes. So Tony Wright, who did the artwork for me, did these very simple little drawings, like two spears going across for a 'T'. They were almost like dictionary illustrations."

The idea for the photographs, she continues, came as a result of her reading true-crime books, with their inevitable "scene of the crime" photographs, and seeing how similar photographs in *Cannibal* could add to its sense of fun. "When you open to the center of those true-crime books, there are always these pictures, and half of them make no sense whatsoever. They'll have the picture of the childhood home and the family picture, and they always have the living-room scene of the crime, and it always looks different from what the guy was talking about in the book.

I'm surprised that nobody's thought of doing this with fiction when, in this day and age, it's a totally visual society, with TV and MTV and people going to the movies."

The photographs feature a number of New York models, art, and publishing figures—even Janowitz herself—all posing in various scenes in the book. Andy Warhol, in one of his last modeling stints, posed as the museum's curator. The book is dedicated to Warhol, who not only was a personal friend of Janowitz's, but who, as a filmmaker, bought the options on the Eleanor and Stash stories from *Slaves of New York*.

"He was always there for me," Janowitz says. "When we said we were having people model for the pictures, he said he'd love to. And he just was very supportive, not just of me, but of many, many young designers and painters. He loved young people, and he loved to support somebody who was creative and starting out in a career. When I think of Andy, I think of a person who truly enjoyed life with a genuine, childlike enthusiasm and, despite what they said about him—that he was detached and uninvolved with life—I have never met a person who was more involved with life. He went out every night for twenty or thirty years, not because he was doing business, but because he truly enjoyed going out and seeing people. He enjoyed going to fancy restaurants or just going to get a hot dog on the corner. If there was one thing that I could learn from him, it would be to keep that childlike joy for things."

Warhol also knew a thing or two about fame, and some of that knowledge seems to have rubbed off on Janowitz. Unlike Earl Przepasniak, her *American Dad* narrator, Tama Janowitz doesn't appear to need fame to make her feel real. It isn't to be taken too lightly or too seriously—but it should be fun. As much fun as modeling for an ad or starring in a video. As much fun as a false but harmless mention in a gossip column. As much fun as knowing people are reading and enjoying your books. As much fun as knowing the literary coin—heads, you're a serious writer; tails, you're rich and famous—and standing it on its edge.

"I write the type of books I'd like to read," Janowitz says. "I think fiction is very often tedious to read. All too often, it's excruciating, boring work to get through. I'd rather read a book where I come away knowing or learning something. I'm interested in the craft and in improving myself and changing and getting better. I feel like I can keep growing for my whole life."

Melonie Sill

ANDERSON FERRELL

"One eye of wanting is pitch black, the other is as bright as the sun. Wanting and death are married, but life is its lady friend. To be free of it is to be it. It is all you are."

—from Where She Was

Fifteen years ago, Anderson Ferrell was working on a tobacco farm in North Carolina. Less than a decade later, as a member of a dance troupe, he performed for a Kennedy Center audience which included the President of the United States. A couple of years later, he decided to forsake a career in dance for one in writing. He was subsequently awarded a publishing contract, with one of the country's most prestigious houses, on the basis of two written paragraphs.

The first thirty-five years of Andy Ferrell's life might be termed a search or quest—he certainly sees them that way now—but you can't help but wonder what it is that drives the spirit, what motivates a man to keep moving despite the fact that he has found a way to earn a living in an artistically challenging career.

Ferrell's answer is an idea that has launched a thousand novels.

"We are nothing but desire," he says.

Stretching out in his apartment near Manhattan's theater district, Anderson Ferrell admits that, by nature, he is inwardly restless. "I'm easily bored," he says, frowning, "and I don't like that about me. It troubles me."

He draws a distinction between restlessness and desire, and it is a crucial distinction addressed in his novel, *Where She Was*. Restlessness, the book intimates, is a feeling; desire is a passion. Both motivate people to take action, but only actions motivated by one's heart's desire will necessarily lead one down a direct path toward true destiny and spiritual fulfillment. Still, as Cleo, the protagonist of *Where She Was*, discovers, powerful feelings of yearning can be elusive to understanding. Are they the results of restlessness, or are they something deeper? How can a woman who has attained everything she set out to attain still feel such powerful yearnings? In the end, when all physical comforts have been satisfied, is the desire for spiritual fulfillment an eternal quest from which we enjoy no rest?

Cleo is a good woman who, due to her upbringing and present circumstance, never looked beyond life's simple pleasures for her own sense of fulfillment and self-worth. She loves her husband and family, works hard on their tobacco farm, and holds steadfast the deep moral convictions which have given her life its meaning. However, a series of incidents, usually vague and occurring almost out of her line of vision, begin to form questions in her mind. At first, the questions are little more than distracting irritations, but Cleo quickly finds that they are not easily dismissed; by the end of the novel, she is obsessed, a woman driven to find answers and meanings to a life which, only a few months earlier, had seemed so peaceful and orderly.

These are feelings that Anderson Ferrell has considered to great lengths. They are the feelings that have driven him, personally and artistically, and they continue to haunt him, even though he says that he has finally found, as a writer, the life he wants to lead.

"I guess you could say that Cleo's psyche and my own are alike," he says. "We're certainly concerned with the same sorts of things, though I would never go as far as she did.

"This woman, Cleo, has everything she knows how to want —in her world, it's all you could want—and she's *young.* Her life was settled early. That's when you start to think about these other issues, these other troubling things."

Ferrell continues, his voice becoming so soft that it blends in with the other sounds filtering through the walls of his apartment building.

"I suppose you could say that, in a philosophical sense, my question is: When we've exhausted our desires, what's left? When your world is arranged just as you would have it, then what? And it goes even beyond material things. When you reach a spiritual plateau, then what? It occurred to me that the only thing to desire is desirelessness. If you can come to that, then you really achieve a state of grace, I think."

He laughs at his next thought. "But then," he goes on, "the biggest part of the battle is still in default because you're left with the pride of having done it, which will undo you every time. You're nothing but desire, but I don't know how to escape it. And if we make the effort and do escape, what will we be? Saints, I suppose."

In *Where She Was*, there are no canonizations, nor are there any openings of clouds, accompanied by brilliant shafts of light, which lead Cleo to a startling satori which forever changes her life. If anything, Cleo's struggle culminates in her experiencing what Tibetan Buddhists call a state of "ordinary mind," in which a person sees the world, in an almost visionary sense, exactly as it is:

> I'll be done with looking, she thought. And because she believed that she was sure of it, a calm came over her so that, to anyone looking, she would have appeared to be a farm woman going about her business. Cleo thought that that was what she was.

It appears to be such a simple, logical conclusion to a journey that found Cleo questioning her own life, turning to different religions for spiritual answers, and ultimately addressing her fears and desires in a climactic passage as frightening as it is eloquent. The struggle, rather than the conclusion, is Cleo's—and the novel's—story.

This, too, is an essential element to Anderson Ferrell's philosophy. *Where She Was*, he suggests, could be interpreted as a long, intricately detailed metaphor with universal applications. It surely applies to the life of the writer.

"I don't think there's anything wrong with struggle," Ferrell says. "All artists are born out of struggle. *Life* comes out of struggle: We struggle to be born—*someone* does."

In Ferrell's case, the struggle to be born, as a writer, ended almost as simply as Cleo's quest for self-determination.

"I had no reason to think that I could be a writer," he admits. "I'd never known a writer. All the writers I knew of—all my friends who had wanted to be writers—planned for it. I had a hard time deciding what qualified me. I knew I wanted to write, but I didn't know why.

"I had become very, very unhappy as a dancer. And a dear friend sat me down and said, 'What would you like to do? If you could do anything, what would it be?' I told him I wanted to be a writer, and he said, 'What do you need to do that?' I said, 'I suppose I'd need a typewriter.' When I came home the next day, there was a typewriter sitting there."

────────────

One of the first dictums any writer hears is to "write what you know" and, for Ferrell, that meant a trip backward in time, to the simpler era he encountered as a child growing up in the Fifties. Ferrell remembers it as a magical period—a time when people kept a slower pace and lived by values which he still admires today.

Born in 1950, Anderson Ferrell grew up in a tiny village (population 300) in the eastern part of North Carolina. The area's economy was fueled by the tobacco industry. Technology and automation were beginning to replace the lifestyle described in *Where She Was*—a standard that had more or less been followed for centuries. Since their livelihoods depended upon conditions of nature and climate, people were more attuned to the land, and because people were working together, performing tedious, repetitious work in confined areas, conversation was a form of entertainment.

"I was growing up down there at a time when it was still rural," Ferrell explains. "I didn't have a television. I'm one of my generation who remembers radio and Jack Benny and Arthur Godfrey and all those shows. You had to focus out for your entertainment and inspiration. What fired my book was my feeling that place is somehow responsible for our actions. Your life is exactly where you are and what you make of it."

Hence, the title of his book. The first three of the book's four sections begin with detailed descriptions of the places of Ferrell's youth, including the town in which he grew up:

Between the station and The Avenue, the places that make Branch Creek a town line the streets that line the railroad. On the west street—three stores for general merchandise. In a town that can support only one well-stocked merchant, the three store owners courteously neglect one thing or the other so that a farmer or his wife might have to go here for a wash bucket, further up for a good piece of fatback, and stop in somewhere else for some screen wire. The stores are evenly spaced along the street, the various necessary places in between: the bank building that is now a jail, the doctor's office where a dope fiend comes twice a week for medicine between this store and that one, a volunteer fire department with two trucks, a barbershop that was once a Holiness Church. Each of the stores has two gas pumps out on the curb—regular and hi-test—hoses stuck in ears like dimwitted monuments to slow living. Across the tracks, outcast, is the county package store and, attached to it, an awning-browed place with a backroom pool table where a beer can be had. The price of the beer is fifty cents and the shame of being seen going in there.

"That's a physical description of the town I grew up in, as nearly as I could get it down," Ferrell mentions. "The railroad that runs down the middle of the town was exactly that way. That farmyard is an actual farmyard that I knew. The book is a work of imagination, but what's real is the description of the place.

"The characters are composites of people I have known. I'm like an actor who looks around and picks up gestures and bits of clothing that he sees in the world and then applies them to the character he has in mind. You know, someone might push his glasses up a certain way and I'll say 'Yes, I can use that.' "

Ferrell used as much as he could remember, filling his novel with the sights and sounds and textures of his youth. He recalls how his grandmother, a Free Will Baptist, would walk him around town on Sunday mornings, taking him from church to church —whichever seemed most convenient, since she didn't drive. These scenes found their way into *Where She Was*, as did memory fragments of the time Ferrell spent alone, wandering around the countryside, admiring nature in its beauty.

When he began writing, he says, he had "this aching desire to put down on paper, to capture somehow with words, the magic that I felt as a young boy in those places. I don't know why childhood is so magical, but it is, and the magic for me was always out in the world. I mean, you fantasize as a child. You see yourself as a fireman or a movie star, but the *real* magic for me was not anything I cooked up myself. I *saw* it. I saw it in a flash of rain or a piece of paper in the ditch bank. There's a part in the book where a character catches sight of a piece of paper in the ditch bank and thinks it's a flower. That's happened to me, where everything down there takes on these extra qualities. They were more than just pieces of paper in a ditch bank—they were rare, rare blossoms."

For all its lyrical description of the larger-than-life elements of the natural world, seen almost in awe through the vision of memory, *Where She Was* is ultimately an ode to the working stiff. The book's poetics can be found in the hum, sometimes melodic, often monotonous, of repetitive labor orchestrated over the ages. Reading Ferrell's book is like looking at the strong hands of your grandfather.

Anderson Ferrell spent a few summers working under the "barn shelter" of a tobacco farm, and unlike many writers, who are all too happy to dismiss their dues-paying days as essential, though perhaps distasteful, life experiences, Ferrell continues to pay tribute to the kind of labor depicted in his novel.

"I love work that doesn't require inner thinking," he says. "I love manual labor, because your mind's free to go. It's as though that repetitive work is an engine or machine that fires the imagination. Because of the dullness of the situation, people's imaginations would spring out, and they would derive pleasure from each other. People would talk and enjoy each other because that was a situation where you'd go out of your mind if you didn't talk. It's interesting that the process that is described in the book really no longer exists. It's terribly automated now, and the social aspects of the work are gone."

Because of the nature of his characters' work, Ferrell could include conversation which moved his story along without sounding pedestrian. Small talk not only performed the usual function of supplying the reader with crucial information about the lives and hopes and beliefs of individual characters, but it also functioned, in Ferrell's book, as a means of further augmenting the author's theme about the way place shapes actions and lives. This was the Old South, yet to be affected by the flint of the Supreme Court's *Brown* v. *Board of Topeka* decision and a Martin Luther King–led Civil Rights Movement, yet it was also a South which could feel on its bare skin a change in the wind's direction, a whisp of something new. It is a change that confuses and angers the people of Branch Creek, as one can gather from this fragment of conversation between townspeople:

"You and me's trading help right on, ain't we, Dalton?" he asked.

"They'll hold up, I believe," said Dalton. "Hazel you can count on. This here bunch of darkies seems right steady."

"It is a-getting worse every year," said the friendly man who had called Dalton's name.

The nodder nodded.

A harmony of woe and sympathy followed, drifted into the gathering pollen haze, curled up into the green-and-white aluminum awning, and floated back, tuned to the well-trained ears of the men—a song sung just for the singers.

"Don't want to work, most of them."

"I'll be forced to get a harvester."

"I think I'll paint my face black and go up there to the Welfare outfit."

"Won't give it to a white man."

These attitudes established, Ferrell introduces his readers to Hazel Balance, the only white woman hired as a laborer on the farm. Aptly named, Hazel is bright, funny, and not at all appalled by the life she leads. One senses that she will adapt to change much easier than Cleo or her husband, Dalton. She is also the book's best storyteller, a person, Ferrell writes, who "knew that stale gossip had to be steamed up a little just like stale bread, before it seemed fresh again."

Ferrell recalls the banter, often laced with humor, that he heard between workers at the tobacco farm, and it was something he wanted to replicate in his book.

"It's been said a hundred times that there's that oral tradition there," he mentions. "This repetitive work allowed the characters the chance to talk, and it's in the telling of a story that people derive pleasure and enjoy each other. The way one says something is *so* important because it's not understood unless it's said well or properly. It's all in the telling."

The "telling," in the case of *Where She Was*, really did involve Ferrell's creating rare blossoms out of scraps of paper. Unlike many of his contemporaries, who are fond of compressing ideas into tight sentences springloaded with imagery, Farrell's prose expands an image, his ideas like sponges dropped into a pool.

> Cleo smelled creek water. It was as if the smell came from his hair and blew around her, a cool smell, a smell so strong Cleo could feel it against the back of her throat, a damp, rich smell as rank as the dirt—a smell that would grow things.

The way the story is told, with all its sensory detail, was not so much a matter of Ferrell's choosing a style as it was a reflection of whom Ferrell perceives himself to be.

"I'm that way naturally," he says. "I'm ill-educated, so I don't have a first-rate mind, but I *do* have good ears and eyes, and I can smell and taste. I can rely on them. It's what I see and feel and taste that forms what I think."

He concedes that this type of writing may be too rich for many readers' tastes, and this played a great role in his restricting the hardcover to its 141 pages. "I kept it short because you can't sustain that for three hundred pages. The reader wouldn't have it. It would entertain me immensely, but I don't know if it would entertain anybody else."

Writing the book, Ferrell continues, was a learning experience. Mainly, he learned about point of view; instead of writing a semiautobiographical novel, told by a first-person narrator, as is typical of first novels, Ferrell drew a story from his imagination and had it presented from a woman's point of view.

"In many ways, this book is like a second novel," Ferrell says, adding that he is currently writing another novel, set in the same location, which is told in the first-person narrative voice. In the new book, Ferrell sees himself "trying to move more toward my own psychological stance in relation to the world. It's about a young man who gets his family to clean off the family graveyard, which has been in a state of neglect for a long time. He does that, and it causes all kinds of problems. On a practical level, I'm trying to learn about the first-person narrative where, with the first book, I learned about using the power of an instant to tell a story."

⌣⌣⌣⌣⌣⌣⌣⌣⌣⌣

Shortly after his graduation from North Carolina State University, Anderson Ferrell packed his bags and moved to New York City.

"I came here to be in the theater, to be an actor," he says. "I had done some amateur theatrics in college, and I could sing, so I thought, 'How hard could it be?' If I had known, I wouldn't have done it. I was so naive, I thought that when I came to New York I had to get an apartment in the Forties or Fifties so I could walk to work." Ferrell laughs at the thought today. "It took me about three years to get into the union. So I think there's a virtue in being simpleminded about these things.

"I started taking ballet, just for the movement. I felt that I should be able to put one foot in front of the other. It was all by accident. I got a scholarship and studied ballet."

He made it to the stage, as a dancer rather than an actor. There were Broadway shows and some concert dancing. He was in a revival of *Oklahoma*, a national tour of *My Fair Lady*, and a musical version of *The Canterbury Tales*. He worked for Agnes DeMille, that tour of duty culminating with his dancing before the President on a night when DeMille won the Kennedy Center Award.

He found that he could indeed make a living as a dancer, but he was still unhappy. "I was not passionate about dancing in the way that you have to be to continue," he says.

He is uncertain how much his days as a dancer contributed to the way he is as a writer. His sentences do have a certain melody and grace of movement which could be attributed to his work in dance, but he is not so certain this isn't the product of who he is, as an individual as opposed to what he has been trained to do.

"What I know I brought to writing from dancing is the idea of imposing discipline upon yourself. There's more outside discipline to dancing than there is to writing, because there are people around when you're dancing, and the music itself imposes a discipline. For writers, there's a discipline from within, and while art is basically illogical, there's a logic to the discipline that the technical training of dance had for me."

The daily discipline of writing offered Ferrell, as an offshoot benefit, the development of artistic standards and a confidence in those standards. He learned about setting standards when he studied in a writing workshop conducted by Gordon Lish. Shortly after his friend bought him a typewriter, Ferrell applied for admission into a writing class at Columbia. He was told that he was not advanced enough in his writing to be accepted into the class he had registered for, and it was suggested that he study under Lish. Ferrell admits that this decision bruised his ego, and that he was initially put off by Lish's aggressive teaching style, but ultimately he learned from Lish exactly what it took to write good serious fiction.

"He was the first one to look you in the eye and say 'This is not good enough, it won't cut it, they won't read this.' In the other workshops I've taken, the approach was to find something positive to say about everything. Everybody was special in their own way. Well, there's special, and there's *special*. I was lucky, because Gordon had high standards, and that was good, because in the early stages, when you have no standards, any sort of standard will do.

"With Gordon, you read only the sentences you earned by *his* standards. The way the class was conducted, he'd say, 'All right, go home and write an attack'—that's what he calls the start of a story. So I dutifully went home and wrote a whole story and was prepared to read it. I came to class the next time and read the first sentence and he stopped me. He said, 'This is wrong. Don't you see why? Here's why it's no good. Next.' That startled me. I had this little story here. But he said, 'I've given you work to do; fix your first sentence.' So I went home and tried to do what he said, and I came back the next week, and I think I got out two or three sentences before he stopped me. 'That was good. The first three were good. The fourth one's wrong, and here's why. Next.' I got mad. I said, 'Don't you see what I'm trying to do? You don't know that on page five . . .' And he said, 'I won't know because I won't read it if you don't *make* me read it. You have to take a reader's head and push it into the page.'

"That's what a set of standards will do, if they're held up to you properly and presented in a clear way so you can understand them and try to approach them. That's what he did. What he wanted me to do was always clear to me. I couldn't always do it, but I knew what he wanted."

Having confidence in one's standards, Ferrell goes on, is more difficult than setting them. "Making art is a matter of being unsure," he says. "I mean, if you were *sure*, you wouldn't sit down to do it. If you knew what the outcome would be, and you knew how to do it, why would you start?

"It's unpopular to say so—and every time I say this to people, they think I've lost my mind—but you have to allow yourself the luxury of failure. It seems to me that risk invites failure more often than it results in success."

Ferrell likes to repeat a story he was told by Agnes DeMille, a story which he believes underscores the importance of belief in one's standards in the face of possible failure. DeMille, Ferrell says, was once asked to do a major ballet. At the time, she was a relatively unknown choreographer, and the head of the ballet, a great impressario, insisted that he have the final artistic say over the way the ballet was interpreted. DeMille refused, arguing that those decisions were the right of the choreographer.

"Why would you want to do that?" Ferrell recalls DeMille's asking the director.

"You might put a mustache on a Rembrandt," the man replied.

"I might," she told him. "Don't hire me." At that moment, DeMille told Ferrell, she knew she had come into her own.

"I think that's true in writing," Ferrell says. "I think you really come into your own as an artist when you can rely on yourself. When you're willing to fail on your own terms—even if success is right there in front of you, to be had *if* you do something someone else's way—you have a *life*. You're living when you can fail your way, rather than succeed in another way."

Writing, Ferrell intimates on a number of occasions throughout our conversation, is such an internalized, personal endeavor that he sometimes has a difficult time seeing a larger picture. He will succeed or fail on his own terms, regardless of what is being done by others at the moment. Great works of literature, he says, don't influence him one way or another; if anything, they serve as inspiration.

He uses Flannery O'Connor, one of his favorite writers, to illustrate his point.

"She had an artistic life that I envy," he says. "I can't envy her work or abilities, because that's useless. I'm a different person, living in a different time. What I *do* envy—and what I try to arrange for myself—is the kind of quiet life I think she must have had, to be able to quiet herself down there and be able to do this great work.

"You can't add anything to perfection. There's never any satisfaction in it whatsoever. When you do see things that are perfection, all you're left with is the desire to try again. That's what I feel. No matter how badly it's gone that day, it makes one want to try again."

DEBRA SPARK

Debra Spark is a fiction writer who, at this point in time, is best known for her editing of *20 Under 30*, a benchmark anthology of short stories and novel excerpts written by youthful authors whose work, prior to the volume's publication, was virtually unknown to the large-scale reading public.

Today, the book is well known and generally well received—even, perhaps, taken for granted in some literary circles—but at the time of its April 1986 publication as a trade paperback original in the Scribner Signature Edition series, the anthology was anything but a safe bet to achieve the reputation it currently enjoys. Journalists were just beginning to focus on the national obsession with youth, glitz, and money in the publishing business. *Bright Lights, Big City* was still a fairly new book that was gathering momentum in its sales figures. The public, readers and critics, still preferred to gamble their dollars and tastes on new books by already established authors. Short story anthologies were more popular than ever in literary history, but their pages were filled with the works of time-tested writers, and their editors had reputations almost as large as these books' contributors.

In short, *20 Under 30* was an experiment and a challenge. In her early twenties and fresh out of college, Debra Spark had little to fall back on but the merits of her anthology's works. Even so, Sparks's process of selection for the volume's entries was more modest than ambitious.

"My only true criterion for selecting stories for the anthology was jealousy," she wrote in the book's Introduction. "Any story I enjoyed well enough to wish I had written I included."

Published with laudatory blurbs by Bob Shacochis, Frank Conroy, and Carolyn Chute on its back cover, *20 Under 30* elicited some strong praise and very little criticism from its reviewers. Jonathan Yardley of *The Washington Post* voiced one of the few dissenting opinions, complaining that the volume's stories sounded alike. ("You could have said that this was a collection of stories by a 27-year-old writer named Henry Smith and readers wouldn't have known the difference," he told an interviewer a year after the book came out.) Phillip Lopate, writing for *The New York Times Book Review*, called the book a "wonderfully enjoyable reading experience," concluding that "it is heartening to see talented literary apprentices learning their craft and producing spellbinding stories. We should be hearing from the writers in this excellent collection for a long time to come." It took very little time for readers to cast their decision on the anthology's merits: By the end of 1986, the book was in its sixth printing.

As predicted, a number of the book's contributors have gone

on to establish their own literary reputations—a fact that gives Spark her own modest pleasure.

"A number of people have done really well, which is nice," she says. "Being included probably wouldn't have made any difference for some of these writers—they would've done well anyway—but I'd like to believe that it was slightly helpful."

Spark says she pays very little attention to the brouhaha over young authors which has appeared in the book's wake. Much of the debate, she believes, centers more on journalism than criticism, with the bulk of the attention being devoted to *who* is doing the writing than on *what kind* of work is being written.

"It's something I try not to follow too much," she admits, "although you would think that maybe I would, having done the anthology. It would be nice if I had certain thoughts about the whole phenomenon, but part of me retreats from it. So much of it is surface stuff and has little to do with the writing itself. I don't think the reading public has the same sort of interest in it. Readers are not so knowledgable about the scene. They pick up a book because they have enthusiasm for the book. It's all the same to them if the book is by a young author or an older one."

Although she has yet to publish her first book, Debra Spark has covered a lot of ground and has written a substantial amount of fiction in her brief career. Born in Boston in 1962, Spark is the daughter of a physician father who once considered a career in photography. She has a younger sister and brother, as well as a twin sister, studying to be an urban planner/architect, who Spark characterizes as "a fine poet herself." Hers was a family of readers.

Spark never seriously considered writing until she was attending classes at Yale. After graduating with a degree in philosophy, she attended the Iowa Writers' Workshop as a graduate student. She recently completed a two-year teaching term at the University of Wisconsin.

In August 1985, at the age of twenty-three, she published her first short story in *Esquire*'s "Summer Fiction Issue." Less than a year later, *20 Under 30* was published. She is presently working on a novel and a collection of short stories. She seems surprised by the reception she has received to this point, but she is cautious about taking it too seriously.

"You know, the attention is quite superficial because the praise you're getting really has nothing to do with what your day-to-day life is like. It seems that if it's given out so easily, it could be taken back, so in a way, I think it's good not to pay too much attention to these things."

Right now you are known more for 20 Under 30 *than for your writing. How did you evolve as a writer?*

For a long time, I thought I would be a photographer. My father did a lot of photography when he was in college and he almost went to work for *Life,* but he decided he would be a doctor. We had a darkroom in the basement, and I did a lot of theater photography when I was in college.

I think I was always interested in writing for stupid reasons. When I wrote papers, I would get them back with the comment, "Oh, you write so well," and you know how you like things when you think you do them well. I wanted to be good at what I did, and that's probably why I didn't go into photography: I was okay, but I was never really good. I didn't have the talent that some people have, and I would have had to have worked very hard just to be competent. The best photographs involve one's being pushy, and I can't stand that. I remember having a few experiences on the street, where I'd be taking a photograph and someone would notice me and get angry, and I'd have to deal with him. Or lots of times I was too embarrassed to take the picture, although I thought it would be a good one. I don't think I would have ever gotten over that.

I'd always had this vague interest in writing, but I'd never done it. Then, one summer, I decided that I wanted to take a fiction-writing class. To get into the class, you had to write a story, but

I hadn't written a thing that whole summer. I'd worked at a summer theater, and on the train, coming back to school, I wrote my first story, just to get into the class.

I took this class and actually felt quite disillusioned. I felt that I was terrible, that my work was horrible. I surely would not have gone on if it weren't for the teacher. His name was Donald Faulkner. He pulled me aside at the end of the class and told me that it's always very exciting for a teacher if he has even one student he thinks could go on to be a writer, and he said he thought I could be a writer. We were in a coffee shop, and I remember dancing out of the shop, thinking, "Oh, great, oh great!" I thought I was writing this embarrassing stuff—and I *was*, actually—but he encouraged me anyway.

Then I took a class with John Hersey. It was a small seminar and he'd meet with us once a week. We had to write a story each week, which was wonderful for us. He was very encouraging, and he taught us things such as sticking to the same point of view—which would have taken me years to figure out if I had been writing on my own.

You started out wanting to be a photographer, wound up being a writer, but majored in philosophy at Yale. Why did you do that?

I don't think I would have been a very good English student —especially at Yale, with all of its literary criticism, which is of no interest to me. I really loved studying philosophy. I was fascinated by it.

How did you feel about the Iowa Writers' Workshop?

It was exciting for me. I was eager to have contact with other writers and get feedback on my writing. I think my experience there was different than for most people because of Rust Hills being there. He took a real interest in my work, and that made my experience quite unusual, I think. He also gave me very good advice and was incredibly helpful in terms of showing me how to fix things in a story and do revision writing. Prior to that, no one had ever really expressed interest in my work. Donald Faulkner and John Hersey had said, "Keep doing it," but no one had said, "This is a good story." Which was fine, as I hadn't *written* a good story. So I was quite surprised. For a little while, I didn't know exactly what to do, because I was almost embarrassed by all the attention he was giving me yet, at the same time, I was so happy to have it. Rust bought my first story out of workshop.

"Summer of the Dead Frogs"?

Yes. That was really the first story that I had ever finished to my satisfaction. Even so, like everyone there, I was terribly nervous about submitting it for discussion. In fact, after I'd put the story up in workshop, I wanted to go back and steal it off the shelf and say there had been a terrible accident or something. *(laughs)*

I was the youngest student at workshop the first year I was there, and I was around people who had put a lot more years into writing than I had. And here the first story I had written gets snapped up by *Esquire*. I had never had a story published in a literary magazine or even in college, so I think I felt almost apologetic, as I was getting what everyone else wanted. After that story came out, people wrote and asked for work, but it wasn't as if I was John Gardner, with a backlog of ten novels I could pull out and say, "Here they are; I'm glad you asked." *(laughs)*

Were you working on 20 Under 30 *at the time?*

Yes. When I was in college, I got the idea to put it together. At first, I thought I'd put together an anthology of unpublished writers, but I realized that that wasn't quite feasible. If the writers were good, they might have been published before the book came out. Then I thought about putting together an anthology of stories by young writers. I just used "under 30" as an arbitrary cut-off point. I was working on it and collecting a few things when I was in college, and then I got a few more stories at Iowa. I wrote a number of people—writers and editors and agents—and for each of the stories in the book, there's a slightly different story about how I acquired the piece. I'm not even sure how many stories I read. I never stopped and counted.

Subsequent to my story coming out in *Esquire*, I met Tom Jenks. He found me an agent who was interested in the project. By the time I was through with my first year at Iowa, the book was all done. We never sent it out, because Tom knew I was working on it. When he moved to Scribner's, he called my agent and asked if he could buy it.

Were you surprised by the response to the book?

I was surprised by everything in those days. . . . *(laughs)* It sold very well. It's still selling well but, as best as I can tell, that's my mother's and sister's doing: If they go into a bookstore and see it face-down, they turn it over. Or they'll go: "Where *is* that book?" *(laughs)* That's one nice thing about my family: They've been endlessly supportive.

L. M. L.

EMILY LISTFIELD

Fade In:

1. MANHATTAN SKYLINE AT DAWN. SUMMERTIME.

Sharp cut to:

2. EXTERIOR. A ROOFTOP. MEDIUM SHOT. DAWN.

Two young women, virtually no more than silhouettes, stand near the edge of the building, looking out at the sky.

WOMAN (VOICE-OVER) New York at dawn. Imagine it. We stood on the lumpy tar roof determined to see New York at dawn. It used to be so much easier to stay up all night, Carrie says, have you noticed that? Age, I say, joking, joking of course. We did not feel ourselves to be aging at all. We were young, so young. Young with New York lightening up before us, for us, as if it were a movie set being gradually lit for our benefit alone. New York beneath and around and above us, the granite and glass. Vulnerable, attainable even, our New York, our city.

Cut to:

3. EXTERIOR SHOTS. NEW YORK STREETS. ESTABLISHING.

A quick series of brief shots of Manhattan's East Village. (We hear loud, rhythmic music—salsa, reggae, rap.) In a series of takes, we see the run-down, partially abandoned buildings of Alphabet City; the shooting gallery of the Bowery; happy children (though obviously impoverished) calling out to each other in Spanish; people walking down crowded sidewalks; customers dining at local eateries.

Sharp cut to:

4. EXTERIOR. EMILY LISTFIELD'S APARTMENT BUILDING. LONG SHOT. ESTABLISHING.

Emily Listfield lives in one of a series of apartment buildings set well off the streets of the East Village. Considering the almost frenzied activity taking place only a block or so away, these buildings, set in a park-like atmosphere with trees, benches, and walkways, are a haven.

5. EXTERIOR. INTERVIEWER STANDING IN FRONT OF BUILDING. CLOSE-UP.

INTERVIEWER Writer Emily Listfield lives in the East Village section of Manhattan, in a rather secluded apartment complex set just off one of the city's main thorough-fares. There is something almost symbolic about this: While she is, in every respect, a New York writer, she is not a part of the mainstream, either in her day-to-day life or in what she chooses to write about. Her two books, *It Was Gonna Be Like Paris* and *Variations in the Night*, are literary love stories, set in New York, which depict not only human relationships but the times in which they occur. In both novels, relationships appear to be doomed as much by the times as they are by the characters involved. Both novels have been very controversial. Historically speaking, love and the human spirit have endured the times, but Listfield suggests that this is not necessarily the case today.

6. CLOSE UP. COVER OF *THE NEW YORK TIMES MAGAZINE*

A couple is seated on a curb. The man is looking off in the distance, to the left of the photographer, his body turned away from his partner. The woman, wearing sunglasses, stares directly into the camera. Both are emotionless. The headline reads: "Alone Together: The Unromantic Generation. By Bruce Weber."

INTERVIEWER (V.O.) In the April 5, 1987, edition of *The New York Times Magazine*, writer Bruce Weber presents evidence to back Listfield's claim. In preparing his article, Weber interviewed approximately sixty people, ranging between twenty-two and twenty-six years of age. His purpose was to examine the 1980s relationship in comparison with the way relationships were carried out when the author was a young man. The young people today, Weber wrote, are very similar to the way he was when he graduated from college, with one major difference: Today, they are *planners*, people who carefully map out their adult lives in such a way that relationships have to be fit into their plans, and not vice versa. For Weber, it is a less-than-pleasing, if not startling, discovery.

7. INTERIOR. EMILY LISTFIELD'S APARTMENT. MEDIUM SHOT.

Interviewer and Emily Listfield sitting and talking on the couch.

> INTERVIEWER (V.O.) *Variations in the Night*, published in 1987, finds Emily Listfield examining a relationship between a woman named Amanda, one of Weber's "planners," and Sam, her Midwestern boyfriend—a man who, Listfield writes, is accustomed to reducing everything in his life to calculated equations. On the surface, it is a very basic story about two people seemingly incapable of expressing their feelings to each other, but beneath this surface is a sense that these people may be the products of their cultural or social environments. These are the types of themes that Emily Listfield finds compelling—themes that she hopes to build her career upon.

> LISTFIELD I think I'm very much a relationship writer.

> INTERVIEWER *New York* relationships.

> LISTFIELD Do you feel that they're so different?

> INTERVIEWER Yes. I do.

> LISTFIELD *Booklist* gave this review saying the relationship in *Variations in the Night* was very "New York." I'll show it to you.

Camera follows her as she gets up, walks over to her bookshelves, and retrieves a sheet of paper. She hands it to the interviewer.

> INTERVIEWER (reading) "A true 1980s relationship . . . Oppressive New York ambience. . . ." I guess that's where I was heading: It's a 1980s New York relationship.

> LISTFIELD Well, I think it's a relationship between guarded people—people who have always had trouble talking. That was the point. It's exacerbated by New York and the times.

But I think there have always been people who have trouble communicating their feelings. The genesis is the same anywhere, but the way people deal with it may be different. In the book, Amanda has defense mechanisms that are different from someone's defense mechanisms in, say, Duluth. Or Los Angeles.

INTERVIEWER (holding up book) In here, they'll think or talk a relationship to death.

LISTFIELD Yeah. In New York, to make a date with somebody you have to take, like, six analysts into account. (*laughs*)

Cut to:

8. EXTERIOR. NEW YORK STREET. NIGHTIME. LONG SHOT.

It is very late in the evening. The streets are almost bare. A couple walks up the sidewalk, away from the camera. Though they are walking close to each other, they are not touching.

WOMAN (V.O.) It was as if they were touching hands on cither side of a prison wall. Though each determined that this time, this evening, they would break through, feel skin on skin, when they got together something stiffened and they were a marionette couple. Only sometimes, in the night, did the awkwardness disappear and so both came to long for the anonymity of darkness, for the freedom it could bring. But more often than not, they were unable to melt into each other and they had clumsy marionette sex too.

Fade out and cut to:

9. INTERIOR. LISTFIELD APARTMENT. MEDIUM SHOT.

Interviewer and Listfield talking.

INTERVIEWER To follow along this theme of the book's being a story of a relationship of the Eighties, there was some criticism about what was perceived to be a rather cavalier attitude about sex, on Amanda's part.

LISTFIELD It's funny. I've felt like some of these people have been offended by what I've written, and I don't see this as an offensive book. Now I was really prepared for controversy with my first book, because of its subject matter and the way it was written. Some people really took offense to the drugs in it. But it made some of the notable books lists that year. I was really unprepared for controversy this time. I thought it was a safer book—not that I meant it to be, but I didn't see it as offending people.

INTERVIEWER AIDS has changed the national consciousness in terms of the way we see casual sex.

LISTFIELD Sure, it influences things. People are being more careful. People are definitely looking at relationships differently, and long-term, monogamous relationships obviously make a lot more sense. When I wrote It Was Gonna Be Like Paris, no one had heard of AIDS, and today, Sarah would not be sleeping with a junkie. I don't know. . . . I'm real suspicious about too much backlash: I would hate to see people go back to the society of the 1950s, and people still have sex, even though there's AIDS. A lot of the reviews of the book mentioned the sexual promiscuity, but I didn't see that coming. For one thing, she only slept with two people in the whole book; I didn't see that as being highly promiscuous.

INTERVIEWER Apparently, some reviewers would take issue with you on that.

LISTFIELD That's become a major issue, and I find it scary. You have this type of "Nancy Reagan backlash" now, where every celebrity is going on television and saying "Just say no." And then there's the big media thing which implies that women, thirty years or older, are just angling for a husband because there's supposed to be such a scarcity of men. I wanted to show a woman who's completely different, and I thought there was an important point to be made. Yes, she has sex, but that doesn't make her promiscuous, and it doesn't make her irresponsible. It's true that I didn't mention birth control, but I didn't write any graphic sex, either.

INTERVIEWER It's probably a matter of the sexual double standard here. After all, Amanda is the one who is more or less controlling the direction of this relationship. Maybe there's more politics behind the reaction to this book than you'd think at first glance.

LISTFIELD I *do* subscribe to the theory that the person is political. I mean, if you write about the changes in a male/female relationship, where maybe the woman is less committed than the man, after a hundred years of people's seeing it the opposite, that *is* political. No, it's not writing about war and it's not writing about apartheid, but that's not what I set out to do. Even so, it always comes up as being politically correct or incorrect. People want to take the edges off writing, but you can't change what you're writing about— not if you're writing about real people.

INTERVIEWER Is your next book going to be about a relationship?

LISTFIELD Yes. It's the story of a first year of a marriage.

INTERVIEWER Do you have a working title for the book?

LISTFIELD *Slightly Like Strangers*.

Cut to:

10. INTERIOR. LISTFIELD APARTMENT. MEDIUM SHOT.

Emily Listfield is sitting at her desk, typing a draft of the novel. The desk and typewriter are located in the corner of her dining-room area.

INTERVIEWER (V.O.) Emily Listfield is reluctant to give away too many details of the new book, which is due to be published in fall '88. She does say, however, that it's a story about the secrets that people keep from their spouses, of the little pieces of their pasts that keep them "slightly like strangers" to their lovers.

11. INTERIOR. LISTFIELD APARTMENT. EMILY LIST-FIELD. CLOSE-UP.

As she answers the question, camera pulls away, settling on ME-DIUM SHOT.

INTERVIEWER What is it that you find so compelling about writing about relationships?

LISTFIELD (brief pause as she considers question) It's interesting. . . . Someone else asked me that question recently. . . . I'm really fascinated by it because I don't think many people do it—or do it well. You're writing about the shifts between two human beings—the shifts in self-discovery and power and the different points of communication and how they discover it, whether it's through sex or silence or talking to each other. I find it very fascinating. European writers write about it, but I don't think it's a very "American" thing.

INTERVIEWER John Updike has been doing it for years.

LISTFIELD Right. I think everyone—not just writers—has a couple of obsessions that are pursued from all different angles. These obsessions don't change that much throughout a lifetime. It's harder to write about something with elusive ideas than it is to write about something with a slam-bang plot. When you're writing about relationships, you really risk running into Judith Krantz–type writing—or becoming, on the other hand, too abstract. But I do think you can make language fit your subject. You can change sentence structure so it mirrors what's going on in a relationship.

Cut to:

12. INTERIOR. CROWDED RESTAURANT. MEDIUM SHOT.

Camera moves in until it focuses on a single couple, seated at a table, menus on the table before them. Each is looking in the direction of the other, but they aren't *seeing* each other. Neither person speaks. They are waiting.

> WOMAN *(V.O.)* For years, whenever Amanda had imaged lovers, intimacies, all she could see was this: arguing, scenes, disharmonies, and finally, silence. It was all she could see. But she and Sam did not argue, had never once argued. Instead, they went round and round and round, dancing the minuet, porcelain figures who rarely broke their painted-on smiles.

*Slow fade and
cut to:*

13. INTERIOR. LISTFIELD APARTMENT. EMILY LIST-FIELD. CLOSE-UP.

Emily Listfield is typing at her desk.

> LISTFIELD *(V.O.)* I always knew I wanted to be a writer. I mean, I don't remember making that decision. It was always something I wanted to do.

14. INTERIOR. LISTFIELD APARTMENT. LISTFIELD AND INTERVIEWER. MEDIUM SHOT.

> LISTFIELD I kept notebooks full of scraps for ideas and stream-of-consciousness stuff. The writing was pretty self-centered. I went to Colgate and studied English and journalism. I think I learned a lot from studying journalism. I also started writing poetry when I was in college, but I felt that it wasn't for me.

> INTERVIEWER There's a feeling of poetry in some of your work.

(reading) "The color of hot summer afternoons when it is piercing yellow outside, almost white, but you don't care because you are lying inside with all the blinds closed so it is an even grayish tan and the sun is just a rumor. That is the color Amanda wanted all of her mornings to be."

Those two lines have an element of objectivist imagery to them. They're very specific, yet they're carrying a lot deeper meaning to them.

LISTFIELD It's funny, because the managing editor at Bantam really liked that line, too, and his only question was: Is that a sentence? (*laughs*) The hardest thing is to get not just the rhythm, but the *feeling*. I know how I want something to feel, and choosing language to get that feeling or mood is very important to me. That's one of the most interesting things about writing to me. That's what I like about writing when I can do it, and I'm frustrated when it doesn't work.

INTERVIEWER Do you work at your typewriter? In long-hand?

LISTFIELD I write at a typewriter, and I'm a constant rewriter. My first drafts are awful, and the only way I can conquer my fear of writing is to get the ideas on paper and then go back and back and back. So I really rewrite a lot.

INTERVIEWER And you've always lived in New York?

LISTFIELD Yes. I was brought up in Manhattan.

INTERVIEWER How do you do it? New York is an expensive city. How can you afford to pay that kind of attention to your work and still be able to afford the cost of living here?

LISTFIELD Oh, God. It was like I'd do anything to pay the rent, and it isn't as if I needed a lot of money to pay it. I was living on Third Street. No one had heard of the

East Village then, and it was just a slum at that time. Cab drivers wouldn't take me home. You know?

Camera stays on her as she continues to talk, though we can no longer hear what she is saying.

> INTERVIEWER (V.O.) Emily Listfield recalls a time, in the late Seventies, when she was trying to pay the rent by writing press releases for two East Village punk bands. Then there was a very brief stint for a rock 'n' roll club on the Bowery; on her first night on the job, the club caught fire. There was also a job that found her writing fifteen-word capsule reviews for a home video magazine that was published out of the editor's apartment; it was the kind of job, Listfield says, where the first key you'd wear out on your typewriter would be the exclamation point. In between, there were jobs waiting tables.

15. EXTREME CLOSE-UP OF COVER OF *IT WAS GONNA BE LIKE PARIS*

The cover photo is of a blond woman, dressed in black, leaned up against a wall on a Manhattan rooftop. The woman is wearing sunglasses, looks bohemian.

> INTERVIEWER (V.O.) When she finally did score on her big dream—finding a publisher for her first novel—the experience turned out to be a nightmare that reached its nadir when her publisher went out of business shortly after the novel came out.

16. INTERIOR. LISTFIELD APARTMENT. LISTFIELD AND INTERVIEWER. MEDIUM SHOT.

> LISTFIELD It's really a funny "New York story," I'd gone away for a month to finish the book, and when I came

back, I had a finished draft but I didn't know what to do with it. I knew no one in the literary world, and I was at a complete loss. Out of the blue, I took it to New Directions. I just walked into their offices. They were very nice to me. They liked it, but their list was full. They thought I could sell it to an uptown publisher, and they said if I didn't sell it to one of them, I should bring it back and they'd publish it. At that time, it was an odd book. I mean, there wasn't a *Bright Lights, Big City* or *Slaves of New York*. Anyway, I was waiting on tables at the time, and there was a man, a writer, who I'd been waiting on for a long time. He didn't read the book, but he told me to take it to this editor uptown. The editor loved it and wanted to buy it. So I was celebrating, you know, because she was a pretty big editor there, and at the last minute, the head of the house vetoed it, saying it was too weird and that no one above Fourteenth Street would ever publish it.

INTERVIEWER Talk about depressing . . .

LISTFIELD I know. I was really depressed, and then I said, "I'm going to get a good agent. I'm never going through this again." I got the names of three agents from the editor at the house that rejected me. I received such a good response that I was able to choose the one I wanted. Being recommended really helped, and once you have an agent, you're doing okay. She sold the book within five months. Still, I had real difficulty when Dial Press was absorbed by Doubleday. It was an absolute nightmare. It was set to go to press four different times. One time, it was bumped because they had a book coming out that was too similar. Another time . . . (long pause) Writers fantasize, before they've published a book, about the first time they get a carton of their own books. It's a really big moment, just to see that book in print. Well, the publishing date was set, everything was printed in the catalog—everything. And then the carton of books arrived. I was having a cup of coffee and skimming through the book, and I saw such major errors that they had to scrap the entire run of the book. So much for that big moment. *(laughs)*

She continues but we no longer can hear what she is saying.

> INTERVIEWER *(V.O.) It Was Gonna Be Like Paris* was eventually published, months later, to good critical notice. At twenty-six, Emily Listfield was considered to be a promising new writer. The novel is as different from *Variations in the Night* as Bessie Smith is different from Whitney Houston. The prose in *It Was Gonna Be Like Paris* is flat and abrupt—reflective, perhaps, of the way the world is seen in the lethargic drug-haze of characters whose bodies are moving at a faster pace than their minds.

Fade out and
cut to:

17. INTERIOR. WOMAN DANCING. EXTREME CLOSE-UP.

Scene starts out with tight camera shot on woman. She is dancing frenetically. She is *working out*, in every sense of the expression. Camera focuses on her upper body, catches her sweating like an athlete. She is pushing herself to her limit. Her heart could burst.

WOMAN *(V.O.)* More wine? Yes, yes, I'll get you both some more wine. A new album. Faster. No, the next song is better. Faster. Drink, drink. Laugh. Faster. Stay. Here, I'll dress up for you—hats, scarves. I'll paint my face. I'll make you laugh. Just stay. Cigarette. Another cigarette. Faster, louder. Talk to me. Anything will do. Faster, though, faster. Tell me a story. No pauses, please, no silence. Here, this is my gypsy look. Have you seen the new book? Do you like my eyes? Yes, yes, I know you've been here before, but I'm sure there are things that you haven't seen. More wine? Don't yawn. Maybe I have some speed you can take. Don't yawn. Stay. Faster. Drink, talk, stay. We need rock 'n' roll. Stay. Another butt. Fast. Fast. Faster.

Camera pulls away until we're in a MEDIUM SHOT. The woman continues to dance. She is completely alone on the dance floor. The music stops; she continues.

Slow fade and
cut to:

18. EXTERIOR. STREET SCENE. LONG SHOT.

Emily Listfield walking up the sidewalk along Bleecker Street. It could be a Saturday afternoon: The sidewalks are very crowded.

INTERVIEWER (V.O.) Like *Variations in the Night, It Was Gonna Be Like Paris* is the study of the relationship between a man and a woman. There is a marked contrast between the types of relationships depicted in the two books, as well as the ways the stories are told. In *Variations in the Night,* Emily Listfield's writing style is as controlled as her characters. In *It Was Gonna Be Like Paris,* the style is as fragmented and disjointed as the lifestyles of Listfield's disaffected characters.

Cut to:

19. INTERIOR. LISTFIELD APARTMENT. LISTFIELD AND INTERVIEWER. MEDIUM SHOT.

INTERVIEWER (V.O.) The contrast is effective. People are out of control in *It Was Gonna Be Like Paris,* yet there is fire—as well as lots of smoke—in the couple's love affair, a feeling that is almost totally absent in the relationships in *Variations in the Night.*

LISTFIELD The two women in the two books are almost completely opposite, and that was very conscious on my part. In the first book, I was very concerned with the issue of how passion fits into daily life. At first, Sarah opted for the passion and sacrificed her daily life. In the second book, Amanda is terrified of that, so she cuts herself off for a lot of life. She uses her cynicism as a barrier. The books are flip sides of the same problem.

INTERVIEWER Where do you fit in? Are you more like one than the other?

LISTFIELD There are pieces of myself in both women, there's no question about that, and even though they're completely different, they both represent a part of me. There's a part of me that's an observer, that's detached, like Amanda, but I don't think I have as much trouble expressing myself or showing affection as she does. I don't know. . . . Maybe the writing helped me work that out. But I think it's very simplistic to say "This is me or this isn't me." There are pieces of me in both books.

She continues, but we can't hear what she is saying.

INTERVIEWER (V.O.) It's a feeling that Listfield places in the detached observer of "Porcupines and Other Travesties," a short story which appeared in the 20 Under 30 anthology, a story which finds her narrator looking at the unhappy love affairs endured by herself and her friends. Even in the middle of love affairs, Listfield's characters are lonely, unhappy. The story concludes with the protagonist saying "I do not like her. I am nothing like her. I am just taking my own sweet time." Presumably, she is speaking of another character, but it's obvious that she could be speaking about herself.

The interviewer now speaks directly to Listfield in her apartment.

INTERVIEWER Up to this point, your writings about relationships have been fairly cynical, inasmuch as your protagonists always end up unhappy. You've dealt with passion on two different levels. What can we expect of your third book?

LISTFIELD Hopefully, coalescence. *(laughs)* I want it to be more optimistic because I *do* believe there is a balance, and you have to believe in it before you can find it. It's funny. The ending of *Variations* has struck so many people so many different ways. One person will tell me "It's so cynical," while another will say "It's soooo rosy." You know? I think it depends on how *you* feel about relationships— how *you* see them—when you decide what's going to happen to these characters at the end of the book. It's almost been a litmus test for other people. But, yes, the third book will be more optimistic.

Slow fade and
cut to:

20. EXTERIOR. STREET SCENE. MEDIUM SHOT.

The Interviewer, on the street, concluding his report, speaking to the camera.

INTERVIEWER Bruce Weber's article in *The New York Times Magazine* supports many of Emily Listfield's theories about the nature of modern relationships. Writing about his conversations with young college graduates, Weber says: (reading) "Career-minded, fiercely self-reliant, they responded to me, a single man with a good job, with an odd combination of comradeliness and respect. When the interviews were over, I fielded a lot of questions about what it's like to work at *The New York Times.* How did I get my job? Occasionally, someone would ask about my love life. Considering the subject of our discussions, I was surprised it happened so rarely. When it did, I told them I'd come reasonably close to marriage once, but it didn't work out. Nobody asked me why. Nobody asked if I was lonely."

Slow fade and
cut to:

21. EXTERIOR. MANHATTAN PREDAWN.
ROOFTOP. MEDIUM ANGLE.

This is the same scene we had at the onset of this program.

WOMAN (V.O.) New York at not quite dawn, the smell neither day or night, but somewhere shifting below, our New York, a paste-up of toy structures to be moved about in the unclaimed hour when everything, yes everything seems possible, how could it not?

We will make it, Carrie says. Yes, we will, I say, and know that it is true, how could it not be? The streets are empty still. Of course we will make it, we will, but later, now it is time for sleep, breakfast perhaps, but sleep, sleep. We are both suddenly too tired to wait for the red pink entry of the day. Well, we almost made it, Carrie says, as we climb down the fire escape.

Slow fade to black.